ALSO BY LINDA S. GODFREY

*Real Wolfmen: True Encounters
in Modern America*

AMERICAN MONSTERS

AMERICAN MONSTERS

A History of Monster Lore, Legends,
and Sightings in America

LINDA S. GODFREY

JEREMY P. TARCHER/PENGUIN
a member of Penguin Group (USA)
New York

JEREMY P. TARCHER/PENGUIN
Published by the Penguin Group
Penguin Group (USA) LLC
375 Hudson Street
New York, New York 10014

USA · Canada · UK · Ireland · Australia
New Zealand · India · South Africa · China

penguin.com
A Penguin Random House Company

Most Tarcher/Penguin books are available at special quantity discounts for bulk purchase for
sales promotions, premiums, fund-raising, and educational needs. Special books or book excerpts
also can be created to fit specific needs. For details, write: Special.Markets@us.penguingroup.com.

Library of Congress Cataloging-in-Publication Data

Godfrey, Linda S.
American monsters : a history of monster lore, legends, and sightings in America /
Linda S. Godfrey.
p.   cm.
ISBN 978-0-399-16554-2
1. Monsters—United States.   I. Title.
GR825.G564   2014   2014012009
001.944—dc23

Printed in the United States of America
1   3   5   7   9   10   8   6   4   2

Book design by Meighan Cavanaugh

To my uncle, World War II army veteran LaVern Blado,

who fought far more terrible things than

the monsters in these pages

ACKNOWLEDGMENTS

This book is deeply enriched and indeed made possible only by so many who have left their helpful paw prints upon it.

My deepest thanks and appreciation to my Tarcher/Penguin editors, Mitch Horowitz and Gabrielle Moss; my agent, Jim McCarthy; and an awesome raft of fellow authors, researchers, and investigators: Stan Gordon, Brian and Terrie Seech, Lon Strickler, Ken Gerhard, Scott Corrales, Preston Dennett, Tal H. Branco, the indomitable William Kingsley, the encyclopedic William Hancock, Sean Viala, Chad Lewis, Terry Fisk, Kevin Nelson, Noah Voss, Bart Nunnelly, Scott Marlowe, Mark Hall, Charlie Carlson, Matt Lake, Laney Hanzel, Dr. Phylis Canion, Phyllis Galde and *FATE* magazine, C. R. Rober, Jonathan D. Whitcomb, Roy Mackal, Mark Moran, Mark Sceurman, adventurous friends Kim Del Rio and Sandra Schwab, the ever-refreshing Media Mavens Breakfast Association, and all of the eyewitnesses who generously and bravely shared their encounters with the world.

CONTENTS

———

PART TWO

MONSTERS BY SEA

PART THREE

MONSTERS BY LAND

Introduction

Newsday, June 1, 1995, the *Milwaukee Journal Sentinel*:
"Rat Tales: 'Psychotic' Rodents Seize Office Building."

*New York—rats in the elevators, rats in the halls. Rats in the
ceiling, rats in the walls. The rodents strolled into offices in
broad daylight, sending terrified workers running screaming
from the building, workers said.*

*"They were rats the size of small cats—very big," said John
Owens, an office of employment services worker.*[1]

This real-life news clip describes the chaotic scene in the New York
City Human Resources Administration building after it was in-
vaded by hordes of supersized rats that workers claimed were "acting
un-rodent like." The city employees accused building administrators
of turning the rodents into psychotic mutants by using cheap poison,
and the health department denied using anything out of the ordinary.
Most people would agree, however, that these rodents had earned the
title of monster rats.

The story made me think about the creatures we fear and what it
is that makes them cross the line from animal menace or transient
nightmare to true monster. Perhaps the scariest thing about these New

York rats, next to their huge size, was the sense that they were not behaving as ordinary rodents should behave. Is that enough to make them monsters?

It's hard to say. The meaning of the word "monster" has been stretched, inflated, popped, stuffed, and reconstructed over the centuries until the word has become as ephemeral as most of the unknown beasts to which it refers. It originally denoted a creature that appeared as a divine omen of doom but has evolved to include anything fantastical, oversized, cruel, grotesque, or even just unfamiliar. This single word now encompasses such a vast range of possibilities—mythic beasts, predatory animals, nasty humans, otherworldly entities, oversized show trucks, energy drinks, and even microscopic flu viruses— that to examine every one of them would require a book large enough to qualify as a monster all on its own. Since I'm not magically qualified to produce a book like Harry Potter's living, monster textbook, I'm forced to winnow the number of beasts I can include here down to a manageable size.

For starters, I'll limit most of my roster to animal-like or humanoid creatures large and semisolid enough to see with the naked eye. I'm going to give general preference to creatures seen in the New World in fairly recent times, except for pertinent historic and mythic examples that lend context to modern sightings.

It will also help the cases of creatures in question if they display qualities odd enough for orthodox science to have declared them outlaws, mistakes, or altogether nonexistent. Things walking on two feet that would normally locomote on all four are one excellent example.

I will happily omit individual members of *Homo sapiens* who became famous for gruesome acts unconnected to monster accusations. While some monster compendiums include human serial killers such as John Wayne Gacy, Ed Gein, or Jeffrey Dahmer, this book will not.

Although I could make a good case that murderous humans are the true monsters of the world, their stories involve criminal and psychological puzzles very unlike cases that consist of glimpses of nine-foot-tall hairy creatures or ginormous flying things. The concept of human monsters creates an entirely different fear factor than what we feel when confronted with anomalous beasts. Analysis of these dark minds is better left to biographers and criminal psychologists.

Animals already known to science won't be addressed here, either, except when it's possible or, in some cases, confirmed that one has been mistaken for a bona fide monster. Bears, for instance, may now and then be mistaken for Bigfoot. And Komodo dragons may be taken for traditional dragons, although they do not breathe fire. On the other hand, microscopic creatures like viruses may kill enough people to qualify as monstrous, but we know very well what they are and they're not likely to be mistaken for werewolves. I'll leave them to medical texts.

So what's left? In short, the monsters I am looking for *look* like monsters. And I believe most people would say their characteristics are obvious: Most monsters are bigger than they ought to be. They hiss, growl, howl, drool, and scream. They threaten us with fangs, claws, sharpened beaks, and even sharper appetites. They are covered with fur, scales, feathers, or leathery skin, and their eyes may glow. They stare and glare, chase us on park trails, hurl their bodies at our vehicles, attack our pets and livestock, and generally menace us in every way they can—and yet remain incomprehensible.

Maddeningly, they also thwart our every attempt to capture them bodily or on film or video. They leave footprints that cannot be proven to match any known animal, and the few hairs or stool samples that they grudgingly offer for DNA or morphological analysis always seem to be contaminated or inconclusive. They are masters of confusion and the very embodiment of the ancient, traditional trickster entities found in so many cultures.

If all of this is true, then why should we even try to decipher what monsters are and what they want? The only real reason—beside normal curiosity—to study unknown creatures, I'm afraid, is that they appear to have equal interest in *us*. They seem anxious, as they've demonstrated by centuries and legions of eyewitness reports, to get in our collective faces and shake our cherished concept of reality. I, for one, would like to know what they're up to.

On top of that, the monsters seem to like our world. They've been here for a very long time and show no sign of leaving. And they're mobile. Just when a sightings flap ends in one locale, it often crops up elsewhere. If the beasts were better at minding their own business, most people probably would be very happy to leave them in ancient history books or ignore them altogether. But humans are wired to solve mysteries. And given that so many people keep seeing mysterious creatures, investigation is inevitable.

The hunt is further complicated by the fact that monsters come in so many types and sizes. I'll try to sort the wide variety into general categories, but observant readers will probably notice that many specimens could belong in one area as easily as another. The *chupacabras*, or "goat suckers," for instance, have been described as having scales like a lizard, a wolf-like face, and bat-like wings. It's nearly impossible to pin a creature down to an anatomical type when normal methods of scientific classification don't apply.

I apologize in advance to those whose favorite monster is not covered within these pages. I've tried to brew most creature categories with an aromatic blend of new and old, but again I must plead space limitations. Also, please keep in mind that many of these creatures have had whole books devoted solely to them. I owe much to other researchers who have dedicated themselves to the pursuit of the kongamato or the Mothman and published their incredible findings in full. I'll refer you back to them whenever possible.

I cannot apologize for the fact that I have not solved the mystery of monster appearances. I've been stalking the creatures I like to call unknown, bipedal canines ("werewolves," to use the word most often seen in headlines and book titles) for more than twenty years. I know a bit more about these creatures now than I did in the beginning but still not enough to say what they *are* with any certainty. That is generally how things go in the pursuit of monsters. All I can hope is that this book will add enough to the world of published cryptid and creature lore to advance the general cause.

And who knows? Scientific breakthroughs happen! Perhaps by the time this book reaches publication, Bigfoot's genome will have been mapped and accepted by scientists, and a live Loch Ness monster will wash up on the beach for all to see. *Chupacabras*, if not pigs, will be seen to fly, and mermen will show biologists how to create gills in ordinary humans. Consider this book a preparation for that admittedly slim possibility. But most of all, think of it as a way to fan your sense of wonder about all we have yet to discover in this universe, especially among those things that *appear* to be alive and are prone to making appearances when we least expect them.

PART ONE

MONSTERS BY AIR

Fear of winged creatures swooping at our vulnerable heads is an instinct most humans will admit having experienced. Who hasn't ducked at the approach of a fluttering bat, or started at the sudden aerial dive of a red-tailed hawk or a great horned owl? Keeping an eye on the sky is not an irrational habit; the human race has been forced from its beginnings to contend with attacks from predators lurking overhead. And if many eyewitnesses are to be believed, there's still good reason to keep looking up. Consider one harrowing incident from America's heartland.

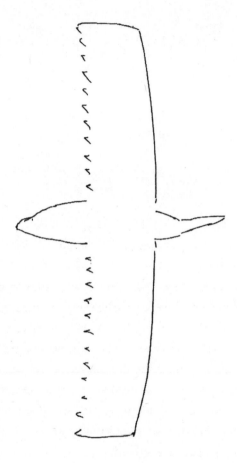

Eyewitness sketch by John Bolduan of the great bird
he sighted in northern Wisconsin.
(Used with permission.)

1

Feathered Fiends

THE WEBB LAKE BIG BIRD

At about 11 a.m. on a bright, warm day in June 2005, Minnesota light-fixture retailer John Bolduan decided to enjoy a bike ride on a country road while on vacation near Webb Lake in northwestern Wisconsin. The family cabin where he was staying was part of a private resort and vacation-home development with very little noise or traffic, an ideal environment for bicycling and observing the local wildlife such as deer and grouse.

Bolduan didn't know it, but he was about to encounter something far wilder. As the six-foot-two, forty-five-year-old man pedaled leisurely past a grassy meadow about three-quarters of a mile from the development's golf course and clubhouse, he spied what looked like a very large bird—larger than any bird he had ever seen—picking its way through the field. Bolduan estimated the feathered behemoth stood only about fifty yards away as he braked to a stop, transfixed.

"I didn't know what it was, so I stopped for a closer look," said Bolduan. "At first I thought it was an emu, an Australian bird that can

get up to six or seven feet tall that some farmers in the area were rais-
ing, but as I got closer, I knew it wasn't an emu."

Using the height of the grass to compare his own size with that of
the bird, he discovered that the bird stood significantly taller than he
did—at least seven feet tall, perhaps eight. Its huge body was entirely
visible above the grass, and Bolduan guessed that the body length was
between five and six feet long, not counting the neck. The body appeared "very bulky," he added. Bolduan's mind raced as he tried to
classify the bird as some known animal: Its head, neck, and beak reminded him vaguely of a sandhill crane, but he knew at the same time

Eyewitness John Bolduan next to the field where
he observed the huge bird. *(Photo by author.)*

that the enormous avian was much larger than the cranes that migrate to the area for Wisconsin's milder seasons.

The bird seemed unaware of his presence, and he quietly continued to inspect it. It was covered uniformly in silvery-gray feathers with no visible markings, but its unbelievable size was what made him want an even closer look. He kept one careful eye on the bird as he slipped off his bike and waded into the field as quietly as he could. He estimates that he was within about seventy-five feet of the creature when it finally "spooked" and took to the air, an action that appeared to require some real effort on the creature's part.

"The size was then truly apparent as it flew away," said Bolduan. "The wingspan I estimate must've been eighteen feet. It was at least three times as large as any large eagle I had ever seen. It was so gawky as it flew away, the flapping of those huge wings was slow and seemingly laborious. The wings seemed to roll as they flapped, like dropping a big rock in water and seeing the waves roll from it. It was not graceful."

Bolduan confirmed the length of that wingspan when I visited the site with him in June 2013. When the bird flew away, there was a short period where he could observe it flying over the road. He noticed that the wingspan was at least as large as the twenty-foot-wide country lane, which we remeasured to make sure.

"Not only was the wingspan large," he continued, "but the wing itself must've been two feet wide as it flopped over the horizon. It almost looked like the size of a small airplane or ultralight aircraft—in fact, there is a small airstrip there where small planes take off and land, and this bird was the size of a Piper Cub as it flew over the trees." The bird then headed off above an adjacent farm and flew toward the airstrip, he said.

John watched the bird disappear into the distance, as the rolling, wave-like motion of its wings again convinced him that he was, in

Eyewitness John Bolduan points out the road flown over
by the huge bird as he watched. *(Photo by author.)*

fact, watching a live animal and not some type of aircraft. "I know it
was an actual animal," he said. He added that he thought briefly of
running to the exact spot in the field where the bird had stood to see if
it had left any evidence but was afraid that it may have been tending a
nest and that disturbing the area might cause the creature to rush back
and attack him.

"I regret the way I approached the bird," he said. "I should have
stayed behind the trees and observed it instead of clumsily walking
onto the field and scaring it away. It was a rare opportunity of detailed
discovery blown. Because I did not know about such large birds, I took
no care that day, thinking it was something known. I assumed the
world around me was explained completely, but I found out that it's
not. I'll probably never see it again; I hope someone else does . . . and
reports it!"

He remained adamant that the bird appeared entirely physical and was not any sort of paranormal phenomenon. He decided for his own peace of mind that it must have been some sort of "mutant" crane or stork that had somehow grown incredibly larger than any others of its species. "I just told myself that's what it was," he said, "because I didn't know what else to think." But deep down he believed that wasn't true, John told me.

"From what I see online, there should be no storks in our area and they don't get this big. Is it an undiscovered North American stork of very large size? I don't know."

There was one more aspect, nearly mystical, to Bolduan's unusual experience. Almost immediately, he found himself dealing with profound changes and unexpected developments in many areas of his business and personal life. Even though he did not believe the bird was any sort of phantom or "spirit" creature, it has occurred to him that perhaps his sighting of it took place as either a warning of things to come or as a message of hope and encouragement. He still wonders about that. "Seeing it changed my life," he added.

I'd have to categorize John's encounter as one of the strongest eyewitness accounts of anomalous, large birds that I've seen anywhere. Most such reports describe only creatures already airborne, usually at a height that prevents the witness from seeing details like feathers or markings. It's also difficult to accurately estimate the size of any object that's observed only in the sky because there are seldom any adjacent objects for comparison. John was able to figure out the bird's size while it was still on the ground. He also had the rare opportunity to watch the giant bird take flight, which allowed him to make a wide range of observations about the creature.

Why would such an unusual beast decide to set down in a rural area of Wisconsin? Like any bird, it was probably searching for habitat to meet its physical needs: water, food, and a private place to rest. One glance at an aerial map reveals why wading birds would enjoy John Bolduan's favorite vacation spot as much as he did—the town of Webb Lake in Burnett County is almost completely surrounded by small lakes and marshes. In fact, the nearby town of Grantsburg is home to a famous wildlife and bird sanctuary known as Crex Meadows.

But what would attract such a massive specimen? The area's sparse human population might provide one advantage for an elusive creature. The area is also about fifty miles south of the shores of Lake Superior, with its rocky, often desolate coast and wind drafts that could help support the wings of a bird too big for its britches. Beyond Superior, of course, lies Canada, with even more lakes and vast acres of wilderness. The big bird may have simply been headed for its summer home.

John's conclusion that this was no ordinary wading bird seems reasonable, since no crane or stork of that size is known to exist in this day and age. It's true that Wisconsin is home to ordinary sandhill and whooping cranes, but both species feature distinctive head markings that John should easily have noticed. In flight, the whooping crane can be identified by its striking black wing tips, and John did not see these markings, either.

The size of these known cranes doesn't measure up, for that matter. The whooping crane is the taller of the two known birds—the tallest bird in North America, in fact—and stands about five feet tall at most. Its wingspan, however, measures only seven and one-half feet and its plumage is mostly white with a bright red crown. On the plus side, if we are rooting for cranes as possible explanations, cranes do have the rectangular wing configuration that Bolduan particularly noticed and emphasized in his sketch (reproduced on page 8) of the bird that he saw.

There are really few other viable candidates. The trumpeter swan, one of the largest living water birds in the world, beats either type of crane size-wise, since the very largest of them can sometimes reach a body length of five to six feet and a wingspan of up to ten feet. It still falls short of the eighteen-foot wingspan described by Bolduan, however, and while its all-white plumage might be mistaken for a "silvery sheen," it has a very recognizable black face and bill that most people would have no problem identifying as the mug of a swan. Its wing configuration is also quite different from the elongated rectangles shown in the eyewitness sketch.

Bolduan told me he has spent countless hours poring over books and online images of large birds and has never found any depiction that matches the size and other characteristics of the one he followed into that grassy meadow. Whatever it was, and despite the fact that it seemed to be doing nothing other than catching a few rays and minding its own business, its astonishing size makes it technically—in my book, at least—a monster of sorts. And even though this giant bird behaved itself quite nicely, there are numerous examples of other flying gargantuans from prehistoric times to the present about which the same could not be said. Some may be no more than ancient myth, but others are modern reports from eyewitnesses every bit as credible as John Bolduan.

His story, then, provides the perfect launching point for our aerial survey of things that come from the sky. Let's hope for safe landings.

Big Birds of the Past

It may be hard to swallow the idea that seven-foot-tall cranes with bodies as large as a human's and a wingspan the size of a small airplane's really exist, but archaeological evidence shows that people have either observed or at least contemplated similar beasts—and myriad variations—around the planet for millennia. Often these birds were thought to be spiritual beings. Religions worldwide echo the Native American beliefs explained by Michael Edmonds in a 2000 issue of *Wisconsin Magazine of History*:

> Because some birds—notably waterfowl, cranes, and raptors—could fly high out of sight into the heavens, which were the domain of powerful spirits, they were considered particularly effectual spiritual agents.[1]

It seems natural that people would want to identify themselves with these impressive creatures. And the human obsession with powerful birds evidently began early in the development of civilization. In early January 2013, a group of British archaeologists announced their discovery of a huge cache of clay figurines in a Greek Stone Age site believed to be at least seven thousand years old. Among the figures were unmistakable representations of human-bird hybrids![2] The exact purpose of these little sculptures found amid equally recognizable human figurines isn't known. They might have symbolized deities or served other cultural purposes now obscure to us—or perhaps, as I like to speculate, they were actually depicting a creature that these people knew all too well from personal encounters.

While most of the giant, winged predators that actually existed in prehistoric times are now believed extinct, there are a few actual mega-avians left in remote corners of the world—the Peruvian or Andean condor with its ten-foot wingspan, for example, or the not-long-gone Washington's eagle, which has been thought extinct for only a little more than a century. (More about that one later.) There were many other big birds that we know of through fossil records and early historical sources, making it likely that our distant ancestors may have had run-ins with birds large enough to inspire legends and even belief in their divinity.

The relative handful of endangered, geographically isolated species that remain to this day, however, cannot begin to explain the hundreds of reports of huge, unknown flying creatures seen across the Americas over the past several centuries. We may consider that these sightings are not merely the invention of fanciful, uneducated early settlers or inebriated woodsmen because similar descriptions of giant birds show up in Native American legends that predate European settlement. The winged things come in a great variety of shapes and sizes, from undead ringers for leathery, prehistoric pterosaurs to enormous, carnivorous bat-like beasts. They all come and go as they please, leaving us to wonder—as we hide the small children and pets.

THE CHILEAN ROC

As I've already noted, the very same monstrosities—differing only in name and detail—flutter through ancient legends worldwide. There are numerous references to fantastic flyers in the New World, both from Native American tradition and from Old World legends brought by immigrants. One example made popular and disseminated by the writings of thirteenth-century explorer Marco Polo is the huge creature called the roc or *rukh* in Middle Eastern folklore. While many New World cultures came up with their own wholly indigenous avian gods and monsters, the Middle Eastern roc contains many core elements of the widespread legends.

The mythical bird was so large that it blocked the sun as it flew in the daytime and was said to attack people by dropping large boulders from its talons. Some researchers believe the legend may be based on an actual giant bird—even though that actual bird couldn't fly—that once lived on islands south of Madagascar. Although this flightless bird is now generally accepted as extinct, a live specimen of *Aepyornis maximus* was seen as late as 1658 by a French admiral. Researcher Roy Mackal notes that the Arabs were familiar with these isles long before Columbus and thus would have known about the ten-foot-tall birds in time to have incorporated them—and their huge, football-sized eggs— into Arabic folklore.[3]

These bygone creatures of Madagascar are also known as the great elephant birds, and their skeletal remnants resemble something like a giant emu. Mackal says that native inhabitants of these islands claim the great elephant bird survived into the mid-1800s and possibly even to present times.[4]

The ancient Middle East may seem a very long way from modern North and South America, and it is, geographically. It's doubtful that a flightless bird could have made it from Madagascar to the Americas. And while a bird big enough to blot out old Sol sounds implausible at best, a mid-nineteenth-century New World appearance of a bird that was anything but flightless brought these old legends to life.

In 1868, a crew of Chilean workmen reported seeing a huge flying creature whose vast proportions darkened the sky as they took a dinner break outdoors one afternoon near Copiapó. The men at first assumed the bird was a massive cloud as it approached them in a strangely direct flight path. By the time the men realized it was a living thing, they could also see it had gray feathered wings, a long body covered in shiny scales, and large, reflective eyes. Its head was covered with bristles, perhaps some type of stiffened plumage.

The fearsome creature sailed far above the terrified men, evidently not finding them interesting enough to merit a closer swoop. We know about the incident only because an anonymous reporter contributed his account of it to a July 1868 issue of the journal *The Zoologist*.[5] As in all types of cryptid sightings, a creature this large may also have been seen by other people, but no one else dared to report it.

STORK UNCORKED

Although John Bolduan had a much better basis of comparison by which to judge the bird's size than do most witnesses, and therefore might be considered a very credible judge regarding the gigantic size of the Webb Lake bird, skeptics still may insist that his sighting was merely a misidentification of some large species, perhaps a nonnative variety that lost its way or was out of place for other reasons.

Exotic bird species in both public and private collections do manage to fly away from their keepers now and then. At least one such escapee, an African marabou stork, took a powder from the rhino yard at the Brookfield Zoo on July 30, 1977, after keepers failed to properly clip its wings. The stork had been brought to the zoo about fifteen miles west of Chicago, Illinois, from Kenya only two weeks earlier. On its home turf in Africa, it survived by scavenging carrion alongside of vultures.

The marabou is the largest African stork, can stand up to five feet tall, and boasts a maximum wingspan of about twelve feet. This zoo specimen was a little smaller, standing four and one-half feet on stilt-like three-foot legs, and with a wingspan of seven to eight feet, depending on the newspaper account. The marabou is nicknamed "the undertaker stork" due to its cloak-like black wings, white belly, and fuzzy topknot on a bare head and neck. It has the long pointed bill common to the stork family. All of these features—the size, coloring, and huge bill—made the Brookfield stork very easy to spot.

It enjoyed a wide tour of the area; a superintendent at the Brookfield Zoo told *Milwaukee Sentinel* reporter William Janz that he received at least fifty calls from people who had seen the bird flying over Indiana, Illinois, and northern Wisconsin.[6] Some people even claimed it was snatching small children, although no one had any proof and it's likely that people were confusing the big stork with several other great bird appearances the previous week in the same area. It's possible that the stork flew other places, too, where the residents didn't think of reporting it to a zoo in Chicago.

The wandering stork finally landed a good seventy miles away in Lake Geneva, Wisconsin, where it settled to roost seventy feet up in a dead oak tree in a field. The bird was described as being shy of nets, so authorities shot it down with a tranquilizer gun. The poor thing broke its wing in the fall. Despite treatment with antishock medication and antibiotics, it died soon after its return to the Brookfield Zoo. (A media spokesperson for the zoo told me that this event would have been handled much differently had it happened today.)

Although the final outcome was tragic, the reports prove that the big stork was on the wing and covering at least a tri-state area from Saturday until Sunday evening, when it first landed on the dead oak. Could it also have flapped as far as Tennessee?

Someone did report a giant bird in the summer of 1977 (although the witness allows that it possibly may have been 1978) flying near Interstate 81 between Bristol and Knoxville, Tennessee. The bird was headed in a northwest direction—perhaps deciding it had gone too far south and was trying to get back to regular meals—at a level lower than the treetops. Researcher Scott Maruna published the account in the blog *Biofort* in 2006.[7]

The witness wrote Maruna that the bird's wingspan was at least double that of an eagle's, and added that although he was familiar with eagles, herons, buzzards, and large owls, this bird resembled none of those. He pulled off the road to watch it, as did a number of other cars drivers who spotted the giant bird, but no one could identify the creature. The writer added that it was definitely not a prehistoric or "reptilian" type of flyer. He did not mention its color or any markings that might have nailed its identity. But perhaps that missing marabou took an even bigger vacation than anyone guessed. In my own opinion, we humans tend to underestimate the vitality, perseverance, and stamina of all members of the animal kingdom. Read on for more examples of oversized flyers that left human observers scratching, and in some cases covering, their heads.

Bigclaw

The year 1977 was great for great birds. Although we'll never know for sure whether the Brookfield stork was the same bird spotted in Tennessee, we can pretty much rule it out as the culprit in several other scary appearances in central Illinois that July. These appearances occurred mostly in the weeks preceding the marabou's daring escape, but because the stork's adventures were chronicled in many newspapers in the eastern half of the country, it was blamed for all sorts of things it couldn't have done—such as snatching away children—in its short window of freedom. Also, many of these appearances involved not one but two large, unidentified birds that became known by the collective nickname Bigclaw.

Bigclaw drew national publicity after a horrific encounter that would give any parent nightmares. On July 25, 1977, residents of the little burg of Lawndale, Illinois, noticed two unusual and very large birds menacing their skies. The birds evidently had their eyes on three children playing in the backyard of one Lawndale home and eventually they descended for an attack. One of the birds latched on to ten-year-old Marlon Lowe and began to flap away with the fifty-six-pound (some sources say seventy-pound) boy clutched in its talons as his terrified mother, Ruth Lowe, chased after them, shrieking at the bird. Little Marlon was also screaming at the top of his lungs, and the bird finally dropped the boy after a short flight of about ten yards. Luckily, it hadn't been able to lift him more than a few feet off the ground and Marlon was not seriously hurt.

Marlon's mother was not the only adult to witness the attack. At least four neighbors had scrambled to the yard and were able to agree on a description of the birds. The marauding avians had ten-foot wingspans, white neck rings, and long beaks. Their wings and bodies were black, with an estimated body length of five to six feet.

The same description was offered by a person who wrote to the Phantoms & Monsters Web site on June 19, 2012. He claimed to have seen the two birds when he was a child, the day before Marlon was grabbed, as he and several young companions hiked along Spring Creek near Lawndale. The birds were following them closely, he said, dipping as low as ten feet above their heads. "I have never disclosed this story publicly," he said, "but I feel it should be known after seeing the shows on the TV and the ridicule endured by Marlon and his family."[8]

Authorities tried to convince the family that the birds were turkey vultures, but neither the description nor their size estimates match those of this smaller, common scavenger bird. The wingspan of turkey vultures averages between five and six feet and they weigh in at little more than five pounds. They lack the distinctive white neck ring observed by witnesses and feature bald red heads that would certainly have been noticed. They also sport gray wing tips and so would not have appeared solid black. This incident undoubtedly spurred some of the previously mentioned phone calls to the Brookfield Zoo's bird expert, since the marabou stork escaped less than a week after Marlon's unexpected ride. And it didn't help that the two large black birds kept showing up around central Illinois. One was spotted over McLean County on July 28, and a mail carrier reported seeing two large birds he called condors as he drove his daily route between Armington and Delavan on July 29. The carrier, James Majors, said that he watched in disbelief as one of the birds snatched and successfully carried off some hapless creature that it had just grabbed from a field. He claimed the birds had ten-foot wingspans.

The pair of giant birds continued to generate evermore sensational publicity, their wingspan growing to a purported twelve feet in the process. A Tuscola, Illinois, freelance writer for fishing and sporting publications such as *Bass Magazine* named "Texas John" Huffer, even managed to film the pair as they flew over Lake Shelbyville on July 30, the same day the marabou stork took off near Chicago. Huffer must have discovered the tree where the pair roosted, because he told reporters that he had seen droppings the size of baseballs at the tree's base.[9] He also heard the birds make a weird cry he described as a clacking noise that struck him as "primeval," even though the birds did not look prehistoric to him.[10] Even with Huffer's ample film footage to examine, however, local officials and experts clung to their statements, that the birds were nothing more than normal-sized turkey vultures.

"The turkey vultures are around Lake Shelbyville all year round," said veterinary student Kent Froberg in an article in a Bloomington-Normal newspaper, the *Daily Pantagraph*.[11] In the same article, however, Froberg sounded less than certain about the turkey vulture identification when he added, "And, it's always conceivable that somebody has illegally imported a bird that got away from him. Of course they wouldn't report it. There are any number of big birds throughout the world."

Bigclaw remained unfazed by its star treatment and swooped over

Bloomington the afternoon of Sunday, July 31. Mrs. Albert Dunham glimpsed one of the pair from her rural home after first mistaking it for an airplane. Her description tallied very well with that of the Lawndale residents: black body, white neck ring, long bill, and giant size. Since she viewed it from the upper story of her house, it was only about twenty feet above her, she said, so that she was sure of what she saw.

Her husband, Albert, and a neighbor gave chase. The neighbor tried to shoot it with a tranquilizer gun but missed, and Albert Dunham followed it to a landfill, where they were joined by a photographer from the *Daily Pantograph*. The newspaper's August 1 article quoted on page 23 noted ruefully that the story's lack of accompanying photograph showed that the bird eluded capture on film.[12]

A local radio station, WJBC-WBNQ, offered a $500 award for the physical capture of one of the freaky flyers, stipulating that the bird had to be a real, living specimen with a wingspan of seven feet or more, and that the bird must not be hurt in the capture. There was also a photo contest with a top prize of fifty bucks. The contest deadline was August 4, and the station's plan was to display the bird at the McLean County Fair. Not surprisingly, no Bigclaw was displayed.

BIG CLAWS ACROSS THE COUNTRY

There have been so many sightings of large, unidentifiable feathered birds in the Americas that to describe them all would fill a separate book. This section, therefore, will have to look at a mere sample from a variety of states. And to give the reader fair warning, we haven't even started on the other varieties of monstrous flyers. But consider these encounters:

PENNSYL-AVIANS

Greenville, Pennsylvania, is a small town set in the northwestern part of the state where several riverways merge. In June 2001, a Greenville man claimed that a bird with a fifteen-foot wingspan made a stopover at a pond near his house, according to an article by Brian and Terrie Seech in *Mysterious Mercer County*.[13] The man reported that the bird he saw was covered in brownish-black feathers and did not resemble the eagles, vultures, or storks that often flew around his property. The bird had perched itself a few hundred yards away from the man's house, and he was able to observe it for around a quarter of an hour. He also said that a neighbor saw a huge unknown bird in the same area the day after his sighting.

South Greensburg, also with "green" in its name but located in an urban setting just southeast of Pittsburgh, had a sighting of a similar creature a few months later, on September 5, 2001. A man driving on Route 119 heard very loud flapping overhead. According to longtime Pennsylvania researcher of the strange, Stan Gordon, the witness reported that he looked up to see what was making this noise and saw a huge, dark, giant bird with a ten- to fifteen-foot wingspan flying fifty to sixty feet above the highway.[14]

South Greensburg can boast an even more recent sighting—and possibly two. On August 26, 2010, just a few minutes past 8 p.m., in waning daylight, four people enjoying the hospitality of a friend's patio heard a loud swooshing sound that one of them interpreted as a gust of air aimed straight down at them. According to Stan Gordon in *The Gate to Strange Phenomena*, one witness shouted, "What the hell was that?"[15]

The bird was only thirty to forty feet overhead, and it was still light enough for the four people to see it clearly as it veered toward the road in front of the house and then just kept going. The witnesses said that it had a wingspan of ten feet or more, and that its massive wings displayed a rolling motion as they flapped up and down. It flew with its short beak and oval head pointed downward as if scrutinizing the ground below, and its bulky body looked as if it would stand about five feet tall when perched. Its feathers were a uniform dark brown or black, and it had a two-foot-long pointed tail. The stunned witnesses said they were too amazed and fascinated by the sight to take a picture, even though they all had cell phones with cameras.

Something very similar revisited the South Greensburg area on New Year's Day 2013, according to Stan Gordon's UFO Anomalies Web site.[16] The incident occurred in full daylight at around 3 p.m. as two women and a boy took an afternoon walk through some snowy woods. The three had noticed one tree that seemed to have a lot of foliage left. They were walking toward it and were within about twenty to twenty-five feet of it when the two women saw what looked like a very large bird unfolding and flapping its huge, black-and-gray wings with a sinuous rolling motion as it walked behind the tree. (The boy was looking elsewhere and did not see it.) They estimated its wingspan as between six and seven feet. But in the few seconds that it took for them to reach the tree, the creature seemed to disappear! It was simply gone, and it left no tracks.

The witnesses were baffled. The trees were not dense enough to have hidden it, said the women, and they were sure they would've seen it fly away. They drew a sketch of a huge, feathery wing with a blue-tinged, dark hue. A local game warden speculated that it may have been a great blue heron or a sandhill crane, although neither of those birds have much of a liking for snow. The wildlife expert also admitted that it was strange that the women would not have recognized one of those birds at such close range and that it left no tracks and was not seen flying away.

Was it a real creature? Many wild animals are experts at quickly removing themselves from view, and it's marginally possible that the bird was somehow hovering just enough above the snow when it was spotted so that it would not have left tracks. If only one woman had seen it, perhaps the idea that her eyes were playing tricks on her might be the most logical explanation. Two people, however, were unlikely to have seen exactly the same light trick. Gordon mentioned the word "phantom" in his headline for this article,[17] and that designation opens up a world of other possibilities for this creature's origin.

Is there some open gateway to an unknown realm of spirit birds in Pennsylvania? According to *Mysterious Mercer County*, Pennsylvanians have encountered giant birds in a plethora of counties, including Clinton, Potter, Lycoming, Tioga, Cameron, McKean, Westmoreland, and Erie. The creatures must be coming from somewhere, and their sheer numbers are enough to make anyone open to the idea begin to wonder if somewhere there is a hidden world where giant birds crowd the skies and occasionally cross into our space. Or perhaps they're just on a flyover from a distant state known for its large species of wildlife, as in the next example.

ALASK-AVIANS

Alaska is a very big state, and many of its fauna are a bit oversized, too. In October 2002, however, a creature deemed startlingly large even by Alaskan standards terrorized citizens and stumped scientists in the state's southwest region.

Although the bird was described as looking more like a humongous eagle than a flying reptile, a Reuters story on CNN.com[18] said villagers in Manokotak and Togiak still compared it to the flying creatures in the 1993 film about resurrected dinosaurs, *Jurassic Park*. Others mistook it for a small airplane at first. Local authorities began telling residents to keep their children indoors.

Area pilot and air service company owner John Bouker spotted the bird while he was flying at a level of about one thousand feet. "He's huge, he's huge, he's really, really big. You wouldn't want to have your children out," said Bouker, according to an article on Uncoveror .com.[19] He added that his passengers had seen the creature as well.

The consensus among local biologists and bird experts seemed to be that this bird with a fourteen-foot wingspan was actually just a specimen of the Steller's sea eagle. The sea eagle would have had to have flown from its native habitat in Japan, a feat judged not impossible by the scientists. Its wingspan reaches only up to eight feet, however, and it bears very distinctive black-and-white plumage that was not mentioned by any of the witnesses. I find this conclusion unsupported by the witness description, and I believe this case should remain in the unsolved mystery file.

TEX-AVIANS

In 1975, two years before the big bird flaps in Illinois, newspaper headlines declared that a giant bird was terrorizing the southern part of another big state, Texas. Sightings stretched from San Benito to Brownsville. The sky invasion was in full swing by the time newspapers began to break their stories.

The 1970s Texas big bird flap actually began in November 1974, when students at an elementary school playground in Robstown, Texas, saw a giant bird the size of a car surveying them silently as it swooped overhead. The local media jumped in to report the event with gusto, as KRIO radio in McAllen borrowed a page from central Illinois radio programs and offered $1,000 to anyone who could bring in the big bird.[20]

The first sightings around San Benito came in late November and early December 1974, starting with a self-declared sober citizen who told police chief Ted Cortez that he and two youths had witnessed a supersized bird.

Not long after, two San Benito policemen, Arturo Padilla and Homero Galvan, witnessed the creature separately while they were driving in squad cars. Both officers estimated the bird's wingspan at around fifteen feet. Padilla told a UPI reporter that the white bird looked like some sort of giant stork or pelican, and added that although he was a hunter he had never seen anything like it.[21] A TV station in nearby Harlingen provided possible proof when they aired footage showing twelve-inch-long, three-toed prints resembling bird tracks found by an area resident in a farm field.

San Benito has a history of large, anomalous birds. Texas author Ken Gerhard noted in *Big Bird!: Modern Sightings of Flying Monsters* that since 1945, three decades before the 1970s sightings, there have been numerous sightings of an even larger bird with a wingspan of twenty feet. This older San Benito bird boasts truly weird characteristics: a beakless, cat-like face with prominent eyes and dark plumage with a white belly.[22]

Gerhard goes on to list no fewer than twenty separate incidents of big bird sightings (including those already mentioned) that occurred across the state of Texas during the 1970s. Descriptions vary quite widely, from an enormous eagle-like bird to something that looked part avian, part human. Perhaps Texas really was the source of some of the oddities glimpsed farther north, but that shaky conclusion still begs the question: Where did all the Texas sky strangeness originate?

The most logical course would be to keep looking southward to the coastal shores of South America, the mountain cliffs of the Andes, and what remains of the Amazon rain forest. Interestingly, the year that the Trans-Amazon Highway opened was 1972! This paving of a wide swath of rain forest land is widely regarded as the landmark event that started the ongoing deforestation of the Amazon. It made formerly pristine areas accessible to hunters, ranchers, and other developers and greatly disturbed wildlife populations. One study found that as few as six passing vehicles per day on a given stretch of road were enough to cause birds to alter their normal flight paths.[23]

Keep in mind that Brazil harbors around 15 percent of all of the plants and animals on Earth. It contains the world's largest wetland and is home to many diverse species of flora and fauna, huge numbers of which have yet to be discovered by modern science. If there was a perfect homeland for huge birds anywhere on the planet, Brazil and the Amazon rain forest would probably be it.

I'm only speculating here, but it doesn't seem such a large stretch to wonder if, when the big highway slashed through the rain forest ecosystem in the early 1970s, the disruption may have spurred a few flying creatures to head north in search of quieter surroundings. The fact that the sudden, large-scale displacement of South American wildlife (logically including birds) was followed almost immediately by the appearance of all sorts of unknown, giant flying creatures over Texas and other parts of the United States seems like the sort of coincidence that might be ripe for further study.

Kentuck-avians

Kentucky author and researcher B. M. Nunnelly reveals in his book *Mysterious Kentucky* that his home state is a haven for not only champion racehorses but also other creatures less well-known. On a windy day in mid-October 2005, says Nunnelly, a Bullitt County resident and two passengers in his car all saw a massive bird standing in a cow pasture. Because the bird was standing next to an Angus bull of known size, they felt they were very accurate in their estimation that the bird stood between four and one-half to five feet tall. As the three people watched, the creature took advantage of a strong wind gust to launch itself back into the sky. The witness told Nunnelly that when the bird spread its wings it was twice the width of the seven-foot-long bull, giving it a wingspan of fourteen to sixteen feet.

The witness also said that the bird's head resembled that of a falcon and that the bird was covered with feathers: black on its back and wings, and brown on its belly, with a white tail and wing tips. The witness added, "The talons were very dark and I didn't look at them very well, but the wings were just like a predatory birds, not a scavenger's— as if made for speed. They were in a triangle, unlike the box [shape] that vultures' wings form."[24]

Interestingly, *Mysterious Kentucky* also notes a newspaper article from the *Cincinnati Enquirer* in early September 1977—the same year that Bigclaw appeared over Illinois—detailing an attack on a five-pound puppy in Burlington, Kentucky. The puppy managed to get away after a large bird dropped it in a pond, but it suffered very serious wounds made by what appeared to be large talons. Unfortunately, the only witness to the event was a seven-year-old boy who described the little beagle's assailant simply as a big bird.[25]

Area wildlife experts thought that the culprit may have been a bald eagle, but it sounds very reminiscent of incidents involving large birds in Illinois that same year. While Burlington is just south of Cincinnati, Kentucky also shares a border with southern Illinois. As I've often observed, unknown creatures seem oblivious to the imaginary lines that divide our states and countries.

FLORID-AVIANS

Big birds, just like their smaller cousins, evidently enjoy a southern vacation now and then. Another of those giant, black-winged birds showed up north of Tampa Bay in the early 1990s with the same telltale white ring around its neck as the Lawndale, Illinois, child snatcher.

A young boy was involved in this incident, too, but this time the eyewitness rode safely on a school bus rather than clutched in giant talons, and he observed the big bird from the bus window instead of from direct contact with the bird itself. The boy said that he was very familiar with vultures and that this bird was quite different, particularly since he estimated its wingspan at ten feet. This account came from Scott Marlowe's *The Cryptid Creatures of Florida*.[26]

There are many other states whose citizens have, from time to time, glimpsed giant stork-like or predatory birds, and we'll be discussing more of these and other types as well. There are some indications in the lore of our native people that similar creatures have been around since very ancient times past.

THE PIASA PUZZLE

Bigclaw, giant storks, and other feathered monsters of the Americas may claim prehistoric precedent in a famous piece of Native American rock art found on a bluff overlooking the Mississippi River near Alton, Illinois. Carved into the rock by the Illini people is a depiction of the flying creature they called the Piasa. The name translates roughly to "the bird that devours men."

The rock art, which has been reconstructed on the face of a nearby bluff after limestone quarrying chopped away the original in the mid-1800s, shows a scowling creature reminiscent of the griffins and sphinxes of the ancient Middle East. It combines great feathered wings with a long, snake-like body, giant talons, and a human head topped by antlers. This fanciful combination means that it's unlikely to be a realistic rendering of an actual predatory animal. In fact, it probably resembles a dragon more closely than it does a bird, but its varied features were sure to have carried great significance to its makers.

The original petroglyph actually included two separate renditions of the creature and dates back to at least 1675, when explorers Marquette and Joliet wrote about seeing it on their river journey. A later explorer, John Russell, wrote about his own, 1836 discovery of a cavern very close to the art site, which he said was filled with a jumble of ancient human bones.[27] He suggested that the cave had been the lair of the unknown, monstrous bird and that the bones were those of its victims. According to the native tradition, the Piasa was large enough to haul away a deer, but it developed a taste for human flesh and began to devour entire villages until a heroic chief found a way to defeat it.

The most interesting connection between the Piasa and the giant birds of present-day America, in my view, lies not in the similarities of its appearance but in its location. In many cases, the common denominator seems to be the proximity to the Mississippi River. Alton, Illinois, lies along the Mississippi, and so do locations of a number of the other giant bird sightings:

The first encounter discussed in this book was John Bolduan's sighting not far from the Mississippi in northern Wisconsin. Then there was the incident in Lawndale, Illinois, where a young boy was almost carried away by a big, winged thing just a few miles east of that mighty river. Travel a little farther south and you come to yet another

big bird–related place: Cahokia, the site of a large, prehistoric metrop-
olis of a sophisticated people known today as the Mississippians.

The Mississippians were skilled and prolific artists, and birdmen
were amply represented among their creations. The birdman, in fact,
is used as Cahokia's official emblem by its present-day site administrators. It's likely that the Mississippians would have approved that logo
since there is evidence that the falcon was associated with the highest
dignitaries of these people. In 1967, excavation of a large mound in
Cahokia revealed the remains of a man whose corpse had been draped
with twenty thousand seashells at burial. Archaeologists deduced that
the shells had once been sewn to heavy fabric cut in the shape of a
falcon whose head and body were fitted precisely over the corresponding areas of the man's body. His burial mound was also crammed with
the skeletons of scores of ceremonially killed people, leaving no doubt
as to the importance of this man who was so strongly associated with
a giant bird of prey.[28]

The Mississippi connection is not limited to giant raptors, however. Yet another mysterious flying thing (covered in chapter 2)
showed up in 2006 near the Mississippi River community of La Crosse,
Wisconsin, located between the Illinois sightings and Bolduan's. Why
does the Mississippi River seem to be a locus of both new and ancient
big bird sightings? It may be something as simple as the fact that large
birds of prey often perch on high cliffs or bluffs, the better to spot their
meal tickets, and this river is lined with such formations. Large rivers
are also attractive migratory routes for, say, something making a
yearly trip from South America to Canada. Birds that look like giant
waterfowl would naturally gravitate to the best water sources.

That would be a tidy explanation if we were indeed dealing with
mere, known birds of prey. The Illini people's Piasa, however, along
with the falcon burial at Cahokia and the growing number of present-

day sightings of unexplainable avians, suggest that something truly mysterious and awe-inspiring may long have haunted these riverbanks. Perhaps there is something in the water.

THUNDERBIRDS

The roc and Piasa birds, with their flashing eyes and dragon-like features, may sound ludicrous to modern ears, but Native American lore is rich in large, legendary birds. The most widely known of these home-grown horrors is the Thunderbird, whose eyes shoot lightning bolts and whose flapping wings boom like cracks of thunder with each mighty flap. The Thunderbird is especially central to many culture stories of Wisconsin's indigenous people.

According to Michael Edmonds, the Ojibwe made offerings to this often beneficial creature to ask for good weather and to protect them from storms. The Lakota believed that the Thunderbird orchestrated the weather from beyond the setting sun, and the Ho-Chunk counted on the Thunderbird for battlefield success.[29] A "good spirit" in the form of a big bird was also described by the famous Sauk warrior Black Hawk, said Edmonds. Black Hawk stated that his people often had seen this creature, which had wings like those of a swan but ten times larger.[30]

The Thunderbirds of native lore usually bore a close resemblance to eagles and other modern feathered birds of prey. We know this both from historical descriptions like Chief Black Hawk's and from petroglyphs, figurines, effigy mounds, and other artistic depictions by indigenous people of North and South America that clearly refer to the Thunderbird legend.

Although some investigators have portrayed Thunderbirds as resembling survivors of supposedly extinct species such as the smooth-skinned, hammer-crested pterodactyl, the overwhelming number of Native American Thunderbird depictions, from the Southwest's Navajo people to the Passamaquoddy of New England, show a raptor-like bird with feathers, a formidable tail, and a short but curved and sharp beak. The main difference between the Thunderbird and known birds, though, is the Thunderbird's unthinkable size. Its massive dimensions, however, are appropriate to its huge role in Native American mythology.

The Lakota of the Black Hills, for instance, call them Thunder Beings, or *Wakinyan*, to emphasize their divine nature as givers of life and governors of the weather. Their reputation is double-edged, however. They're revered for the belief that they bring spring and healing rain, but feared for the death-wielding power of their great talons and beaks, and for the dangerous thunderstorms they can whip up.

Researcher Steve Mizrach believes that in many tribes the Thunderbird was also seen as a sort of trickster spirit, since it was equally able to send gentle rains or destructive storms. In addition, says Mizrach, "Some Indians claim that there are good and bad Thunderbirds and that these beings are at war with each other. Others claim that the large predatory birds [that] are said to kidnap hunters and livestock are not Thunderbirds at all."[31]

Mizrach also notes that most Native American people "describe the Thunderbird as a *spiritual*, not just physical, being. It is not seen as just a large, predatory bird that inspires stories. Rather, it's an integral part of the Plains Indians' religion and ritual."[32] Thinking of the Thunderbird as a spiritual being, of course, leaves a lot more leeway in the interpretation of its appearance. A somewhat similar big bird, the culloo, may be found in the lore of some northern tribes.

The Micmac Culloo

In the tale that follows there figures a remarkable bird, a monster in size, into the form of which certain sanguinary chiefs, who are wizards, powwows and cannibals, are able to transform themselves, retaining their intelligence, and able at will again to resume the shape of men. The tradition of such a bird is not a fable, though the bird itself is fabulous.[33]

The bird described here by Silas Tertius Rand in his book *Legends of the Micmacs* was called the culloo. The Micmac, or Mi 'kmak, people of the regions of Nova Scotia and New Brunswick were some of the first Native Americans encountered by European explorers. As Rand retells the story after hearing it from a Native American speaker, a huge bird-like culloo tries to snatch a sleeping Indian family from their tepee. A brave young boy pursues the beast into its own territory, where it is known as an old chief and magician. He slays it and takes another, younger culloo captive, subdues it, and learns to ride it through the air, after which he and the young culloo undertake many adventures on behalf of the Micmac people.

As noted earlier, anthropomorphic birds—creatures half avian and half human—are depicted in the very oldest human artworks. There seems to be something in the human soul that identifies itself with birds, and perhaps this helps explain encounters such as that of Jackie, from Nashville, Tennessee, who called in to the radio show *Coast to Coast AM* while I was a guest on a 2007 program. Jackie, who didn't give her last name, said that she was a security worker at a place that required her to patrol a fenced yard. She was on duty one night when she saw what she called "bird people."

"One of them was walking toward me," she said, "and then was standing and looking at me. It was about four feet tall, and its face was humanoid but its body was shaped like a bird's. Its face was flat and gray and its eyes were little. It had a bird-like nose and a small mouth and seemed very intelligent."

Jackie was not sure exactly how many of the creatures were there, and she felt that the experience had a definite mystical quality about it, as if she couldn't remember everything that she should have. The next evening she was on alert for the bird people again but she didn't see them. She did say that she heard something after the experience that sounded halfway between birdsong and a human singing.

I was unable to reach Jackie to interview her further. Even though her sighting almost seemed more like a subjective experience than a meet up with natural animals, I found the creatures in her story reminiscent of those described by many native cultures. I suspect that other legends around the world have originated in a similar manner. That's not to say they don't represent some type of reality. The culloo seems especially similar to Jackie's "bird people."

But there are two other known birds whose existence supports the notion that the Thunderbird, the culloo, and similar legendary creatures may have been inspired by physical animals, as well.

GIANT CONDORS AND WASHINGTON'S EAGLE

Could all of these strange birds, perhaps even the legendary Thunderbird, have been condors, as the Illinois mail carrier thought? California condors are very large birds with wingspans that range up to ten feet, and they do have black plumage—but no white neck ring. The Andean condor does sport a fluffy white neck ring but lives much farther south, not that it couldn't make an occasional foray north.

Since condors are a type of vulture, their heads and necks are bare, the better to plunge into bloody carrion. In addition, the California condor's normal range is far west of places like Lawndale, Illinois, and by 1977 they were nearly extinct! By 1982, their worldwide population was still only twenty-two birds. Intensive breeding programs have brought the population back above one hundred closely monitored birds, but it seems highly unlikely that a pair of such a highly watched species could have migrated to central Illinois and caused the Bigclaw flap or similar sighting sensations without having been recognized for what they were.

The California condor may still be the basis of most legends of great *spirit* birds. It would fill the Thunderbird bill in size and general description. This condor is sacred in its own right to the Native peoples who inhabited the wide-open, mountainous planes of the American West. It's a much better candidate for the origin of Thunderbird legends than any out-of-place great bird such as the African marabou, which is not indigenous to North or South America. There's yet another very large bird of the Americas, however, whose characteristics are similar in many respects to those of the Thunderbird. And it also has an association with the Mississippi River.

The Washington's eagle, named after the first US president, was a huge variety of eagle whose existence as a unique species is still somewhat contested. Some experts insist it was only an oversized bald eagle, and no official specimens have been captured for at least a century or so. There is some evidence that it once soared over North America alongside golden and bald eagles, however, including a portrait painted by the great artist and naturalist John James Audubon.

Audubon had undertaken a personal quest to find the great bird after he spotted it several times between 1814 and 1821—first in the Great Lakes region of the upper Mississippi and later near the Green River in Kentucky. Audubon finally bagged a specimen near Henderson, Kentucky: an adult male the naturalist shot as it gorged itself on the carcasses of some slaughtered pigs. He described all of its physical features in great detail and then painted the bird in a pose that made it appear to be scanning the horizon from a tall cliff.

Some objected that Audubon's prized specimen was nothing other than an underdeveloped bald eagle. The Washington's eagle was a rich russet brown, nearly the same dark brown of immature bald eagles before they develop their distinctive white heads. But the wingspan of Audubon's specimen measured a staggering ten feet, much larger than the bald eagle, whose wingspan may reach seven and one-half feet at most. It doesn't seem likely that an immature bald eagle would have surpassed that measurement by such a degree.

Ornithologists who believe Audubon really did find a different species of eagle assume that it must have gone completely extinct shortly after Audubon painted the portrait. There have since been modern-day reports, however, of giant birds that look suspiciously like

Washington's eagle. Scott Maruna posted one of the most compelling accounts in *Biofort* on October 23, 2006.[34]

The eyewitnesses who contacted Maruna identified themselves as Mr. and Mrs. William McManus, residents of Minnesota. They wrote that one morning in late winter 2004 they had spied a massive red-brown eagle perched in a tree north of Stillwater, near a channel of the Mississippi River. They estimated that it stood about three feet tall and boasted a much larger wingspan than that of any bald eagle they had ever seen. This was no momentary glimpse. The couple watched the mysterious raptor for about two hours from about sixty yards away before it finally took wing after they finally approached it. They also declared that they had a very good look at its head, and that it was the head of an eagle and not a condor.

Zoologist and cryptid researcher Karl Shuker defended Audubon's case for the Washington's eagle in an article for *Fortean Times* magazine, noting the artist's familiarity with various species of birds and his very detailed diaries chronicling his observations.[35] If the Washington's eagle did live for untold centuries in North America before its alleged extinction, it's easy to imagine that its great size and its preference for lofty perches would've identified it with sky deities in the minds of Native Americans. And the fact that the Thunderbird is most often described and depicted as a massive eagle makes it a much likelier possibility than either the condor or the crane-like gray bird that John Bolduan saw in northern Wisconsin—although Bolduan's sighting occurred only about an hour's drive from the McManuses eagle sighting.

The Washington's eagle's true nature seems a bit ambiguous in retrospect. Was it a real, previously unrecognized species or an uncharacteristic boo-boo on the part of Audubon? This sense of uncertainty ties neatly into the notion of the Thunderbird as trickster spirit put forward by Steve Mizrach, and the thread of ambiguity looms large in some older examples of sightings.

The Giant Bird of Hickory Creek and Other Historical Big Birds

Still related to running water but a state away from the Mississippi, a bird large enough to create a mini-tsunami in a country creek brought a high tide of excitement to Benton Harbor, Michigan, in the mid to late 1890s. Benton Harbor's *News-Palladium* ran a series of articles in the early 1960s on the recollections of longtime resident and amateur ornithologist Harvey Seasongood, who divulged some rather amazing bird sightings made decades earlier.

In a January 31, 1963, article by Ben Nottingham, the eighty-four-year-old Seasongood claimed to be the last living person to have seen the creature locals called the Great Henhoten.[36] The writer does not explain the origin of that name, but it means something like "many standing houses" in the Germanic languages. That may seem a puzzling title for an unknown, massive bird, but Seasongood insisted that what he saw was a real animal regardless of what people called it.

Seasongood told Nottingham that he was ten years old in 1889 when he last glimpsed the creature gliding over Hickory Creek near his family home south of St. Joseph. He described its plumage only as "speckled," and its head as hook-shaped. He said that the bird dangled its head and very long neck downward as it flew, and although he did not give any measurements he said that the size of its wings was "awesome."

He observed that the bird always flew in from the north and then perched in a nearby swamp in a sycamore tree. Its visits were always followed by extremely heavy downpours that often washed out small farm buildings such as chicken coops and hog pens. Seasongood explained that in his opinion, the bird was simply able to sense changes in air pressure, which allowed it to follow the air currents for easier gliding. Area farmers, however, began to blame it for bringing on the destructive storms with its oversized wings.

Other folk fables began to grow around the bird, such as the idea that its gaze could curdle milk and turn hen's eggs sterile. The tales grew to Paul Bunyanesque proportions in a yarn about a superstrong blacksmith (name unknown) in nearby Stevensville who managed to catch the great bird by attaching a two-hundred-foot-long chain to his anvil and swinging it up and around the bird's tail. The bird emitted such a loud shriek that the smith was rendered permanently deaf. He allowed the bird to fly off unharmed, except for the loss of one great tail feather, which landed on the farm of Herman Zick. Seasongood claimed that the giant feather smashed four rows of grapevine arbors on the farm. The feather was too heavy, in fact, to remove from the vineyard until several men sawed it into four pieces—a process that took two days. Even more unbelievably, the bird's shriek was alleged to have stopped the flow of Hickory Creek for a full thirty seconds. According to Seasongood's tall tale, this created a persistent water vortex that moved into the St. Joseph River and then into Lake Michigan, where it was responsible for the sinking of the steamship *Chicora* in January 1895. He added that as of 1963, the giant bird had not been seen for well over a half century, and that he believed it was a remnant of some unknown species now gone extinct.

My personal opinion is that while Seasongood obviously invented an imaginative tour de force of folklore in the telling of his bird yarn, he still may have based it on memories of an all-too-real creature that did appear now and then in the late nineteenth century. It sounds to me like the amateur ornithologist was also skilled at watching people and that he observed area residents becoming more and more fearful and superstitious about the great bird. He was evidently adept at collecting folktales, since another of his contributions to the newspaper was a story about a phantom ice skater on Hickory Creek. But when he talked about his personal observations of the creature rather than its fantastic exploits, its characteristics are much more believable and seem very similar to other historic eyewitness reports of giant birds.

Other early newspapers around the Midwestern United States also reported citizens who claimed sightings of megabirds, and it's hard to know whether young Seasongood knew of them and had been influenced in that direction. For example, the earliest American giant bird incident, described by authors Janet and Colin Bord in their book *Alien Animals*, occurred in 1868 in Tippah County, Missouri. In what sounds like a precursor to the Lawndale, Illinois, incident almost a century later, a schoolteacher was aghast as a huge bird she compared to a large eagle seized an eight-year-old boy while her students played outdoors at recess. She and the other students screamed and shouted until the great bird dropped little Jemmie Kenney, but he died from injuries suffered in the fall and from deep wounds inflicted by the creature's talons.[37]

The Bords also mentioned an 1882 sighting of a whole flock of mammoth, buzzard-like birds in Cameron County, Pennsylvania. Their wingspans appeared to be a whopping sixteen feet or more, reported Dent's Run resident Fred Murray.[38]

At least one resident of the area around Coudersport, Pennsylvania, believed the Black Forest region of that state harbored similar great birds in the 1940s. Local historian Bob Lyman wrote a book called *Amazing Indeed* about these and other creatures. According to a 1976 issue of *Pursuit*, Lyman wrote researcher Curt Sutherly about the book before it was published, saying that the book "will tell about the actual Thunderbirds that all reference books agree do not exist.

They are wrong. They [the Thunderbirds] have always been in our Black Forest and are here now. Several are reported each year."[39]

Lyman included his own 1940 sighting of such a bird, which he said occurred a few miles north of Coudersport. He described the bird he saw as brown-feathered and standing upright, with an estimated height of about four feet. Its most impressive feature was its wing-spread, which covered the entire road from shoulder to shoulder. Lyman measured that road later and discovered it was twenty to twenty-five feet wide. Despite the great length of the wings, he said, they were no more than one foot in width. Those proportions seem a bit unlikely, but there really are no hard-and-fast rules when it comes to the anatomy of unknown, giant birds. At any rate, the wing size was no impediment to the creature's movement as the bird sped off through the dense timber surrounding the road, maneuvering easily through the trees. Lyman also mentioned other eyewitness sightings of the huge bird and speculated that the long-winged creature was a northern relative of South American condors.[40]

Teratorns Return?

While I've already mentioned that some researchers think that large condors are a likely source of giant bird sightings, there is one more very large bird in the fossil record that once sailed the American skies. Actually, I should refer to them as birds, plural, that all belonged to a group of extinct predatory flyers called the teratorns. The teratorns were relatives of both modern vultures and storks, and their slim, sharply hooked bills indicate they probably lived on small, fresh prey rather than carrion. Their legs were shorter and stockier than today's wading birds, and some were so large that scientists argued at first that they should not have been able to fly. The later discovery of additional specimens showed these birds did have muscular tendons used in flight, so that they almost surely used those wings to fly. Teratorns came in varying sizes, but the king of them all was *Argentavis magnificens*. As its name suggests, it lived in Argentina, although not recently, and it was magnificent with a weight of around 160 pounds and a wingspan of nearly twenty-four feet.

When I said this giant species hadn't lived in Argentina recently, I wasn't kidding: *Argentavis magnificens* ruled the roost about six million years ago, so it would be miraculous indeed if some of them survived to the present day to migrate across the United States and perplex modern humans. Still, between Argentina and the United States and Canada lies that massive rain forest of the Amazon. The cliffs of the Andes are not far away either, so that if there was a continent where massive prehistoric birds had any chance to survive, South America would probably be it.

Author and *Fortean Times* researcher Mark A. Hall seems hopeful in his 2004 book, *Thunderbirds: America's Living Legends of Giant Birds*, that a small, relict population of teratorns may someday be shown to be responsible for sightings of Thunderbirds. After laying out his case that gigantic birds do occasionally show themselves in North America, Hall says, "There is little doubt about the ornithological identity of the predatory hawk-like Thunderbirds. Fossil finds known since 1952 have demonstrated the past existence of such a formidable creature. Similar birds might survive in the Americas and around the world.

"The fossil genus of birds *Teratornis*," he adds, "has been linked with the legend of Thunderbirds for more than fifty-five years."[41]

One of the best parts of his well-researched book is a map showing likely migratory routes from the southern United States northward, based both on appropriate geographical features conducive to such migration and actual sightings of giant birds over many decades. It shows two paths that might be taken by such creatures. One of them starts over Texas, proceeds over the Ozarks, and then runs up through the whole length of the state of Illinois before it continues to northern Wisconsin. The other takes a path northward along the western foothills of the Appalachian Mountains, crosses diagonally over Pennsylvania and New York toward the northeast and finally ends up near Canada.

Hall notes that although the birds themselves may be unusual, "the distribution of these birds is *not* unusual [emphasis mine] and the habits they exhibit are what would be expected of birds of this kind. The habits that are indicated by the known reports and the Indian lore are those of a migratory bird of prey. The birds are annually on the move in the East, in the Central states, and in the West."[42]

Of course, there is still no definite proof as to whether the giant birds following these logical migratory routes are teratorns, vultures, storks, condors, cranes, or supersized eagles. Some, all, or none of these species might be involved in these sightings—and there are always other possibilities considered anathema by mainstream science. But at least these great birds on our present suspect lineup have one thing in common: despite their size, they all still look like modern-day birds. And while that similarity to the mundane may not seem particularly comforting right now, it will after we get the next, much creepier section down our gullets.

Consider that there have been many other sightings of unknown sky denizens whose existence seems even less likely than that of massive eagles or other great feathered birds. Flying things with furry bodies, pointy teeth, hairless wings, and a variety of other anomalous parts zoom in and out of our airspace right alongside the more conventional creatures. Batmen—and not the costumed kind—are tough to define and identify, but the curious and the brave have been trying for decades and perhaps even centuries.

2

Batsquatch

WISCONSIN'S MAN BAT

Bats are, for the most part, helpful, harmless creatures that eat insects and play a big role in the environment. Even in their normal, fairly small sizes, however, they tend to creep people out because of their nocturnal ways, tiny fangs, and fuzzy faces that many consider plug-ugly. Zoom a normal bat up to twenty times its size, however, and it will do far more than just creep people out—it will inspire sheer terror, as a man in his fifties and his twenty-five-year-old son discovered in western Wisconsin.

On the evening of September 26, 2006, around 9:30 p.m., the men were driving home from a music rehearsal in the Mississippi River city of La Crosse. The son was at the wheel as their pickup truck rolled up the hill on Briggs Road in a rural area between La Crosse and Holmen. They were just passing a private shooting range on their right when a great, dark thing flew out of the black night and almost completely blotted out their windshield with its immense wings. As the men braced for a collision, the creature's appearance scared them even more than the prospect of an imminent crash. The dark thing's bat-like wings unfurled to a span wider than the truck—the men estimated it at between ten and twelve feet—and were attached to a human-sized, furry, roughly bat-like body topped by a canine face; large, sharp fangs; and pointed ears. The creature's extended arms and legs ended in prominent clawed feet. The men could clearly see its rib cage as it bore down on their truck. "It looked hungry," said the older man, who goes by his Cherokee name of Wohali.

His son swerved to avoid the creature, which shot upward at the last second before impact and disappeared over some nearby trees. As it left, it emitted a piercing shriek.

"Both of us had feelings of nausea and we were very afraid," wrote Wohali in a letter he sent me recounting the incident. "Well, this site is about three city blocks from our home [at that time] and when we got home we were both sick. My son threw up six or seven times, and I gagged and was sick all night. I've been living in this valley all my life and have seen some strange things—after all the Upper Mississippi River Refuge is the largest in the county. . . . It hides lots of strange creatures. But I've never seen anything like this."

Whether Wohali and his son were sickened by fear or by the sound of that piercing shriek—certain sound wave ranges have been shown to cause physical illness in humans—the men were profoundly affected. "I hope I never see it again," Wohali added.

He didn't, but a few others may have. Another man reported that he and one of his neighbors had each had a run-in with the creature I call Man Bat a full year before Wohali and his son were nearly run into the ditch on Briggs Road.

This man, whom I'll call Bill, lives on French Island, which is part of the city of La Crosse and reachable by bridge. It lies about six or seven miles directly south of the Briggs Road sighting. In summer 2005, between June 15 and 25, he began to hear what sounded like some sort of large animal traipsing around on his roof at night. People in this neighborhood started to complain that their pets were disappearing, and Bill lost two of his own animals in one week.

Bill's friend "Jim" lived only a half block away. Late one evening that summer, Jim had stepped outside for a bedtime cigarette when something massive swooped into a tree in his backyard. The branches on the very large tree shook wildly enough so that he knew it was something bigger than an owl or another normal nocturnal bird. The creature was hidden by thick foliage and when Jim tried to approach it, the hidden intruder quickly flapped over to Jim's garage, where it ran along the roof before launching itself into the darkness. He never did get a good look at it, but Bill remembers that Jim was "extremely freaked out."

Bill also observed the strange "shaking tree" phenomenon and began sitting out on his deck at night, hoping to see the creature. For a while he noticed nothing except motion-sensor lights switching on for no apparent reason, as well as unexplainable lights in the sky that would shoot in one direction or another in moves too fast and erratic to have been airplanes. Finally, one night he was lucky enough to catch a glimpse of the tree shaker. He watched in disbelief from inside his house as a five-foot-tall creature with long hind legs slunk quietly out of a tree and climbed onto his children's playground set.

The yard was too dark to make out details of the creature's appearance, but Bill said that it moved smoothly and naturally, and that "it seemed very sly." He was sure, however, that it wasn't a bat. He said, "It kind of resembled the way Gollum [a stealthy, humanoid creature from J.R.R. Tolkien's *The Lord of the Rings* books-turned-hit-film series] would walk around on all fours. It had to have been only about five feet tall at the most. It looked almost hairless, and its eyes didn't glow. The hands and feet looked bigger than normal, and its legs were longer than they should have been for a usual biped."

The man stood higher to try and get a better look, and as he did, the creature lifted its head as if looking directly at him, then quickly scuttled away into the shadows. "I felt extremely uneasy for the rest of the night," said Bill. "I had this feeling like I wasn't supposed to see that." In fact, he added, he had the distinct impression that it was unhappy he had observed it. That begs the question, if you are an unknown creature of the night that's trying to remain hidden, why dive-bomb a vehicle or hang around a crowded neighborhood and risk detection? Of course, no one ever said anomalous creatures had to make sense. And they seldom do—to our way of thinking, at least.

BATSQUATCH OF TACOMA

The La Crosse Man Bat was not the first of its kind to be seen in the United States. Long before Wohali and his son narrowly missed having to clean up the biggest ever windshield smear, people in the western part of the country began to encounter something that came to be known as Batsquatch.

The state of Washington is best known in the world of strange animals for its numerous sightings of the nine-foot-tall lumbering humanoid most often called Bigfoot or Sasquatch. In the last decade or two, however, it's also become a hub for sightings of slightly smaller furry humanoids with the unlikely addition of wings. Batsquatch first came to public attention in an article published on April 24, 1994, in the Tacoma, Washington, *News Tribune*.[1] Reporter C. R. Roberts, who is still with the paper as a business columnist, wrote a dramatic account of eighteen-year-old Brian Canfield's nighttime encounter with a nine-foot-tall winged creature.

The teen, Roberts wrote, had been driving home to a small community known as Camp One at 9:30 p.m. the previous Saturday when his pickup truck's engine suddenly failed. He'd been having trouble with his carburetor but had his foot on the accelerator at the time so that the carburetor shouldn't have been a problem. Canfield didn't even have time to pull over before his car just stopped, and as he sat there trying to figure out what his mechanical problem might be, his headlights revealed a second reason for concern. Only thirty feet down the road, a huge and horrific being was descending out of the dark sky. It landed hard enough to whomp up a cloud of dust.

Roberts quoted Canfield's reaction: "It was standing there staring at me, like it was resting, like it didn't know what to think. I was scared. It raised the hair on me. I didn't feel threatened. I just felt out of place."

Roberts interviewed Canfield only a few days after the encounter, while the incident was still fresh in the teen's mind. Roberts told me in a phone interview conducted for this book that the one thing he took away from his talk with Canfield was that the boy absolutely believed in the truth of his story. Roberts also said that he cross-interviewed Canfield and performed background checks, but that he found only positive, favorable reports regarding the teenager's character and behavior. Roberts also noted in his article that, for what it's worth, Canfield had never seen a UFO, did not listen to heavy metal music, and was not into role-playing games. These characteristics are not necessarily associated with people who sight strange creatures, in my experience, but Canfield's denial of them does help paint the picture of a serious, conservative young man.

Canfield's memories were vivid. "Its eyes were yellow and shaped like a piece of pie with pupils like a half moon," he said in the article. "The mouth was pretty big. White teeth. No fangs. The face was like [that of] a wolf." It was covered with fur, he added—fur that appeared blue in his headlights. Although that could have been an effect of the artificial lighting, Canfield reported to investigator Phyllis Benjamin, in an interview conducted one year later, that the creature actually was a bright blue color, comparing it to the intense hue of the NBC peacock.[2]

Roberts asked Canfield whether he had any other sensory impressions during the episode. Canfield replied that he remembered hearing the wind and smelling gasoline from his leaky carburetor as he and the creature stared at each other for several minutes. Canfield said he felt the creature was bewildered and that it didn't mean to hurt him.

Finally, the creature looked away and unfolded its giant wings. Canfield was astounded to see that they were at least as wide as the road. The creature evidently decided it was time to go. With a turn of its head for a last peek at Canfield, it flapped away and in the process displaced so much air that Canfield's truck rocked back and forth. He sat numbly and watched as it headed for Mount Rainier.

Strangely, Canfield did not have to send for a tow truck. His engine restarted itself about the time the creature was out of sight. He wasted no time in heading home. He said that he had a hard time catching his breath as he fought off his shock in order to tell his parents what had happened. His mother, Sandra, told Roberts that her son was so frightened that night that she could see his hair standing on end. She managed to calm him enough so that he could draw a rough sketch of what he had seen and then she, Canfield's father, and a neighbor drove back to the site to see if the creature was still in the vicinity. It was not and had left no discernible trace.

Canfield took some guff from schoolmates for his report, but he did come up with a name for what he had seen: Batsquatch, a perfect homage to the Sasquatch. The name stuck and has since been used to describe many other similar unknown creatures around the United States and the world.

"It did happen," said Canfield in the article. "I'm willing to put my life on it," he said, adding that he wished the encounter had never taken place.

Another Tacoma-area family reported an encounter with a large, bat-like creature in July 2011, according to the publication *The Gate to Strange Phenomena*. The October 2011 issue quoted a report the family sent to the blog *Lights in the Texas Sky*:

"We lived near Tacoma, Washington, on several acres of mostly tree-covered land with a creek. We have seen and heard a strange nocturnal, bat-like creature. This thing is huge, [with] light gray skin, no fur, feathers or scales. It silently swoops down at you with giant bat wings."[3]

The family noted that the creature made a distinctive sound they compared to that of a "jungle monkey or bird." They consequently dubbed the beast the monkey bird. It was not as large as the other bat-like creatures discussed here so far, with the wingspan of only about four feet—although that is still very large for any North American bat. The biggest bat native to the United States is the greater bonneted bat, with a wingspan of two feet at most. Asia's Malayan flying fox bat has a wingspan of about six feet, but it wouldn't normally be seen in the wilds of Washington.

Escapes, as I've noted previously, do occur both from zoos and, more frequently, from private exotic animal keepers, so a flying fox on the lam cannot be entirely ruled out. The weather would've been temperate enough in June that a tropical species could survive outdoors. If the sightings really were of some caged beast gone rogue, however, the escape was a double one since the family observed two of the creatures together on one occasion. They also wrote that two of their cats disappeared without a trace.

Author and investigator Paul Dale Roberts has also been following Washington's fanged flyer. In an online 2009 article for *Unexplained Mysteries* titled "Batsquatch Sighted at Mt. Shasta," Roberts described the creature's features as resembling "the head of a bat, red eyes, purple skin, and wings of a pterodactyl."[4]

Roberts had received a call from two men who had been hiking around Mount Shasta in mid-March 2009, when they observed a giant creature sailing out of a crevice. The pair compared its man-sized body to that of Hulk Hogan, adding it had bat-like wings spanning an estimated fifty feet! The head was like that of a bat, the man said, and did not resemble a pterosaur at all. The creature ignored the men and soared off out of sight.

Bat Men of Pennsylvania, Missouri, and . . . Chicago?

Pennsylvania fairly teems with giant avians, perhaps because the state lies on that big bird migratory route proposed by Mark Hall, and witness descriptions of at least one creature reported there sound suspiciously similar to a Batsquatch. A 2011 report by researcher Stan

Gordon in his "Unusual and Unexplained" column in the journal *The Gate to Strange Phenomena*, describes what a witness called "the freakiest thing I ever saw."[5]

The sighting began as so many of these incidents do—with a driver wending his way along a dark, lonely rural road in the early hours of the night. This particular witness was driving through Butler County, between Chicora and East Brady, early on March 18 of that year, when he noticed what seemed to be a living creature about fifty yards ahead of him on the road. This area is not far from the Allegheny River, a major waterway. The witness, a very credible-sounding businessman, switched on his high beams and kept driving.

The tall, muscular creature rose from a hunched position and then bounded across the road in only three steps, passing in front of a road sign before it disappeared into nearby woods. Judging by the creature's height relative to the road sign, the witness figured it stood eight feet tall. He knew the creature was not human because he could see its features fairly well in his headlights, and it had long wings on its back; clawed forelimbs; long, flat pointed ears; and hind legs jointed like those of most quadrupeds. Its light brown skin was smooth rather than furry. The creature never even bothered to turn and look at the witness, as if it had more pressing business.

A very similar creature showed up in Pacific, Missouri, on October 27, 2009. Again, the man bat enlivened an otherwise quiet evening drive for two people traveling along Viaduct Road at about a half hour before midnight. This time, however, the beast was airborne at an altitude they estimated at 150 feet. The scary thing about this sighting is that the creature appeared to be following their car, keeping up with them at speeds as fast as forty miles per hour. The winged creature was man-sized, the witnesses said, and its fur was brownish gray. It was apparently too far away for the witnesses to make out any details such as head shape or eye color. The episode was also recounted in *The Gate to Strange Phenomena*, which cited a post on the Phantoms and Monsters Web site, written in October 2009, as the source.[6]

Most residents of big cities are used to the nocturnal appearances of bats. The sight of a giant, possible Batsquatch flying over Chicago on August 22, 2011, however, understandably surprised a married couple from the southwest suburbs who happened to catch a blurry image of it on their smart phone camera. They were on 63rd Street near Pulaski Road when they stopped to take a photo of an area landmark, a stereotypical statue of a Native American atop a tobacco store. It wasn't until they got home that night and examined the four photos taken by the husband that they realized they had captured something besides the retro-style statue.

"At first I didn't think nothing of it," the husband wrote in a report posted online at UFO Casebook. "I figured it was a plane or something. But just for the heck of it I enlarged it. It looked something similar to a bird or a bat, but then again it doesn't. So I have no idea what it could be."[7]

The photo was included with the post at the URL noted in the above citation. While it's hard to tell the exact size, the figure does feature a roughly bat-like shape with discernible, spread-out limbs on a substantial body and what may be a head.

By itself, that photo might be dismissed as a fluke. But about a month later, a half-dozen students living in the University Park neighborhood claimed to have seen a bat-like creature launch from ground to air, as it made a giant whooshing sound—a noise almost universally reported in sightings of giant flying things. Their description of it tallied up with many of the others: a six-foot-tall, humanoid, dark-colored body with glowing eyes and huge wings.

Yet another Chicago Batsquatch showed up in mid-October of that year near the University of Chicago when a group of people spotted what they said looked like a man with bat wings only about twelve feet overhead. One woman described it as reminding her of a huge sugar glider, a small marsupial that glides on wing-like membranes, similar to the North American flying squirrel. Unlike the sugar glider, however, this creature displayed the trademark glowing red eyes of a Batsquatch, and was the size of a human.

These incidents were all reported in *The Gate to Strange Phenomena* January 2012 issue and were gathered from accounts made to MUFON, the Mutual UFO Network, which reports all manner of unexplained flying objects—metallic or furry.[8] I would think that if anyone in Chicago reported seeing a flying humanoid, many other people should have seen it as well. Batsquatch, however, probably suffers from the same malady as many of its cryptid brethren—severe underreporting of its true numbers due to the fear of public ridicule.

TEX-MEX BAT BEASTS

Batsquatch appears to enjoy southern climes just as much as it does *el norte*. In late March and early April 2009, sightings of man-sized bats began floating out of the state of Chihuahua, Mexico. Xavier Ortega wrote about several eyewitness reports of events that occurred in that time frame on the online site Ghost Theory.[9] One involved an elderly man taking a bedtime stroll at about 10 p.m. when he glimpsed a dark shape in the distance. At first glance, he thought it was a person standing on a fence—certainly an unusual circumstance—and draped in a long cape, which some have suggested may actually have been folded wings. The elderly man bravely shouted at the creature and it moved swiftly to a nearby hill.

Another of those spring 2009 reports came from a resident of La

Tena. He described the creature he saw as humanoid with a female body. She stood over six feet tall and had two pairs of wings, small arms, and large red eyes.

The final report made around this time in the state of Chihuahua came from an officer of the law and described a decidedly more aggressive beast. While most unknown flying creatures skedaddle as soon as they're sighted, a police officer in Guadalupe named Leonardo Samaniego claimed that a human-sized, winged thing dropped out of the tree and landed heavily on the hood of his squad car. The officer observed the same female body shape as did the witness in the previous encounter, as well as the large red eyes and cloak-like folded wings. At this point the encounter grows *truly* strange; the officer said that he passed out after he observed the creature placing one clawed hand against the windshield. He woke up later in the car, clothing askew, and called in to the station.

UFO buffs might wonder whether the officer was the victim of some sort of abduction; the missing time coupled with messed-up clothing are classic characteristics of alleged kidnapping of humans by alien beings. Add to that the fact that many cryptid sightings are accompanied by UFO appearances in roughly the same time and place and it begins to put a whole new light on possible origins of Batsquatch and other unknown creatures.

Ortega noted that the spate of sightings had incited mass panic in many parts of Chihuahua, until many people were staying indoors at night to avoid the creature. I would have, too.

Chihuahua has its own ancient association with birdmen and flying humanoids, as evidenced by pottery found in the Casas Grande–area archaeological site in the northern part of the state. The once resplendent walled city sheltered as many as four thousand inhabitants and flourished between 1050 and 1500. Only ruins remained by the time of the first Spanish explorers. Archaeologist Christine Van-Pool wrote in *Archaeology* magazine about her study of the artwork that decorated certain pots found in those ruins:

> Then I examined a group of vessels with images of dancers that appear to be in the process of transforming into spirit beings and traveling to the spirit world. . . . They also all wear headdresses, suggesting that they are involved in ceremonial activities. The headdresses usually depict a horned and feathered serpent or a macaw head.[10]

It seems, however, that the mask wearers are more than mere ceremonial dancers. The caption for one of the photographs accompanying the article states, "In the drawing, below, from a painted vessel, the shaman has transformed into a macaw-headed man. With animal companions sitting on his leg and nestled under his arm, he flies through the spirit world to commune with spirit beings, then returns to the natural realm."[11]

Keep in mind that this is a centuries-old piece of artwork. It's unlikely that those ancient ceremonies once used to (allegedly) turn shamans into macaw-headed beings are still used today, but who knows for sure what kind of continuity exists in shamanic practices, or to what extent those practices worked? Could it be that shamans in the region of Chihuahua are still trying to communicate with the spirit world via their own transformation into creatures of flight? That is a wholly speculative question, but one that pops into my mind every time another ancient corollary is found for a modern sighting—especially when contemplating why so many unknown flying creatures have been spotted north and south of the Mexico/Texas border.

Texas is almost as rich in Batsquatch sightings as it is in oil, although some Texas Batsquatch reports are even more difficult to sort out than those of most unknown creatures. One such puzzler came from the November 2006 issue of *FATE* magazine, submitted as an original eyewitness report.[12]

As the witness, Max A. Rodenfoe from Lytle, Texas, explained, he was sitting on his back porch at about 2:30 a.m. on June 23, 2005, having a cigarette, when he spotted something making its way toward him in the clear night sky. Rodenfoe first thought it was some type of aircraft, but as it approached he realized he could hear no buzz of engines. As the airborne body came to within about a hundred feet of him, he estimated its wingspan at fourteen feet and wondered if it was some type of remote-controlled glider. He couldn't stop himself from exclaiming aloud, and at that, the beast above him turned its head and stared at him with eagle-like eyes that he felt were distinctly predatory—perhaps evaluating his suitability as a meal.

He bolted for the house and grabbed his gun, but when he returned the creature had disappeared. Rodenfoe had stared long enough at the creature, however, to describe it in detail. He noted that its head, as in many Batsquatch reports, looked canine or wolf-like, although he saw no ears. The body was covered with thick, shiny black fur, with an added fringe of longer hair that made a soft fluttering sound along the edges of the bat-like wings. Rodenfoe also noticed curled digits at each end of the wings. He estimated its total body length was about six feet, with the rear end of it tapering back to a tailless point. I was unable to locate Rodenfoe for further questions.

Batsquatches never need feel lonely in the Texas sky; apparently a wide variety of anomalous flying creatures patrol the state from the Panhandle to the Mexican border. *Pursuit* cited a 1983 *Daily Texan* article that described a few of them. It listed a big, feathered bird type similar to those mentioned earlier here, a prehistoric-looking giant pterosaur—one of which displayed a hump on its back similar to that of a Brahma bull—and something that resembled a big penguin, although it did not say whether the penguin-like creature waddled or flew.[13] We'll get to the Texas pterosaur later in this section.

There's only a fine and spotty line separating Batsquatch and our next group of freaky flyers. The exact characteristics of giant flying humanoids with glowing eyes tend to blend and overlap so that sorting them into well-defined categories becomes almost impossible. Part of that difficulty may lie in the fact that most of them are entirely creatures of the night, when visibility ebbs and shadows play tricks on our eyes. The pale glow of moonlight may change the colors and textures of objects, and sounds seem amplified when heard in the quiet of the night. Despite all these impediments to the clear discernment of their features, the creatures tend to lump themselves into rough categories based on wing type, size, eye traits, and other bodily features. For example, there's a group of airborne anomalies that tend to be more owlish than batty.

3

Moth-mania

MYSTIC MOTHMAN

The Mothman of Point Pleasant, West Virginia, and Gallipolis, Ohio, is one of the most famous monsters in the world. It stands immortalized as a bigger-than-life, twelve-foot-high statue in Point Pleasant, which presides over an annual festival featuring tours, music, speakers, and monstrous souvenirs aplenty. Those who miss the fest can always visit Point Pleasant's year-round museum devoted to Mothman lore. Ubiquitous on Internet monster sites, this unknown winged thing has been studied, investigated, and portrayed in word and film by luminaries of cryptozoology and the entertainment industry to a degree reached by very few mystery creatures.

Despite such star treatment, researchers and investigators have never come to any universally accepted conclusion about the true nature of the beast. Its name suggests a humanoid/moth chimera, but the dozens if not hundreds of people who claimed to have seen it during the early to mid-1960s originally described something more akin to the "big birds" we discussed earlier. The earliest sighting may have occurred in 1961 on West Virginia's State Route 2, in the colorfully named Chief Cornstalk Wildlife Management Area a few miles south of Point Pleasant.

The witnesses to this possible Mothman precursor were a father and daughter who happened to be driving through the area late one evening. They slowed their vehicle after spotting a large figure poised smack-dab on the center line ahead and were surprised to see what looked like some type of unknown humanoid. They realized it was not an errant human traveler when it snapped out a pair of wings so wide that the tips, as described in so many cases, reached either side of the road. Luckily, the daughter, who was driving, didn't have to worry about hitting the creature because it simply sailed straight up into the air and vanished into the night, in a manner very similar to the departure method of the La Crosse Man Bat.

Five years later, Roger and Linda Scarberry were driving their friends Steve and Mary Mallette around a former military munitions facility on the outskirts of Point Pleasant that was known locally as the "TNT bunker area," when the two young married couples saw something much scarier than the abandoned buildings. First they noticed bright red eyes shining out of the darkness, and then a gray thing the size and shape of a tall man emerged from the shadows. Exactly as the father and daughter did in 1961, the foursome decided very quickly that the bipedal creature was not human when it revealed huge wings attached to its back.

Scarberry "whipped a U-ey," to borrow 1960s-era teen slang, and tried to speed away from the bunker area, but the creature began to sail easily after them. It kept up with the automobile, even though Scarberry later admitted reaching speeds of up to one hundred miles per hour in his efforts to outrace the creature. As it flew, the creature emitted ear-splitting squeaks that reminded the two couples of a huge mouse.

The thoroughly frightened couples drove straight to the sheriff's office to report the creature, and the officials took them seriously enough to investigate. No flying humanoid was to be seen, however, and the teenagers endured serious ribbing from everyone they knew when the incident became public. The two couples stuck by their story, which became a national sensation through newspaper and magazine articles and, later, through several books, movies, and TV shows.

The couples did not feel quite so alone, however, when other people began reporting the same creature. A Charleston news reporter intending a word play on the popular comic and TV character Batman dubbed the winged thing Mothman, and the name was instantly picked up by the press and public alike. The sightings multiplied. Investigator and author John Keel claimed to have interviewed at least one hundred witnesses during the year following the TNT bunkers encounter. And people's descriptions remained remarkably consistent in their details, Keel noted in a 1990 edition of *Strange Magazine*.

"They always said the thing was taller than a large man—in other words he was maybe seven feet tall, and that it had fiery red eyes. Nobody was ever able to describe the face. The eyes dominated the face. The wingspan was always only about six feet wide. But they couldn't tell you whether it was covered with fur or feathers or scales or what.

It was just an awesome apparition—a big, dark, black thing with fiery red eyes. It was some kind of occult apparition. It was very selective in the people that it picked out. It picked out people who were about to die. And some of them did die during that period, on the bridge, and so on. It picked out attractive young women, for one thing."[1]

The Scarberrys and Mallettes did not come to any harm, however, and Keel's opinion that the creature was an occult apparition remains controversial. But forty-six area residents, some of them witnesses or relatives of witnesses, did die about one year later when the Silver Bridge, which crosses the Ohio River at Point Pleasant, collapsed on December 15, 1967. The accident, caused by the failure of a supporting I-bar pin, occurred around 5 p.m.—the worst possible time—as a full load of rush-hour vehicles all plunged helplessly into the icy river. The Mothman sightings slowed after that, but the legend lived on. John Keel wrote a best-selling book about the events called *The Mothman Prophecies*, which was made into the 2002 Richard Gere film of the same name.

Keel's first articles about the Mothman, however, appeared in the late 1960s in magazines and journals such as *The Flying Saucer Review*, and Keel later strengthened the Mothman-UFO link in other writings such as the September 2007 issue of *FATE* magazine, where he noted, "There had been countless UFO sightings up and down the Ohio River all year [in 1966]."[2]

Keel added in the *FATE* article, "The region was not only haunted by strange aerial lights, the homes of the witnesses were plagued with poltergeists and other supernatural phenomena. Television sets were burning out at an alarming rate. Telephones were going crazy, ringing at all hours of the day and night with no one on the other end. Some people were getting calls from mysterious strangers speaking a cryptic language."[3] More disturbing, mutilated dogs and farm animals began showing up about the same time as the UFOs, according to Keel.

Keel famously refers to these locations where multitudes of strange things occur, usually after being jump-started by the appearance of UFOs, as "window areas." In *The Complete Guide to Mysterious Beings*, Keel says, "Point Pleasant, West Virginia, is a typical 'window area.' There are hundreds of others throughout the United States, each marked by continuous UFO activity over long periods of time, bizarre monster sightings, and the mysterious comings and goings of unusual persons."[4] Keel added that he knew of other Mothman-like sightings as late as 1969 that went unreported by the press. Other investigators have noted that reports of similar creatures in the area surface now and then to this very day.

Mothman may even have had its own brush with celebrity. In an article on connections between UFOs and rock-and-roll stars published in *FATE* magazine in February 2006, writer Sean Casteel revealed an eerie story about legendary rock guitarist Jimi Hendrix. Casteel explained that the story came from a writer and bass player named Curtis Knight who had been a member of an early band Hendrix had played in, and who later wrote a book published in 1992 called *Jimi Hendrix: Star Child*.

The event took place during a heavy snowstorm in upstate New York—well before Hendrix's iconic 1969 performance at the Woodstock festival—after Hendrix and his band became stuck on the road on their way back to New York City after a minor engagement. The windows had frozen shut, Casteel said in the article, temperatures were dangerously cold, and the car had begun to fill with poisonous carbon monoxide. Two band members had already succumbed and were unconscious when Jimi peered through the falling snow to see a strange, cone-shaped craft descend to a nearby spot. A humanoid entity exited the craft, and Knight claimed Hendrix later described it as "kind of like a cross between a feathered creature, maybe like Mothman, and an angel."[5]

I would have loved a more complete description of the creature. Unfortunately, Hendrix died in 1970, long before the book was written, and he was no longer available to confirm, deny, or elaborate upon his former bandmate's story. Whatever the entity was—alien, angel, Mothman, or carbon monoxide–induced dream bird—it unfurled large wings as it circled the stranded vehicle, somehow melting the snow to free the stuck car and very likely saving the lives of all the band members. One can only wish that Point Pleasant's Mothman had been able to do as much for the people who died in the collapse of that town's doomed bridge.

HALL's BIGHOOT AND AWOL OWLS

Other researchers have taken a more pragmatic, if still theoretical, view of the Mothman phenomenon. Investigator Mark A. Hall's *Thunderbirds* suggests the sightings were due to an unknown or supposedly extinct species of gigantic owl—perhaps a larger variation of the great horned owl or a New World version of the European eagle owl. Hall brilliantly nicknamed this possible relict bird Bighoot.[6] His theory makes some sense; owls do glide silently at night and their large, round eyes will reflect red or a reddish orange as did Mothman's glaring peepers.

Hall backed up his idea by citing a known giant owl species, *Ornimegalonyx oteroi*, which lived in Cuba as recently as ten thousand years ago. This owl would have stood almost three and one half feet tall, with a correspondingly wide wingspan. Ornithologists believe, based on fossilized skeletal remains, that it could fly only short distances, rather like present-day wild turkeys. Animals continually defy the limits imposed upon them by human experts, however, so perhaps a few hardy individuals could have made it from Cuba to the mainland or vice versa, with (big stretch alert) the very toughest specimens managing to survive to the present day.

Perhaps we needn't reach so far into the past to find a culprit that comes closer to some descriptions of Mothman, however. European (or Eurasian) eagle owls, *Bubo bubo*, can and do escape from captivity. Although they are not native to North America, it's feasible to assume that one or more may have been smuggled here from Europe at some point. Consider what happened fairly recently in mid-April 2006, when Scotland went all atwitter over an eagle owl that escaped from its owner's yard tether just when it was probably ready to feed, since it had not eaten for several days.

"Lock Up Your Pets . . . Eagle Owl on the Loose," warned the headlines in the Wednesday, April 12 edition of *The Scotsman*.[7] The article went on to advise residents of West Lothian that eagle owls stand three feet tall and have wingspans of five feet. They are also armed with sharp four-inch talons.

"Eagle owls are capable of carrying away cats, dogs and other small pets," the article continued. "Earlier this year, an escaped eagle owl in Norfolk attacked five dogs over a fortnight before being captured. . . . Parents should be careful, as it is not an impossibility that it may swoop on small children and prams. . . . The bird is brown with a white chest and has prominent ear tufts and vivid orange eyes."[8]

Weirdly, the eagle owl also barks or growls if threatened!

The newspaper's warning was more than just precautionary—the owner told police this particular owl, named Fergus, had picked up a Staffordshire bull terrier—a breed similar to the pit bull and weighing between thirty and forty pounds—on a previous escapade.

Before we return to our comparison with Mothman, I feel it's worth a quick digression to show that European eagle owls are not rare as pets, either. More than two thousand of these fierce raptors were registered in Britain alone between 1998 and 2003, and since the article states that owners "usually" register their owls, we may assume there are probably some who do not register them, so there may be even more of these creatures in that country than authorities know.

Neither was the escape itself a rare event. The article quoted a spokesperson for the Scottish Society for the Prevention of Cruelty to Animals as saying there had been "quite a few" escaped European owls in the previous eighteen months. Add in all the other European countries with populations of these owls, and it's easy to imagine that at least a few have been brought to American shores.

Still, even the eagle owl fails to come close to the size and humanoid appearance of the creature reported by most Mothman eyewitnesses. Linda Scarberry provided more detailed observations in a handwritten report she made soon after the original incident. Her description sounds unlike the features of big owls or raptors. Here's a brief excerpt from that report, which was printed in its entirety along with many other original reports and newspaper clippings in *Mothman: The Facts Behind the Legend* by Donnie Sergent Jr. and Jeff Wamsley:

> "To me it just looks like a man with wings," wrote Scarberry. "It has a body shape form with (It was a dirty gray color.) wings on its back that come around it. It has muscular legs like a man and fiery-red eyes that glow when the lights hit it."[9]

And yet, reports from other parts of the country tell of encounters with equally mysterious creatures whose features do appear decidedly owlish. Was the Mothman one defined creature, a flock of various weird creatures that happened to be going to the same area, or perhaps a single, amorphous shape-shifter? As is usually the case when we attempt to examine unknown animals, we are left with unproved if tantalizing theories. The guessing game continues.

WASHINGTON BIGHOOT

At least one man has contacted me with what sounds like a possible 1999 sighting of one of these giant owls—in Spokane, Washington. The man worked the late shift as a nurse at a large retirement complex. One night, he stepped out for a break at about 3 a.m., and as he stood breathing the fresh air and scent of nearby ponderosa pines, he noticed loud owl hoots coming from the area of the trees. The hoots seemed to emanate from different positions, as if the owl were moving around or there was more than one owl vocalizing in the pines.

"Each time I would locate the place of the sound with my very powerful flashlight there was simply nothing there. Now it felt very creepy," the man wrote. "I heard it once again on top of the building behind me. I shone my flashlight at the sound and this time I did see a very large medium-to-dark-brown owl with a thick body standing on the edge of the building. . . . I estimate its body height at easily three and one-half feet tall. This thing was huge! It spread its wings fully—I am guessing its wingspan at six feet—and sailed off the building, out into the stands of trees about forty yards away, and disappeared into the darkness. I never saw or heard it land onto anything, and it never once flapped its wings. Maybe it was my imagination but it seemed to glide just a little bit slower than I would expect to sustain flight."

In light of John Keel's observation that the Point Pleasant creature appeared in tandem with strange lights and other manifestations, I need to mention that this eyewitness also saw a glowing orange "cloud" over a hilltop at the same location but on another date. The so-called cloud's shape was perfectly rectangular and unattached to the other cloud formations in the sky at the time, and it moved through the sky in a perfect semicircle before it passed directly over the man's head at a height he estimated between one hundred and two hundred feet.

Perhaps even more interesting is the actual location of these incidents: Spokane, Washington. Alert readers will recall that the earlier chapter on Batsquatches included a number of sightings of humanoid, bat-like creatures in that same state, near Tacoma and Mount Shasta. It's not inconceivable that a few of the Batsquatch sightings might also have been due to a stray European eagle owl. Or maybe all these large flying creatures are unique and different entities that simply love the same type of territory.

Although I'm willing to entertain theories that the creatures are from other times, dimensions, or worlds, I confess I'd prefer them all to be out-of-place, flesh-and-feather raptors. As frightening as a face-to-face encounter with an actual European eagle owl may be, such an incident still doesn't measure up to the terror of meeting truly unknown, human-sized figures with wingspans wide enough to cover the road, as so many witnesses have described.

I also don't think it likely that Hall's Bighoot could account for all of the many recorded sightings around Point Pleasant and the Ohio River Valley in the 1960s. But it could account for some, and a few historic legends indicate Hall may not have been far off the mark in blaming oversized owls for the Ohio River Valley hysteria. As Hall himself has pointed out, monstrous owls also figure prominently in the lore of East Coast Native Americans.

FLYING HEADS AND OWL PEOPLE

Scary, owl-like creatures in Native American legend suggest a long history of encounters between humans and these unknown flyers.

These occurrences would naturally have been considered important enough to keep tribal memories of the creatures alive in sacred lore. The legends include stories of both giant, man-like owls and, even scarier, of weird owl and human heads that could fly without bodies attached.

The human-like heads, according to folklorist William Elsey Connelly, originally sat on the shoulders of cave-dwelling giants who harassed and threatened to wipe out the Wyandot people of what are now the eastern American states. Eventually the Wyandot were able to cut off the giants' heads, which tenaciously reanimated into fearsome flying things whose bloody hair shone like lightning as it streamed around the big noggins. The heads liked to lurk in mist and fog, emerging furtively to steal children (perhaps with their teeth) and eat livestock, ruin crops, and cause sickness. Only fire and lightning could kill them.[10]

Some researchers have surmised that the legend of autonomous "heads" was caused by misperceptions of large owls that happened to be flying straight at an observer as their bodies trailed, hidden from sight behind their round, flat faces. Under the right conditions, the lined-up head and body made it appear that wings were attached to the sides of the creature's face. The wings may even have looked like hair when seen from the front.

Western Apache lore includes a character called Big Owl that the Apache believe was vanquished by tribal culture heroes, while the Seminole people of Oklahoma and the Southeast talk of humans who can shape-shift into great horned owls and are known as *stikini* or Man Owls! Once transformed, the *stikini* go searching for dinner— human hearts, which they drag out through their sleeping victims' mouths. The *stikini* may be stopped only by arrows that have been decorated with owl feathers and treated with certain herbs.[11]

The Pueblo of New Mexico are advised by ancient tradition not to whip their children. If they do, says the legend, Owl Boy, a youth who in ages past turned into a very large owl, may come and snatch their children away. Might this tradition be based on a long-standing memory of some giant, owl-like bird that actually did carry off an infant or young toddler, similar to the big bird incident in Lawndale, Illinois? If so, it seems all too likely that such a horrifying event would be remembered in some form of traditional lore.

THE CORNISH OWL MAN

The owl man is not a concept limited to the New World. Possibly the most famous example of this legendary creature is the Cornish Owl Man, a feathered beast spotted by several witnesses in 1976 and 1978 near the Mawnan Parish Church on Old Church Road in southern Cornwall, England, an area that is popular with tourists because of its nearness to the coast. I mention the Cornish Owl Man in this book about monsters of the Americas only because it is so similar to the American flying humanoids and therefore lends some interesting comparisons to cases like Point Pleasant's Mothman.

The legend of the Cornwall creature began when two young girls, twelve-year-old June Melling and her nine-year-old sister, Vicki, encountered the unthinkable in April 1976. The elder sister drew a sketch later published in a book titled *Creatures from Elsewhere: Weird Animals that No One Can Explain* that showed a mysterious beast with huge feathered wings, pointed ears, slanted eyes, and a roughly humanoid body with dangling legs below.[12]

Two fourteen-year-olds camping in woods near the church in July 1976 also claimed they had seen the giant "bird." The girls were preparing to go to sleep around 10 p.m. when they heard a loud hiss from the nearby woods. Looking anxiously for the source of the noise, they spied what they described as a man-sized owl standing in front of some nearby pines. It had glowing red eyes, gray feathers, and pointed ears, said the girls, and they both laughed, thinking someone was playing a trick on them. At that the creature rose straight up into the black night and as it ascended, the girls could see huge, black, pincher-like claws on its feet. The girls quit laughing. One of them, Barbara Perry, later drew a sketch with many similarities to June Melling's drawing. The descriptions by both sets of girls are strongly reminiscent of descriptions of Mothman, so much so that the most distinct difference between the Old World and New World humanoid flyers was that the British press never introduced the word "moth" in its articles on the Cornwall creature.

This owl-like man or man-like owl seemed particularly attracted to pairs of young girls. (Many Mothman witnesses were also youthful females.) On July 4, 1976, the day after the teen campers' sighting, two young sisters again seemed to be the creature's chosen witnesses. Jane Greenwood and her sister observed a bird-like creature the size of a full-grown man, with slanted crimson eyes, a huge mouth, gray feathers, and the same black, pincher-like claws drawn by Barbara Perry. It sailed away from the treetops as soon as the girls had taken a good look.

In June 1978, a sixteen-year-old girl spotted the creature swishing through trees in the area of the church, and in early August of that year, three young French girls witnessed "a great furry bird . . . with a gaping mouth and big round eyes."[13]

Could the European eagle owl be blamed for sightings of the monster known as the Cornish Owl Man? As we noted earlier, the eagle owl is large, but not as large as most humans. Its eyes are bright orange, and its talons are black. It also lacks the pointed head and the claws at the end of the wing tips. Still, it seems like the best natural candidate for those who believe that most monster sightings are misidentifications of known animals. This case has, however, an added oddity factor in that the sightings all occurred in the vicinity of the old church. When a strange creature is spotted near a sacred area time and again, speculations about supernatural connections are bound to occur. And Mawnan is definitely a sacred area.

The Mawnan Parish Church dates back to the year 1231, and according to its Web site was used as a place of worship of one kind or another since ancient times. According to the Web site, "The site of this church was already sacred since it is built within the confines of an ancient earthwork, which was still in an excellent state of preservation when the churchyard was enlarged in 1920. It is the situation of this church that is one of its most outstanding attractions. Situated high above [the] mouth of the Helford River, it is a navigational aid to vessels entering the river."[14]

The location on a high point of land and proximity to fresh running water are also characteristics of ancient, sacred spaces—and of hotspots for strange creature sightings, as well. Point Pleasant was located on a river, too, one whose history turned tragic.

As always, the implications can go two ways—toward a phenomenon beyond present scientific knowledge, or toward something that can be explained by known animals. Are these mysterious creatures manifestations of entities conjured in ancient times, emerging, perhaps, to draw on the special energies of these spots, or are they simply unusual but natural animals that need fresh water and prefer to hunt from high vantage points? This same dilemma can be applied when pondering the origins of many of the creatures in this book, and without a way to prove any of the alternatives, the answer must always be left for the reader to decide.

4

Untimely Pterosaurs

LINGERING WINGED THINGS

They're leathery, large, and long of beak, or (to put it mildly) living nightmares! Pterosaurs, whose name means "winged lizards," are also supposed to be extinct—they are thought to have died out sixty-five million years ago. That has not prevented people from seeing huge specimens of these flying reptiles that apparently still flap around now and then in modern times. Sightings are surprisingly widespread for an extinct species, with reports ranging from the most remote corners of Africa to populated areas of South Carolina. Of course, epic migration routes are only to be expected from a creature with a wingspan measuring in the dozens of feet! More baffling than their talent for globe-hopping, however, is their apparent migration through millions of years of time.

One of the largest pterosaurs was Quetzalcoatlus of the late Cretaceous period. It was a true monster in size with a wingspan of thirty to forty feet. The first known fossil specimen was discovered in 1971 by Douglas A. Lawson, who named it for the Mesoamerican sky god of wisdom, creation, and civilization arts, Quetzalcoatl. Ancient Aztec artists usually portrayed this deity as a giant feathered serpent.

That depiction of the ancient sky god actually may not be too far from the true appearance of the prehistoric flying reptiles we know about. While the pterosaurs have long been shown in reproductions as smooth-skinned or leathery, recent research has found that at least some of them had light feathers or hairy filaments that may have been brightly colored.[1] Many pterosaurs also sported large, bony head crests that pointed backward, and most varieties were also equipped with long, sharp beaks specially adapted for scooping up food. Pterosaurs were physically very distinct from birds and bats, and most scientists believe that they developed the ability to fly separately from the evolutionary path taken by birds.

Pterosaurs also came in a wide variety of shapes and sizes. Head crests might be striped, plain, shaped like sails or daggers, or absent entirely. Their beaks were adapted to diverse habitats; some were long and flat, some curved, and others sported an upright, paddle-shaped protuberance near the tips. Wingspans ranged from under a foot to dozens of feet in width.

The larger pterosaurs probably did not fly easily, however. Many experts believe Quetzalcoatlus probably needed either a cliff or a sloped runway to launch into wind currents to glide upon. While very few modern-day sightings describe creatures as large as Quetzalcoatlus, many witnesses have noted that the prehistoric-looking creatures they observed also seemed to have a difficult time getting airborne.

There are more things to consider in the question of whether prehistoric flying reptiles from millions of years ago might still exist. Practical difficulties of flight are one thing, but as we discussed earlier regarding the teratorns, a larger problem is how a breeding population of such humongous flying creatures could remain hidden in modern times. The question grows even more difficult considering that humans have lately dispatched astonishing numbers of mechanical flying things to whiz around the atmosphere of our planet—including ever-improving satellite technology. Wouldn't these giant air beasts be picked up by satellite or at least by radar? That could happen, say some investigators, but unless those reading the radar have been trained to interpret certain blips as prehistoric flying creatures, they probably wouldn't recognize such a signal if they saw one. Some active researchers offer other evidence they consider more viable.

Roving Ropen

Explorer Jonathan David Whitcomb has written two books about his decades-long search for the giant creatures called kongamato by Africans near the continent's center. He and some other researchers refer to them as ropen.[2] Whitcomb believes that there could be some small, very well-hidden populations of pterosaurs that managed to outlive the great dinosaur extinction event that killed off so many creatures of Earth's distant past. After gathering data from expeditions to Papua New Guinea, and remote corners of the United States taken by other

researchers and himself, he's convinced that not only do these creatures still exist but that some of them may also be endowed with a
natural ability to glow in the dark, a trait called bioluminescence. He
bases this conclusion on eyewitness accounts of great gliding birds
that were seen to emit their own light in the night sky.

Eyewitnesses included two American researchers, Garth Guess-
man and David Woetzel, who were on an investigatory trip to an island in Papua, New Guinea, in 2004 when Woetzel observed a strange
glowing object that flew between two nearby mountains. The globular
object appeared to be about one-fourth the size of the full moon and
did not resemble a meteor or any other known objects in the night sky.
Woetzel later published a scientific paper for the *Creation Research
Society Quarterly* describing the event.[3] And perhaps significantly, the
unusual flyby occurred near a village of indigenous people whose traditions included sightings of great, glowing, pterosaur-like birds.[4]

The TV shows *MonsterQuest* and *Destination Truth* also conducted
hunts for living pterosaurs in New Guinea in 2009 and 2007, respec-
tively, without conclusive results. An article in a *Smithsonian* magazine blog, *Dinosaur Tracking*, states that a flying creature caught on
video in New Guinea alleged to be a pterosaur "is definitely a frigate
bird (*Fregata minor*) based on the dark feathers and white patch on the
chest."[5]

These negative results from well-equipped investigations would
seem to increase the odds against any sighting of a huge prehistoric-
looking bird actually turning out to be a living pterosaur. What the
many witnesses describe, however, doesn't exactly resemble a frigate
bird, which is covered with brown feathers, is much smaller than a
pterosaur, and lacks the bony head crest and long beaks. Consider the
following example:

This alleged pterosaur encounter described by Whitcomb was reported by another witness and occurred near Winder, Georgia, in the northeast corner of the state in 2008. The female witness who wrote him about her experience said that she was on her way to work in Athens as she drove along a rural, wooded stretch of Highway 82 in late August of that year. The sun was up, and as she passed through a section of dense forest, something very large burst out of the woods and flew in front of her car across the road from right to left. It flew so low that she almost felt it was "dive-bombing" her car. Because it was not too far above her, she had a very good look at its profile from directly below.

Her description is that of a classic pterosaur with a hammer-shaped, crested head, a long tail, and large, flapping wings. Its color was solid beige, except for some darker brown bands on its abdomen. The long tail ended in what she described as a "heart-shaped pad." She immediately called a friend and exclaimed that she had seen a pterodactyl. He objected that what she saw was probably a great blue heron, but she insisted the dive-bombing creature didn't match any images of herons that she could find. About two weeks later, she saw another one on her way to work from about the length of a football field away and felt she had a better handle on its size this time since it was flying at about her eye level. She estimated that its length was probably equal to that of her car. She again noticed the bony crest and the very long tail and observed what she called a "scooping motion" of its wings.[6]

Her description again brings to mind those images from Hollywood films such as *Jurassic Park*. Interestingly, long tails like the ones she observed are associated with the earliest pterosaurs. That means the creature (or creatures) this Georgia woman saw may be even further "out of time" than the short-tailed or tailless species usually reported around the modern United States. It's also true that all of these bony, leathery creatures are more commonly spotted in the western states than they are east of the Mississippi.

TEXAS PTEROSAURS

Texas seems to be a favorite habitat for pterosaurs, where the wide-open spaces may allow them to soar with the equally giant stork-like birds. As we discussed earlier, the area near Brownsville and about thirty miles north of the Rio Grande experienced a rash of massive airborne creature sightings in the 1970s. While the birds all shared the common feature of abnormally large size, they differed in other important respects such as their beaks, tails, color, and skin—or feather—textures. The following house crasher, however, was no stork.

In January 1976, a mobile home owner near Brownsville claimed that a giant winged creature with bat-like rather than feathered wings smashed into his trailer. Researcher and author David Childress wrote about the incident in the online forum site Educate-Yourself:[7]

Alverico Guajardo had been relaxing inside his home at the time of the crash, and after hearing it, he naturally ran outside to see what might've caused the sound. There was no meteor, no downed tree, and no errant automobile—but there *was* some type of large animal that he could not identify. He fled to the safety of his car and used the headlights to try to get a better look at the creature. It was not dead. According to the article, the house crasher rose from the ground and fixed its bright red eyes upon Guajardo. Most of its body was obscured by long wings that it had wrapped around itself like a cape, and Guajardo watched it for several minutes until it finally backed away into the darkness and vanished.

The creature's truly weird appearance sounds not at all like the long-billed, stork-like Bigclaw.

Were two or more different types of giant winged things harassing South Texas in the 1970s? The creature that smashed Guajardo's mobile home sounds much more like a blast from the Cretaceous past then it does a giant stork.

In the same month, Childress's article reports, a human-sized, bat-winged creature was also seen near Brownsville by two women. Other eyewitnesses to this phenomenon in the area included three school-teachers driving south of San Antonio who saw a huge flying creature with a fifteen- to twenty-foot wingspan in February of that same year, 1976, and an ambulance technician who reported a giant, leathery-skinned flying creature that passed over him as he drove an emergency vehicle in the wee hours of the night one evening in 1982.

Pterosaur Tour

In a more recent sighting, a wrong-way driver arrested for crashing into a light pole two days after Christmas 2007 in Wenatchee, Washington, blamed a "pterodactyl" for the accident. This incident seems easier to dismiss than most eyewitness testimonies since the man's blood did test positive for a minimal amount of alcohol, according to an article in the *Daily Herald*.[8] He also had a lot to gain by coming up with a good excuse for driving the wrong way and crashing his car. In the driver's favor, however, is the fact that, as mentioned earlier, the state of Washington is renowned for sightings of large, bat-winged flying things. And the city of Wenatchee lies along the confluence of two rivers with the Cascade Range as a backdrop—a very typical sort of habitat for big "birds" of prey.

In May 2008, however, a daylight sighting by a sober, non-impaired driver that occurred in the eastern United States on Pennsylvania Route 43 was harder to explain away than the Wenatchee sighting. As reported by Stan Gordon in his "Unusual and Unexplained" column in a 2009 edition of *The Gate to Strange Phenomena*, the creature was so large that the driver assumed at first that it must be an airplane passing over his car.[9] Then he noticed that the wings were flapping in a way that no airplane wings could or should be able to do. The driver was able to pull onto the shoulder for a better look at the creature, which he estimated was cruising a good one hundred feet above the road. Its wingspan appeared to be at least twenty feet, and the wings were membranous, like those of a bat, rather than feathery like a bird's wings. The driver observed other automobiles pulling over, and he saw at least one person snap photos of the creature, although to Gordon's knowledge these images were never made public.

I recently received a vivid eyewitness report from Oregon, submitted by a man who saw three pterosaur-like birds as he was surfing near Brookings in early October 1986. He was riding the waves near the area's main jetty break, he wrote me in September 2013, and recalls that the air was so cold that the wetsuits he and his friends had left to dry atop their station wagon the previous evening were caked with ice by morning. Determined to practice their sport, they broke the ice off their suits and plunged into the ocean at dawn.

"A few hours later," he wrote, "a thick fog enveloped me. I was maybe ten yards out, in seven feet of water, and the surf was still in between sets. For maybe ten to fifteen minutes, the fog had about thirty feet visibility. By 8 a.m., the day turned partially cloudy and later, rainy, with little wind.

"I was six feet tall," he continued, "one hundred ninety pounds' solid muscle, and twenty-six years of age. I worked in car body shop prep. I was just sitting very still, waiting for waves to come, when out of nowhere, whammo! I was buffed off my board—not hit—by three of these things. They seemed intelligent and aware. They did not flap."

The birds were only about six feet off the water, so he had a rather good look at them and estimated that if the birds had been standing, they would have stood about six feet tall. Their wingspans, he said, appeared to be between sixteen and eighteen feet. They were light gray with "orange fins" on the backs of their heads, but he couldn't tell whether they were covered with smooth feathers, scales, or leathery skin as they glided away from him into the fog, heading north.

"I had strange feelings," he added, "and if I had been in one of these portals I have heard about in these days over the radio, I wouldn't doubt it. I was quite disturbed about it since; like not being able to figure out a puzzle."

He said that he resumed surfing and had one of the best sessions of his life. There were only a few others out on the waves that day and no one else mentioned seeing the huge birds, perhaps due to the fog. He painted a picture of them soon after the incident and permitted me to include it here.

Eyewitness art. *(Used with permission of the artist.)*

Of course, we can now only wish he'd been equipped with a waterproof camera. As with other mystery creatures, photographic evidence of relict pterosaurs has been scant. In one curious case so alternately affirmed and disputed that it looks like a classic example of "disinformation" (false evidence planted to confuse an issue), a number of people have claimed to have seen an historic photo of a dead pterosaur shot in Arizona. The trouble is that no one knows or remembers exactly where the photo was published, and none of the alleged sources have been able to verify any such thing in their archives.

The photo's original publication was supposedly alongside an article in the *Tombstone Epigraph* circa 1890 that detailed the shooting of a large flying reptile by two Arizona ranch hands. The photograph, according to those who claimed to have seen it, showed a line of men dressed in characteristic fashion of the old American West standing in front of a shed to which the giant bird had been nailed, its wings splayed open. But searches of old copies of the *Epigraph* failed to reveal the illustration. Some people claim to have seen the photo in some mid-twentieth-century issues of a men's sports magazine such as *Argosy* or *Field & Stream*, and still others have insisted they saw it displayed on a Canadian TV talk show. Several artistic re-creations of the photo exist, which only serve to muddy the already troubled waters. Unless and until real proof of the actual publication of the purported photo shows up, this incident will have to remain filed under "Curious but Confusing."

The list of flying things that get about on wings constructed with membranes rather than feathers continues to grow, however. Batsquatch, Mothman, and the relict pterosaurs seem to share that feature with a host of even stranger airborne terrors. We'll start our look at them with a short flight to the Garden State of New Jersey.

5

The Jersey Devil: Monster of the Pines

My toddler grandson has a mix-and-match animal puzzle with interchangeable pieces that allow him to assemble creatures never before seen on this natural earth. He can combine, for instance, the head of a horse with the body of a kangaroo, wings of a bat, and hind legs of an ostrich. And that would actually be a pretty good start at portraying the infamous monster of New Jersey known as the Jersey Devil.

Mark Sceurman and Mark Moran, authors of *Weird N.J.*, provide the definitive description of this potpourri creature that they've been documenting around their home state for decades: "The tracks resemble the claw prints of a strange bird or the footprints made by a two-legged creature. Actual sightings are less common but those who catch a glimpse describe a weird collection of animal parts: the body of a kangaroo, the head of a dog, the face of a horse, large leathery wings, antlers like a deer, a forked reptilian tail, and intimidating claws."[1]

This bizarre zoological wonder is often associated with a local legend said to date back to the 1700s. And centuries later, something like the creature described in that old legend is still being sighted—and on one occasion, fired upon by police—especially around a part of the state known as the Pine Barrens.

"The Barrens" is a seven-county stretch of dense tree canopy, blueberry farms, and cranberry bogs situated between the sprawling urban area around Philadelphia and the Atlantic Ocean. It supports a unique habitat specially adapted to its sandy soil, which sprouts carnivorous plants and rare species of pines with equal exuberance. And back in the year 1735, or so the story goes, the Pine Barrens also hatched a mystery.

That's when, says one of the many versions of the legend, an Atlantic County woman named Deborah (or Jane) Leeds discovered she was with child. This baby would be the family's thirteenth, a number associated with ill omens. A family head count of thirteen children wasn't unusual in those days before birth control, but the Leeds family could barely feed the children they already had. Deborah allegedly cursed her unborn child for the extra burdens it would bring.

Curses are seldom without consequence in any legend, and when Deborah's due date arrived, the family was shocked to see their new little family member transform itself into a hideous, murdering demon. It sprouted horns and then immediately massacred the entire family. With the bloody deed accomplished, it ran howling into the Pine Barrens, where it hid for almost two centuries. Locals heard its unearthly screeches as it made occasional forays into inhabited areas to steal livestock or terrify unwary travelers. They called it the Phantom of the Pines, and it remained largely unknown outside its rural habitat—until something rousted it from its lair in 1909.

That's when the creature went to town, literally, as it showed up in at least thirty different New Jersey communities in mid-January of that year. When it ventured into Haddon Heights, all the passengers on a city trolley witnessed the creature, which they said looked much like a kangaroo with wings. Pets and farm animals began to go missing in various spots around the southern half of the state, and the depredations were blamed on the creature now known as the Jersey Devil.

Panic set in and authorities made serious attempts to deal with the creature. Although extremely elusive, it did leave footprints on the ground—and on snowy rooftops—that looked like they were made by large hooves. Police hunted the unknown beast with bloodhounds to no avail. In Camden, it lingered long enough that it was seen by both a civilian group of eyewitnesses and a police officer who observed the thing drinking from his horse trough. He fired at it but the creature disappeared unharmed and came back several days later. It was also fired upon in Bristol, Pennsylvania, and hosed with pressurized water by Collingswood firefighters in equally unsuccessful attempts to kill or capture it.

The creature seemed to settle back into its Pine Barrens home with only sporadic sightings after its wild spree of 1909, but area residents say it did not go away and remains at large, even in the present day. Although its description has changed little since 1909, modern depictions of the creature, which has become a popular sports mascot and commercial cartoon figure, may or may not include its original horns. In one 1993 sighting the creature was missing a few more things, as well. Cryptozoologist Loren Coleman documented the remarkable incident reported by a highly credible, off-duty summer park ranger in a 1995 issue of *Fortean Times*.[2]

The ranger, John Irwin, was returning from a date in a nearby community one evening as he drove through Wharton State Forest in a desolate area along the Mullica River when he almost ran head-on into the sight of a lifetime. Irwin was sufficiently impressed that he filed an official account with the park ranger's office. His supervisor, Peter Gentile, related some of that report for the magazine article:

But up ahead, in the long shadows cast by his headlights, he noticed a large, dark figure emerge from the woods and move into the roadway. John, an experienced Park Service seasonal patrol man, thought the figure was a deer and slowed to let it across but as he got closer . . . the creature defiantly blocked the roadway. John had to stop his car to avoid hitting it.[3]

John said that whatever the creature may have been, it was like no deer he had ever seen. It stood fully upright and was covered in dark, matted fur with a shiny, wet look to it. He estimated its height at about six feet tall. It did have a deer-like head, which John saw clearly when the creature turned to stare at him with eyes that glowed red. As a park ranger familiar with wildlife, he knew immediately that this intense red color did not match the usual bright, whitish-yellow shine of a deer's reflective eye membranes.

After a few very long moments, the creature turned and walked into the brush on the opposite side of the road on its hind legs, in a manner that John described as robotic. The creature appeared to be missing its forelimbs, said John, and he also did not see the bat-like wings described by 1909 Jersey Devil witnesses. Could it have been a deformed deer? A sketch John drew of the creature indicates that while it may have been deformed, it wasn't a deer. The sketch showed short pointed ears positioned on the sides of the creature's head rather than the large upright ears that are almost always a deer's trademark. And although he portrayed the animal as walking on hooves, its legs are strangely bent and far larger and more muscular than those of a deer.

Investigator Lon Strickler addressed the question of why sightings of the creature have tapered off in a column on his Web site, Phantoms and Monsters. "There is a stigma attached to the Jersey devil," he said. "People are wary of reporting sightings of this creature (though I think it may be more supernatural than flesh and blood). I'm not sure if the reluctance is because of the fear of ridicule or that the legend has some ominous bearing to it."[4] Those are the same reasons that make people reluctant to report sightings of anomalous creatures everywhere. But perhaps there have been sightings of the same creature in other places where it is known by different names.

As unusual as the anatomy of the Jersey Devil may sound, and despite its legendary origins, there are other mythic beasts around the Americas alleged to sport the same kangaroo-like form, bat-style wings, and proclivity for slaughtering domesticated animals. The aforementioned Batsquatch of Tacoma and other points north immediately springs to mind. But there is another creature reported from Puerto Rico throughout Central America and the southwestern United States that we've already mentioned—el chupacabras—"it sucks goats" or "the goat sucker." Generally observed in places with a heritage of the Spanish language, it's known for its alleged habit of drinking the blood of its prey.

One pair of Tucson reporters had no trouble recognizing the chupa's similarity to the Wharton State Forest Jersey Devil reported by park ranger John Irwin in 1993. Gregory McNamee and Luis Urrea wrote a piece called "Hell Monkeys from Beyond: Chupacabras Comes to the Sonoran Desert!" for the Tucson Weekly in May 1996.[5] Their lengthy article included an account of Irwin's sighting but made it clear that something just as mysterious as the Jersey Devil was either afoot—or perhaps aflight—in their own neighborhood nearly a continent's breadth away from New Jersey, as we'll explore in the next chapter.

6

Challenge of the *Chupacabras*

HELL MONKEYS FROM BEYOND

"Hell Monkeys from Beyond," read the tongue-in-cheek, lurid head-lines in the May 30 edition of the *Tucson Weekly*. "A monster is wing-ing its way over Tucson. It's out there, prowling the night sky, ready to strike without warning."[1] That monster was, of course, the cheeky *chupacabras* I've alluded to several times now, and which we'll finally discuss in more detail.

Descriptions of the Arizona goat sucker evoked a creature that sounded as much of a patchwork mix as the Jersey Devil: part vampire bat, part kangaroo with "a hint of armadillo thrown in for good measure."²

Whatever it was, it had evidently been lurking around Tucson for some time. A local businessman told the reporters that he remembered stories of a creature called the goat sucker when he was a teenager in the 1950s. Described as something like a giant kangaroo rat, the creature was said to creep northward from Nogales after dark to attack anyone so foolish as to be out wandering the desert alone. This man did not claim to have seen the creature, but another Tucson resident, Joe Urrea (perhaps related to one of the two writers?), said that he did encounter it once in the 1950s. He was a youngster at the time and remembers being outside his home, in the yard, when the outhouse door suddenly opened to reveal something that looked like a very large kangaroo. It stared at him and, creepily, seemed to be urging him to come closer. Joe wisely ran in the opposite direction of the outhouse.

The article then went off on a slight kangaroo tangent, as it discussed another 'roo-like creature with a thirst for blood that made headlines in rural Tennessee in 1934. The small community of Hamburg near South Pittsburgh in Marion County was terrorized, according to newspapers, by a large, fast-moving animal that killed and devoured domestic fowl and German shepherd police dogs with equal gusto. A local minister caught a glimpse of the beast as it ran and leaped across a field and declared that its motion looked like that of a kangaroo, an animal that is certainly not part of the normal fauna of rural Tennessee.

Hunting parties began to track it, and near the end of January authorities announced that they had shot not a marsupial, but a very large lynx. Since great cats do have the ability to leap and bound, the original killer kangaroo was declared a case of mistaken identity.

There is no doubt that the lynx was ferocious. According to an article in the *New York Times*, even after the lynx was filled with buckshot, it managed to kill one of the tracking hounds on its way down from the tree where it had been hiding.[3]

Although the attacks on dogs and livestock ended, there is no real proof that people were really seeing a lynx rather than some kangaroo-like creature bounding around the Tennessee hills. It may even have been an actual kangaroo; out-of-place 'roos have been spotted all around the United States. While some are undoubtedly escapees from public or private zoos, kangaroos on the lam are usually not claimed by any known collections. But although their origins are seldom explained, they are occasionally captured. Two different animals were caught in Wisconsin alone in 2005. One, actually a wallaby, was killed, and the other was taken to the Henry Vilas Zoo in Madison, where it became a popular exhibit.[4]

I am not suggesting, however, that sightings of the *chupacabras* or the Jersey Devil may be explained by out-of-place kangaroos. Kangaroos generally lack bat-like wings, and their occasional odd appearances do not cause corresponding waves of *chupacabras* sightings. I will admit that Wisconsin's lone Batsquatch showed up on the same side of the state as the two captured 'roos, but the misplaced marsupials were both already out of the picture in the year previous to the La Crosse Man Bat encounter.

RAVAGING PUERTO RICO

But now I've gone off on my own kangaroo tangent, which may be worthwhile since comparisons to the Aussie hoppers keep cropping up in regard to bat-winged flying things. The iconic and unmistakable physical form of the kangaroo was often cited in the original *chupacabras* descriptions that began in Puerto Rico in the last quarter of the twentieth century, first in the mid-1970s and again in 1995.

The monster responsible for the initial flap was called the Moca Vampire for the Puerto Rican town of Moca, where sightings began. In February 1975, farmers began discovering dead cattle, goats, chickens, and other animals that had been totally exsanguinated, or drained of blood. Investigator Scott Corrales wrote in a 2010 issue of online magazine *Inexplicata* that the cows, for example "were found dead with strange puncture marks on their hides, indicating that some sharp object—natural or artificial—had been inserted into the hapless bovines. Autopsy reports invariably showed that not a single drop of blood remained within the animals, as if it had been consumed by some predator."[5]

No one could figure out what predator to blame. Rumors began to circulate about some type of vampire, since any normal predator would presumably devour at least some of the flesh. All that this creature seemed to want was blood—and certain small bones and body parts that were carefully excised through tiny, almost surgical holes made in various body parts as described. Authorities suggested everything from a native snake to some kind of spirit bird, but none of their explanations fit the eyewitness descriptions—which varied from a feathery creature to something with a round head, big eyes, and hairy tail—or the unusual forensic evidence found in the weird wounds and drained bodies. There were also many remarkable sightings of a variety of UFOs throughout Puerto Rico during the whole period of animal attacks. In the meantime, the elusive predator continued to prowl. The animals it killed numbered in the hundreds by the end of August of that year, after which the creature seemed to disappear.

Two decades passed, and then similar attacks began anew. By the spring of 1995, the animal carnage near the towns of Orocovis and Morovis had grown to unacceptable proportions. As vampiric live-stock killings increased, so did the anxiety of area residents. But by summer's end, the culprit finally showed itself to several eyewitnesses.

Those expecting a massive beast were disappointed, since it stood only about four to five feet tall. But what it lacked in stature it made up in ferocity and weirdness. Most witness descriptions included the kangaroo-like body topped by a rounded, oversized head, with either a cat-like or reptilian face. It walked upright but sometimes featured the same bat-like wings as so many of the other big flying things we've discussed, plus the usual long claws required of any decent monster. Eyewitnesses also said the creature had a pair of long, tubular fangs suitable for puncturing the necks of prey, accented by a row of spikes along the spine.

One of the original Puerto Rican witnesses, Madelyne Tolentino of Canovanas, said she saw the creature at 4 p.m. one day in August 1995, through a glass window as it walked down a narrow street toward her mother's house. She gave an interview about her sighting to members of a local research group the following March, less than a year after the incident. Author Scott Corrales quoted much of the interview in *Chu-pacabras and Other Mysteries*, and Tolentino's description sounds like something truly out of this world. In addition to the characteristics detailed in the preceding paragraph, Tolentino said that its eyes "ap-peared dark gray or black. . . . They were damp and protruding, run-ning up to its temples, and spreading to the sides." She added that "it was walking like a human, on both legs. Its arms were drawn back into an 'attack position,' as though it were a [TV] monster."[6]

She also said that it had three long fingers and three webbed toes, and that its hair was "rather short, and close to its body. Rather well-combed, in fact."[7] She could also see purplish-pink skin in a small area where the fur had worn away and said she checked for visible genitals but saw none. It did have structures on its back that she thought were feathers, but which another witness said looked more like defensive spikes as he later tried to grab the creature. Tolentino said the short beast ran away after she finally screamed.

The fact that its description had become widely known through all types of media didn't seem to bother the creature as it continued to ravage the countryside. At least 150 animals of different types were killed in one town alone in its never-ending quest for the blood of goats and other domesticated animals.

Reports from credible witnesses kept coming over the next decade. In 2004, the creature showed up in Chile on a back road between Santiago and La Serena. The family of Roberto Ayar, a district prosecutor, was on their way home from a vacation when they took a wrong turn into *Chupacabras*ville. On a desolate back road at just about dawn, a strange bipedal creature suddenly appeared in the middle of the road right before the astonished husband and wife, as their daughter slept in the backseat. Scott Corrales translated the attorney's reaction (as told to *La Cuarta* newspaper) for the July 2004 issue of *FATE* magazine:

"I swear to you that I'd never seen anything like it," said Ayar. "It wasn't a dog, rabbit, or any other known animal. . . . It was completely covered in hair and had red eyes. It was bent and had a hump on its back. It had the body of a kangaroo. . . ."[8]

The creature had small hands rather than paws and made quick movements with them as it stared at the family with its red eyes. The attorney described its fangs as being like "two tubes, one stuck to the other." It reminded the family of a lizard as it walked away on its hind legs, and they concluded that it must be supernatural. It did fit the general description of the goat sucker pretty closely, even if it was not caught red-fanged.

THE TEXAS BLUE DOGS MYSTERY

As famous as the creature had become, proof of its existence failed to surface in all but one of the countries where citizens claimed goat sucker invasions. The sole presentation of evidence that the *chupacabras* was a real animal, claims author Alan Brown in his book *Haunted Texas*, may have turned up in South Texas in August 2007. As you'll discover, the animal Brown indicated and that we're about to discuss does not really belong in a chapter on flying creatures. It has no wings. I've decided to put it here, however, because it has been so closely tied to the term *chupacabras*, in both print media and a variety of investigative TV shows, that I think it needs to be examined in that light.

"A few people claimed to have seen the monster over the years," wrote Brown, "but no carcass of the *Chupacabra* [*sic*] was ever found until August 2007."[9] That discovery, whether it was actually a *chupacabras* or not, was preceded by what looked like goat sucker activity in 2005 when Cuero rancher Phylis Canion began finding her chickens lying dead with no visible blood in or around them. Similar fates were befalling other animals in the neighborhood. Friends told her the culprit must be a goat sucker, but Canion had never heard of the *chupacabras* at that time and dismissed that idea as superstition.

Two years and twenty-six dead chickens later, she had reason to think twice about that claim when she found a canine-like creature dead on the highway near her house. Its hairless skin was a bluish color, and its big ears and fangs lent it a creature-from-elsewhere look. The beastie lacked bat wings, though, as well as spikes. It was also smaller

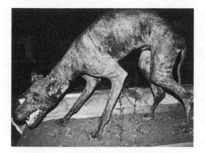

Photo of mounted specimen of the canine creatures found near Dr. Phylis Canion's Texas ranch. *(Submitted by and used with permission of Dr. Canion.)*

than most previous eyewitness descriptions of *chupacabras*. Canion prudently preserved its head in her garage freezer for future testing. And lacking a better name for the creature, she called it a *chupacabras* and even sold T-shirts from her Web site, www.cuerochupacabra.com.

One of these creatures would have been weird enough, but Canion and her neighbors discovered three more of the bluish, hairless animals dead in different areas near her ranch. Texas Parks and Wildlife biologist Ryan Schoeneberg examined one and declared it a dead coyote that had suffered from sarcoptic mange, a disease that causes acute hair loss.

Canion, a medical professional who lived and hunted in Africa for four years and whose home is filled with mounted specimens of various game animals, disagreed. As she said to me in a phone interview for this book, "Animals with mange will have some evidence of hair, with large bald patches that become irritated from the animal scratching at them. These creatures were covered in light fuzz, no hair, no mange, with skin more similar to an elephant's."

She added, "An animal with very bad mange is a sick animal that's unlikely to survive for very long, and I watched one run around my ranch for two years."

The carcasses bore other oddities, as well: blue eyes, odd nodules on each side of the tail that were solid and very unlike a normal dog's anal glands, and only two nipples on each side of the chest. The nipples were not attached to any mammary glands. Their forelimbs were shorter than their hind legs, and their skull case was wide like a wolf's but with a smaller muzzle more like a coyote's.

All of this began to pique Canion's scientific curiosity. A certified nutritional consultant with a master's degree in nutrition and a bachelor's degree in psychology, she had DNA tests done at five different universities, and in every case the results showed an unknown species with both maternal coyote genes and paternal Mexican wolf heritage. Some people still suggested to Canion that the creatures were feral specimens of the Mexican hairless dog also known as a Xolo, short for Xoloitzcuintle.

An article on Mongabay.com interviewed an unidentified "top dog breeder" who said, "The dog looks like it has Xolo genetics. This is not a chupacabra [*sic*]—that's absurd."[10] The breeder added that the animal's head had the right skull for a Xolo as well as hairless skin. The DNA tests did not show Xolo genes, however, and as Canion told me, "You can't refute what the DNA says." She has begun to refer to the creatures as Texas blue dogs, to denote their unique nature.

But what about those bloodless chickens? Could the bluish, naked canines have been responsible? If so, that would imply there were two very different types of large, land-based, blood-sucking predators in the southern and central areas of the Americas.

I asked Canion how the canine creatures could suck an animal dry of blood so immaculately without using a specialized structure like the purported hollow fang of the *chupacabras*. She suggested that like vampire bats, the blue dogs might have made puncture wounds and then licked the blood that flowed out, perhaps in response to a medical condition called pica, when animals ingest things they wouldn't normally eat in order to satisfy a mineral deficiency. In this case, they craved chicken blood. But bat saliva contains anticoagulants that keep the victim's blood flowing, and the blue dogs wouldn't have had that advantage. It's also hard to understand why they wouldn't simply have eaten the chickens.

While other so-called *chupacabras* reported around the United States and other countries since that time actually have been shown to be foxes, coyotes, or raccoons with severe hair loss caused by infestation with mange mites and varying degrees of decomposition, Canion's Texas blue dogs are unique.

My own, extra-unofficial layman's theory is this: Sometime around 2004 near Cuero, Texas, a male Mexican wolf macked on a female coyote, which then bore a really strange litter of pups that looked a lot like Xolos but whose genetic profiles matched those of their parents, the coyote and the wolf. The Xolo is a very old breed thought to have arrived in the Americas during pre-Columbian times with the ancestors of the Aztecs. Interestingly, its hairlessness arose through natural mutation rather than human selection, and according to the online resource center for hairless canines, K9Gems, "hairlessness is one of the most common spontaneous mutations, occurring in every known mammalian species."[11]

The Web page continues, "The first Xolo obviously survived and thrived to reproduce the trait on a wide scale, a rare occurrence for mutations—favorable or otherwise. The Xolo's defining trait must have provided an adaptive advantage, possibly increased resistance to fleas and ticks, and higher tolerance for heat. Because it was a dominant trait it likely spread through Western Mexico's dog population like wildfire."

The site also notes that archaeological evidence suggests that the hairless trait arose 3,700 years ago in western Mexico. If canid hairlessness arose spontaneously once, why couldn't it do so again? Perhaps the Texas blue dogs are really a brand-new breed—all over again!

Many people have written off the original *chupacabras* as complete myth or hoax due to this confusion with naked canines and decomposed raccoons. In my opinion, these misleading cases do not necessarily mean that the Puerto Rican sightings (and some that continue in Central and South America, Mexico, and the southwestern United States) also had to be canines with mange or odd genetic traits. In my opinion, the original *chupacabras* is a genuinely mysterious phenomenon whose name was unfortunately co-opted to explain puzzling creatures in other places.

With this in mind, I asked Phylis Canion whether instead of calling the hairless canids found near her ranch goat suckers, a more accurate moniker might be chicken lickers. All in good humor, she agreed. In Spanish, the new name would be *lame pollos*, which I'll shorten to *el lamepollos*. True, the Chicken Licker definitely inspires less terror than the Goat Sucker, but those naked blue *lamepollos* still pose their own mystery.

Dragons and the American Gargoyle

While it seems really unlikely that so many hideous, membrane-winged creatures could be flitting around the Americas, drinking the blood of farm animals and instilling fear in the general populace, there is one mythic creature that could serve as a sort of catch-all description—although probably not an explanation—for all the beasts we've been discussing: gargoyles.

Gauging the Gargoyle

Gargoyles, strictly speaking, are not living creatures at all, but fancifully carved waterspouts designed to direct rainwater away from the walls of medieval cathedrals and other important buildings. While most of them were intentionally grotesque, bizarre, or even obscene, they portrayed natural animals and humans as well as mythical entities whose more spiritual purpose was to keep harmful spirits outside of buildings along with the rainwater. The rationale of using the likenesses of evil beings to protect a sacred cathedral from harmful spirits might sound counterintuitive, but one could think of it as fighting fire with fire.

While gargoyles varied widely in appearance and could be sculpted to look like almost any imaginable entity, an entry by Chiara Piccinini in the book *Medieval Folklore* notes, *"Hybrid animal types are especially common: creatures constructed of parts of different animals* [emphasis mine], like the 13th-century bird with four legs on Burgos Cathedral, Spain. . . . Particularly common are four-legged animals equipped to fly: cows . . . dogs . . . fish . . . lions. . . . All appear with wings. According to some interpretations, these composite creatures have an overtly negative, if not a precisely diabolical, significance, representing confusion and disharmony."[1]

Flying four-legged creatures made of parts of different animals would describe many of our bat-winged creatures. "Overtly negative" might well sum up the impression many witnesses had of them, and the Mothman, Jersey Devil, La Crosse Man Bat, and *chupacabras* have certainly all sown their share of confusion. I think that "American gargoyles" would be a good and useful term for all of these creatures of North and South America—it gives them a general category of their own while allowing for varying characteristics.

Medieval gargoyles, like all these flying creatures, are also often linked with the dark side of the supernatural, seeming to both warn against evil events and foster them. One eyewitness in a very recent North American sighting said she felt that same sense of ambiguity as she was torn between abject terror and fascination.

THE TOMAH GARGOYLE

Lori Liddell, a resident of the Tomah, Wisconsin, area, described a creature with the same characteristic kangaroo body shape discussed in the previous chapter, in a report about a sighting she witnessed that she sent me on May 8, 2013, only an hour after the incident occurred. She wrote,

About 9:40 p.m. tonight, I heard my dog barking outside like he was scared, so I put my glasses on and opened up the door and there was a creature that looked very similar to a kangaroo about four and one-half feet tall standing on the other side of my car, about twenty-five feet away from my dog. When I opened the door, it turned its head toward me, really creepy, and had this weird yellow eye shine. . . . . I saw the upper body, smaller arms sticking out in front, upper torso, later, brown-colored fur, like deer brown during the heat of summer. It had a bony-looking head, kangaroo-like ears and a thinner neck than I would expect. It was not a deer, dog, goat, anything I can think of, and I don't think it was a kangaroo, either. It was unnatural, like it could be an alien as much as it could be a kangaroo. Very creepy. I looked at it for a minute and decided I needed a flashlight. A minute later when I returned, it was gone. This was in my yard.

Living in the country as she does, Lori said that she had seen many other creatures—raccoons, possums, and deer—whose eyes were illuminated by her yellow porch light, but that none of them displayed that "creepy" yellow color of this creature's eyes.

Lori added that the creature was thin, weighing only between ninety and one hundred pounds at most, and that its head did not look like that of a canine. She kept coming back to its eyes, which she said were not only an unnaturally intense yellow but were "slanted" in shape rather than rounded like those of a deer or most other animals. She couldn't see its back or feet from her position on the porch, and she was not inclined to cross the yard to go closer to where it had stood at the edge of the road.

"It was definitely on two feet," she told me the next day in a phone interview. She did have a good look at the animal's forelimbs, which she said were very skinny, short, and "puny" and were held out in front of it so that she could make out claws on the ends of its paws. After the creature disappeared from view, she summoned her roommate to the scene and the two of them went to look at the roadside area where the creature had stood, examining the ground by flashlight in hopes of finding tracks. The spot was soft and muddy, and yet there were no tracks of any kind. It's possible that the creature had actually been standing on the road surface rather than the shoulder—or perhaps it had wings! Since she didn't see it from the back and the road behind it was dark, we'll never know.

Tomah does lie on the western side of the state, the same side in which the two out-of-place kangaroos described earlier were seen. Could there be some secret kangaroo ranch in western rural Wisconsin with very poor security? Or is this creature representative of something else that has been around for a longer time? There's a Ho-Chunk community known as Blue Wing very near Liddell's residence, and she said that members of that community have told her that a spirit creature they call the goatman appears in the area from time to time. She had the impression that it was not considered a benign entity. If this was what Lori saw, it would go a long way toward explaining her impression that the creature was "creepy" as well as its very strange eyes. It would also place it very squarely in my category of American gargoyles.

THE VAN METER VISITOR

It's true that most people don't think of the Midwestern United States as a mecca for kangaroo-bodied, flying gargoyles. But a trio of investigators have uncovered a little-known chapter in cryptid history that may just change the way people look at one of those states. Chad Lewis, Noah Voss, and Kevin Nelson wrote *The Van Meter Visitor* to chronicle three days of mystifying terror when something not quite human paid a visit on the quiet village of Van Meter, Iowa, in the early 1900s.

The little town with a current population of just over one thousand souls received a truly rude awakening in the autumn of 1903, when they discovered something huge and bat-like had crept out of an old abandoned mine shaft and headed—where else?—downtown. The first hint of weirdness came in the wee hours of September 29 when Ulysses Griffith, a local tool and farm implement salesman returning from a business trip, witnessed a strange unidentifiable light hop from rooftop to rooftop over the town's business area at about 1 a.m. He had no way to investigate at that time and was tired, so he continued home and went to bed.

The next evening at about the same time, the town physician—a Dr. Alcott—awoke to some bright light shining into his darkened bedroom. The good doctor grabbed a firearm and went out to confront what he probably supposed was a burglar. Instead, he was met with the strange form and horrific glare of the classic American gargoyle.

Lewis, Voss, and Nelson described the creature that stared back at the doctor as "half human and half animal," with large, membranous wings and a blunted horn growing out of its forehead. The doctor pumped five bullets into it, but although he fired at fairly close range, the monster seemed unaffected.

The monster was as consistent as it was invincible. It appeared yet a third night, on October 1, at its preferred witching hour of 1 a.m., to a bank cashier named Clarence Dunn. He had headed to the bank to make sure the supposed "burglar" that had been lurking about the town left his place of employment alone. He was sitting inside, armed with a shotgun, when he heard a strange wheezing noise and then saw the telltale bright light beaming through the front window of the bank. He could make out a huge shadowy figure looming just outside, and he shot it right through the windowpane. When he ran to look, though, there was no dead creature lying outside, just a very large, three-toed print in the dirt.

The creature woke up another businessman who had fallen asleep as he guarded his store from his second-story apartment. He fired upon the dark shape he saw sitting on a wooden telephone pole on the street below, and like the banker, believed that he had hit it. Instead, the creature trained its eerie light straight at him and used its large, hooked beak to help it shinny down the pole to the ground, where yet another startled citizen witnessed it standing erect, the light still beaming from its forehead. This man estimated its height at eight feet. The creature then took off, leaping like a kangaroo, according to the last witness, while flapping its wings as if trying to take flight. It may have been scared away from the business area by a train that rumbled into the station just at that time. At any rate, the creature headed straight into an old, nearby mine shaft.

The monster apparently stayed in its underground sanctuary until 1 a.m. on the morning of October 3. A group of men working a late-night factory shift in that vicinity heard strange sounds coming from the mine shaft and then saw not one but *two* of the creatures exit the shaft, their lights ablaze. The pair, one of them slightly smaller than the other, took wing and sailed off into the moonlit night.

The sight galvanized the factory shift eyewitnesses as the whole town of Van Meter woke up and turned up their electric lights. In no time an armed posse organized and stationed itself at the mine shaft to wait for the creatures' return. And return they did, at about 5:45 that morning, right about sunrise. As the pair of gargoyles came closer, the men all took aim and fired, but the only response of the creatures was to release a "putrid" odor that had also been smelled by one of the downtown businessmen. The creatures flew back into the mine shaft after apparently avoiding the hail of bullets and were never seen again.[2]

This story brings to mind not just other bat-winged creatures but cryptids that usually go wingless, as well. The foul odor is a common feature of encounters with Bigfoot or Sasquatch, and the inability to be downed by gunfire reminds me of many incidents involving Bigfoot and werewolf-like creatures.

But what of the strange "horns" that emitted bright light in an era when electricity was still considered a newfangled invention? It seems a little different from the bioluminescence displayed by the ropen of New Guinea that Jonathan David Whitcomb described in his book. The Van Meter creature's lights sound almost like headlamps worn by modern miners, although I rather doubt the men who once worked in a mine already long abandoned by 1903 had such equipment.

Since the creatures left no evidence other than a plaster cast someone made of the three-toed footprint, some have asked whether the whole thing was a hoax. Chad Lewis told a reporter for the United Kingdom's *Daily Mail* that after years of investigation and many visits to the town, he didn't think so. "Lewis says he has found no evidence to suggest the monster was a hoax," said the paper, "although he believes the facts of the story may have been embellished over the years."[3]

The Van Meter Visitor explores a range of possible explanations for this truly weird pair of creatures, covering everything from misidentified natural animals to extraterrestrials. Why such an out-of-the-way little town along the Raccoon River in Iowa should have been chosen for their stopping point is just as mysterious as the migration route of any North or South American gargoyle—whether by way of Point Pleasant, West Virginia, or rural Chile—or for that matter, of any unknown cryptid.

And if kangaroo-bodied beasties can grow horns and fly, why couldn't other sorts of creatures as well? Simply add scales and you have something that closely resembles a better-known fabulous beast: the dragon. And after all of the flying creatures we've explored in the previous chapters, it should not be surprising that I've heard from eye-witnesses who say that dragons indeed exist in modern times.

DRAGONS AND SKY SERPENTS

Dragons—serpent-like, flying reptilians usually of giant size and some-times breathing fire—are another of those mythic animals known to every culture through antiquity. Some, such as Chinese dragon deities, are mostly benevolent, while others, like those in the medieval fairy tales of Western culture, are often destructive treasure hoarders that must be slain by the hero: in other words, true monsters.

"Sky snakes" are no strangers to the Americas, either, and appear to have beaten European settlers to these shores. Pioneers of Nebraska reported a scaled "flying serpent" twisting and flashing fire through the clouds over the Missouri River from 1857 through 1858,[4] and a Bonham, Texas, farmer named Hardin and several field workers said that in June 1873, they spotted what they all described as an "enor-mous serpent" in the sky.[5] They said that the yellow-striped creature was about the same length and width as a telephone pole and that it undulated toward the eastern sky using much the same type of move-ment as would an ordinary snake.

On November 29, 1883, someone reported in a letter to the Frederick, Maryland, periodical, *The News*, that while standing atop a rise on Jefferson Road in Maryland's Catoctin Mountains in the early morning, he saw what he called a "monstrous dragon" diving about in the sky above him. He said it had "glaring eye-balls, and mouth wide open displaying a tongue, which hung like a flame of fire from its jaws . . ."[6]

Many reports similar to these three can be found in newspapers of the 1800s and early 1900s. Some may have been intended as jokes, but not all are easy to explain away. And while sightings of things people tag as dragons aren't as common in these days of modern aviation—perhaps partly due to a greater tendency to see most aerial anomalies as UFOs—I do receive reports now and then in which eyewitnesses use the "D" word. One of the most striking came from near Wisconsin's most cherished area of "frozen tundra."

DRAGONS OF OCONTO FALLS

Green Bay, Wisconsin, is renowned as home of the Green Bay Packers football team. But the report I received was of another "team" that did not wear green and gold. Nor did it field a pigskin—but was every bit as exciting as a Packers-Bears game to the folks who observed their show. I included an abbreviated version of the story in my book *Monsters of Wisconsin* but found new information and additional witnesses when I did a follow-up for *American Monsters*.

A young man I'll call Jim, who was sixteen at the time, had e-mailed me in 2007:

> On October 27, 2007, in Oconto Falls, Wisconsin, some of my friends and I were at a concert at a now-closed-down arcade. It was the same as always, a few of the best local bands, me and some of

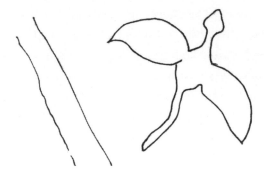

Eyewitness sketch of dragon-like creature of Oconto Falls,
Wisconsin. *(Submitted by and used with permission of the artist.)*

my friends joining them on stage, and hanging out outside after-
wards. While we were outside on the cold, partly cloudy night, one
of the guys that was there from Green Bay said he thought he saw
something in the sky. Most people were skeptical but we just decided to lay down on the grass and on top of vans and trucks and
maybe we could see what it was.

After about fifteen minutes of talking and laughter, those emo-
tions changed to surprise and astonishment as we watched a massive, white/tan dragon fly over the clouds. We knew it had to be a
dragon, because how else would you describe something flying
over that was almost silent, larger than a plane, and had a tail, bat-
like wings, long neck, and a narrow, pointed head, and scales?

I remember noticing the scales because they dimly reflected the
street lights below. We thought we were all seeing things but five
minutes later it flew over again, this time in the opposite direction.
The eight people from Green Bay wanted to stay but they had to
leave. They hoped to see more back home.

Me and my friend K, however, decided to go to my house and

lay in the backyard and watch. My mom joined us, not really believing any of it until as soon as she was about to go back in, another big one flew over the house. If I remember right, her words were, "I'm tired and I'm going to bed, I doubt that it even—holy [exclamation]!"

We saw a few smaller ones after that but I haven't seen them since that night. I believe that they were migrating during that month. Hopefully I will see them again next October. When talking about the incident at school, one of the girls around us claimed to have seen the same thing with her cousin two years earlier.

The description he gave sounds very much like modern-day eyewitness accounts of pterosaurs, except for the scales, and it's interesting that Jim and his friends saw more than one creature. But more important, I was recently able to interview his mother and sister, both of whom remember the night and those creatures very well. His mother even wrote about it in her journal and made a sketch.

The family asked to remain anonymous, but I'll call Jim's mother Janet. She was forty at the time and employed as a housekeeper. She was waiting for Jim to call her for a ride home that night, and when he finally did call, it was to tell her what he and his friends had seen.

"He was describing to me how the light from the city street was reflecting off the creature and he could see the wings, scales, and bone structure of the wings. Being a doubting Thomas, I thought he was telling a big joke, but I ventured down to pick him up and stuck around as he and a few others were laying around on the grass looking up at the sky," said Janet.

She noticed a shadow pass over the parking lot and then saw some type of "fireball," light blue with orange and yellow around it, passing from east to west in the sky. Jim told her they had seen the same thing before the winged creatures came through. At that time she drove Jim and his friend home.

It was between 2:30 and 3:00 a.m. when Jim talked her and his sister, "Jill," into staying outside to watch for the creatures he had seen a few miles away. They all lay on the backyard trampoline and saw another fireball moving east to west, then another west to east on the same path. They joked that the dragons must be spitting fire at each other. Neighborhood geese and dogs began to honk and bark, and they heard a loud "screech" they couldn't identify.

"Then as we were watching the sky," she said, "coming from the west from the river to over our yard, we saw what appeared to be—and this is the only thing we could think of to describe it as—a dragon. It was making gliding movements up and down, never flapping its wings, kind of like how a mermaid is shown when it swims is how I can best describe the gliding movement of its body. It never flapped its wings at all. [Author's note: That's almost exactly what the Spokane, Washington, witness said.] And it looked almost cream colored. The drawing is showing it as we were looking up at the underside. Its stomach reminded me of the underside of a cow, barrel-chested, and from where we were, it looked as large as a cow. I remember the moon was very bright and full that night."

It had a "snake-shaped" head, she said, and a long, pointed tail. She drew her sketch of it when she went in the house later. I asked her if she thought it looked in any way like a prehistoric bird or pterosaur, but after looking up some pterosaur and pterodactyl pictures she said their wing structure was not anywhere close to that of the creature she observed.

She added that she was familiar with cranes, herons, geese, and other large birds of the area and that this creature was much too large and differently shaped to be any of those. The creature was only about twenty feet above her two-story house.

Janet and her family also saw a few smaller creatures they thought were associated with the large one, she said. The smaller ones seemed to tumble and circle one another as if playing, and Janet said they referred to them as babies but she couldn't see them well enough to be sure they weren't bats.

Her daughter, Jill, also wrote out a full statement for me, and she remembered vividly her mother saying that her brother and friends claimed to have seen dragons before she went to pick him up that night. She remembered seeing the dragon even more vividly, and said, "I don't care what the scientists say, it was NOT a pterodactyl. I could see it had pearly, pale scales. And the fireball came from its mouth. After that I went inside because my heart told me, 'No, you aren't supposed to be watching this.'"

Jill also added that she didn't agree that the dragon should be in a book about monsters, and that she didn't want them hurt, "because they didn't harm us. Dragons are the guardians of the earth, and they were beautiful and flew gracefully. I could see they had four legs, too. They were tucked up underneath them like when a bird flies."

Janet also considers the dragons special rather than scary. Every year, she said, her family keeps a watch on the night sky in late October in case the creatures make another flyover. Although the creatures haven't shown up again, she said she did see a truly unidentified flying object a year or two later, a huge, silent, flying V-shape with lights along its sides. And she is glad that she saw the "dragons" at least once.

"I don't know what they were," she said, "but I feel privileged and honored to have seen something so unusual that you just can't explain."

DEER DRAGONS

Another creature described as dragon-like nearly caused a freeway accident near Cottage Grove, Oregon, in June 1996, according to Neil Arnold in *Alien Zoo*.[7] Cottage Grove is a small town in Lane County that's known as The Covered Bridge Capital of Oregon, since it boasts seven of the quaint structures. Two major highways run through the town, and it's surrounded by creeks and river ways, wooded hills, and a reservoir.

The eyewitness was a woman driving through Cottage Grove at night who said that something she at first thought was a deer burst onto the highway, running at a speed the motorist estimated as at least seventy miles per hour—on its hind legs! That would have been startling enough, but then the "deer" suddenly flipped a set of wings from its back and shot up into the sky. The woman thought that the wings didn't seem large enough to lift a creature that size into the air. The dark sky obscured her view of the creature after that.

The brief account in *Alien Zoo* didn't say whether the creature was covered with fur or scales. If fur-covered, it may belong in the Batsquatch chapter of this book, especially since the northern West Coast states are Batsquatch hotspots. I might also refer to it as an American gargoyle.

I do occasionally receive reports of upright deer. A Massachusetts man wrote to tell me of an upright deer that he saw sometime in the very late 1990s or early 2000s near Gordon-Conwell Theological Seminary in South Hamilton. He was a student at the seminary and was driving home one night when he saw something strange just off the road as he approached a small bridge. It appeared to be a deer standing on its hind legs partially behind a tree, staring at him. It looked at him for a few seconds, he said, and then slowly moved behind the tree. I asked him whether it could have been anything else other than a deer.

"The animal I saw did not look like a wolf," he wrote. "The strange thing about it was how tall it was and the erect posture—more like a person and not hunched over. It was just weird. South Hamilton around the seminary is spooky at night anyway. Feels like something is watching you in a negative way."

Since he didn't see wings, I would not really classify it as a dragon or even a gargoyle. Bigfoot comes to mind, or perhaps—consulting Occam's razor to find the simplest explanation—it was actually a deer that was standing up to reach some tasty bark on that tree. As I've noted before, there's nothing spookier than an animal doing something truly unexpected, especially while it's watching us.

Ohio Highway Dragon

Another, more unaccountable sighting came from an Ohio woman who contacted me through my blog in October 2011. She wrote that her encounter had occurred a few years before, perhaps in 2008 or 2009, as she was making a midday, early-summer car trip between Mount Vernon and Martinsburg on State Route 586. As she rounded a sharp curve on the wooded road about five miles from Mount Vernon, her field of view widened considerably, and a dark-colored figure only half a mile or so away grabbed her attention. She wrote,

On the right side of the road I saw a massive winged "bird." It was at least one-half mile ahead of me and it was the largest animal I have ever seen. All I could think was dragon.

It could have been a thunderbird. No eagle could reach this size. I was at least a half mile away and the size was overwhelming. I continued driving but it disappeared back into the trees. It had hovered over the road for at least ten seconds before disappearing.

I wrote the woman to ask for more details, and she immediately answered:

I saw it arched up like you see pictures of dragons with the wings outstretched, then the wings moved slowly down, flapping. The "bird" didn't seem to move—just flapping wings enough to stay at its location in the air. When it moved back into the trees, it seemed to drop a little in the air and swoop back in. I only saw it for maybe ten seconds but it didn't seem to move very fast. . . . I was too far away to see feathers. All I saw was darkness for coloring, either dark brown or black. I didn't see any light colors. I didn't hear anything—maybe because I was too far away. It was like a massive eagle—only dragon-sized.

The sheer size of it blew my mind. I didn't feel fear, just amazement. It just seemed to be in slow motion. By the time I got to where it had disappeared into the trees, there was no movement in the trees and I didn't see anything else. I have seen hawks and eagles flying. In terms of size, an eagle would be a speck in the sky from the vantage point I had. I don't know if I could have even identified an eagle other than [as a] bird from the distance I was. I remember that it was wider with wings flapping than the road it was hovering over. It was a two-lane highway and it was a little to the side of the road and over the road. The trees were close to the road.

Obviously this amazing sighting could also have been included in the chapters on Thunderbirds or pterosaurs, since the witness wasn't close enough to make a definite ID of this flying creature. But her repeated mentions of its similarity to a dragon convinced me to include it here, especially since none of the other sky beasts seen by witnesses boast an iron-clad dragon pedigree, either. And there are other winged creatures whose descriptions sound even closer to those of traditional dragons that do have a long history here.

8

Quetzalcoatl and Other Dragons of the Ancient Americas

We need not look to other parts of the world for examples of dragons in ages past. Flying, long-bodied reptilian creatures date back to prehistoric times all over the Americas. The Aztecs, Toltecs, and other ancient Mesoamericans, however, left some of the New World's best-documented and -illustrated records of flying reptiles in their religions.

Reptilian Gods

We know that one of the most important Mesoamerican deities was a serpent-like being, Quetzalcoatl, or the Plumed or Feathered Serpent. Part human, part bird, and part snake, he wore a unique, symbolic hat that trailed red plumes as he writhed through the sky. The plumes were modeled on the tail feathers of the Quetzal bird, from which he derived part of his name. And of course, as noted earlier, his name is now also associated with the huge, dinosaur-era pterosaur, Quetzalcoatlus.

The Quiché Mayans had their own sky god, Gucumatz or O'uq'umatz, who modern scholars believe to have been Quetzalcoatl's direct counterpart. He was also a feathered, humanoid serpent. Another Mayan sky deity named Itzamna was often portrayed with a humanoid body but a lizard's head and face.

Quetzalcoatl, Gucumatz, and Itzamna were considered creator spirits who first helped bring forth the human race and then bestowed upon their brutish protégés the arts and sciences needed for civilization. Ethnographers, those who study the folklore of indigenous peoples, see the universal serpent creators as metaphors for the societal transition made by early humans from hunter-gatherers to farmers and townspeople. John Bierhorst, editor of *Myths and Tales of the American Indians*, says, "The serpent imparts the knowledge of culture and is thereafter associated with all that culture implies, including wisdom, life, vulnerability to death, and loss of innocence."[1]

Some researchers believe those beneficial "spirit" serpents were something a bit more concrete, however. As TV shows such as *Ancient Aliens* frequently suggest, some "ancient astronaut theorists" think that belief in sky dragons in Mesoamerica, China, and other early cultures may have been inspired by ancestral memories of extraterrestrial, often reptilian aliens who arrived in prehistoric times to literally set up the human race for business by teaching our forebears agriculture, metallurgy, mathematics, astronomy, and other skills.

THE MYSTERY LIGHTS LINK

An alternative view holds that the prehistoric peoples of the Americas were actually seeing living pterosaurs just as modern eyewitnesses claim to do, and that they built their religions and rituals around appearances of the powerful creatures, ascribing qualities to them that we associate today with mythic dragons. Researcher Jonathan David Whitcomb puts forth the case that perhaps it was the glowing bioluminescence of living pterosaurs that the ancients of some cultures mistook for fiery breath.

"What about a winged dragon that could exhale fire?" Whitcomb writes on his Web site, Ropens. "Consider the ropen of Umboi Island. One eyewitness described the glow of the nocturnal creature as red, like the glow from burning embers."[2] Whitcomb also noted that there is a centuries-old phenomenon called the Marfa Mystery Lights, recurring light orbs viewable from a spot on Highway 90, nine miles east of Marfa, Texas. He speculates these lights might be explained by the nighttime flights of predatory ropens hunting bats. He also said, however, "As of late 2010, there still seems to be no direct evidence for the Marfa Lights connection, but at least a few cryptozoologists believe the ropen is a living pterosaur and the Marfa Lights may be related."[3]

The official Web site of Marfa's chamber of commerce testifies that its Native American population knew of the lights long before the first official report by settlers in 1883.[4] It holds a festival for the lights every Labor Day weekend. And Texas is definitely a contender when it comes to top locations for pterosaur sightings. To recap the earlier discussion on that topic, author Ken Gerhard says in *Big Bird! Modern Sightings of Flying Monsters* that he knows of at least seven credible eyewitnesses of living pterosaurs from the Lone Star State, including three teachers and an ambulance driver. True, the major stomping grounds of Texas pterosaurs is allegedly the area around Brownsville, on the southeastern border, while Marfa is situated far to the western side of the state—but such big birds should be able to manage the trip if they simply follow the Rio Grande.

I also can't help but connect those scaly dots between dragons, mystery lights, ropens, and the colored fireballs, and huge creamy-white creatures seen in October 2007 over Oconto Falls, Wisconsin. After all, every major ancient culture in the world believed in something similar to what these unrelated witnesses have seen. Who are we to say dragons are impossible?

FLYING MANTA RAYS

I cannot close this section without a fast peek at a highly baffling, apparent cryptid that does not resemble a traditional dragon. Instead, it looks a lot like the normally oceangoing manta ray—except that eyewitnesses have seen it hurtling its flat self across the sky in places quite far from any saltwater environment!

Lon Strickler's *Phantoms & Monsters* blog has become a hub for reports of this mystifying creature, which looks but does not behave like a known marine animal once nicknamed the devil fish. *Manta birostis* can reach a width of twenty feet and may jump as much as three feet out of the water, but it doesn't have long-range flight capabilities.[5]

How, then, was a creature two people identified as a "stingray" able to swoop over their car on January 25, 2012, above a highway near Hebron, Kentucky, just southwest of Cincinnati, Ohio? It wasn't giant in size, only about one to two feet long, but one of the witnesses, a teenage boy whose mother was at the wheel, said it powered itself through the air by making "swimming motions."[6]

That sighting was near the Ohio River, as was another reported in 2004 on Route 2 between Point Pleasant and Huntington by an artist riding with a friend to an art show in West Virginia. The time was between 6 and 7 p.m., and the sky had already darkened as the pair crossed a set of railroad tracks near Ashton. The artist said he was musing over the logistics of setting up his exhibit when he spotted something flying over the Ohio River to his right.

"It was a grayish, smooth, winged shape. The shape swooped in a figure eight in front of the windshield and then was suddenly gone to the left of us. It didn't fly out of sight, it was just gone. This happened very quickly, but as I am a visual artist, it was impressed into my memory banks!"[7]

He estimated the flat-bodied creature swooping about twenty-five feet or less away was as big as their car, with a wingspan the width of the road, and added that it was almost translucent. It had no distinguishing characteristics such as facial features, limbs, or even a head, just the ray-shaped body and pointed wings. He was sure it was not a bird.

The phenomenon seems to have taken off since the early 2000s with many other similar sightings, exciting some cryptozoologists who have been eagerly following its development. Kurt McCoy, author of *White Things: West Virginia's Weird White Monsters*, wrote on Strickler's blog, "I have no idea what is going on . . . but I think there are enough reports now to say that this represents SOME kind of phenomenon. Folks, we have an emerging Monster tradition! All fresh and relatively new! Something that is most definitely not another manifestation of 'Mothman,' but a phenomenon in its own right!"[8]

I agree with Kurt McCoy; I have no idea what is going on, either, but I believe this newborn monster is only in its infancy and that reports of airborne ray fish swooping over cars, trucks, and other things are bound to escalate as more people become aware of their seemingly impossible existence. This is probably as good a place as any to leave our unexplained flying things and splash down into the world of the wet and wild.

PART TWO

MONSTERS BY SEA

9

Aquatic Aliens: Unidentified Submarine Objects

UFOs, or unidentified flying objects, are rightly thought of as belonging to the skies—hence, the word "flying." And in that case, they would belong in the first section of this book. But anyone who studies the subject soon realizes that strange lights and crafts unlike any known Earth technology are observed nearly as often entering, exiting, and even inhabiting bodies of water as they are seen zipping through the clouds or stars. In that case, they are called USOs, or unidentified submarine (or submerged) objects. I'm placing them at the beginning of this new section as a sort of bridge between the two worlds of air and water. But there's a second question: Do UFOs, wherever sighted, belong in a book on monsters?

The notion of calling UFOs or USOs and their inhabitants monsters may seem novel, but in my opinion these intruders that often look like wrinkled gray dwarves or giant insects rank right up there with America's scariest beasts. They are terrifying enough when we spot them in the upper atmosphere, but something about the thought of them submerged in our waterways and possibly interacting with our marine life—and us—is even more deeply disturbing. First-person accounts of such sightings are quite common. And sometimes, eyewitnesses catch a glimpse of—or endure frightening interactions with—living beings whose appearance many would consider monstrous in or near these craft. On other occasions, the craft itself may be the monster. But whether humanoid beings or sentient vessels, these enigmatic intruders act far more at home in our lakes, rivers, and oceans than should any proper visitor from beyond.

In the mid-1990s, when I was working as a reporter for an area newspaper, I had the opportunity to interview the manager of a small local airport that closed a few years after the story ran. When we had finished talking about my story topic, I asked him if he could tell me off the record whether in his years in the field of flight, both as a pilot and in other capacities, he had ever seen a UFO. He said that indeed, he had, years earlier while serving in the US military at a base in Puerto Rico (yes, home of the *chupacabras*). Saucer-type vehicles would emerge from the ocean as he and other personnel watched them through long-range telescopes. Some of the craft had what looked like windows or portholes, and on some occasions the observers could make out occupants inside those portholes!

Sometimes, he added, they would use cameras attached to the telescopic equipment to take pictures of the craft, and by the next day officials would always show up and confiscate the film. Researcher Ivan T. Sanderson wrote about many similar sightings during the 1960s in Puerto Rico.

Extremely Ancient Aliens?

Many other researchers have discussed the possibility of large, underwater bases of operation used by humanoid creatures with technology far superior to our own. Of course, there are also allegations of under-

ground bases, but that's for another chapter. Some researchers believe both land-based and water-based unknown humanoids are extraterrestrials; others think perhaps they are ancient human beings with a much older pedigree than our own, or perhaps time travelers from our own future.

Encounters with highly developed humanoids based in large bodies of water may not be strictly a modern phenomenon. In the third century BCE, a Babylonian priest known as Berossus wrote about a marvelous being of antiquity: a part-human, part-fish, god-like creature called Oannes that emerged from the Persian Gulf in times past to visit Babylon and teach people about agriculture, religion, the arts, and other knowledge helpful to civilization. Each night, Oannes returned to the sea, where he seemed to maintain underwater living quarters. He did not eat human food, and the Babylonians observed others of his kind as well. Some proponents of the theory that extraterrestrials visited Earth in prehistoric times believe this legend may represent actual events long preserved as myth, despite certain questions about exactly which ancient people received the knowledge and the fact that this work of Berossus exists only in second- and thirdhand accounts from later historians.

In a nutshell, and scholarly quibbles aside, the tale of Oannes gives us a very old tradition of advanced, fish-like humanoids from the sea.

There are similar traditions in other parts of the world. An ancient Chinese tale whose written form dates from 200 BCE to around 100 CE tells of a man named Yu who could shift into the form of a dragon. The tale itself is believed to be four to five thousand years old. As the very brief version of the story goes, while Yu is sitting by a river one day, trying to figure out how to stop a plague of extreme floods, he is given the necessary engineering know-how by a mysterious figure.

Teresa Moorey said in *Understand Chinese Mythology*, "As he watched, a strange white-faced creature, half fish, half man came toward him, bearing a chart with the eight trigrams telling how the river could be quelled."[1] It sounds much like the legend of Oannes. And both sound rather like creatures that today we'd call extraterrestrials.

UNDERWATER BASES

It's hard to know exactly what these aquatic denizens look like, since (except for the experiences of human abductees) they are mostly glimpsed through portholes or not visible at all within their crafts. If we presume they are the same creatures described by the many people who say they have encountered or been abducted by aliens, we might logically guess that they look like the amphibious- or reptilian-type creatures so well-known in popular culture (and which will be discussed at greater length in the next section of the book). But what would such beings want with our oceans?

The Web site UFOInfo tackles the question of what the advantage of an underwater base might be in a succinct post by author Bill Hamilton, who writes, "Are there alien forms of intelligent life that occupy the vast volumes of water that constitute our oceans, seas, and lakes? The largest of our oceans, the Pacific, covers 64,000,000 square miles and reaches a depth of 36,198 feet, a depth that no ray of sunlight ever reaches. . . ."[2]

That is one whopping amount of deep, dark water largely absent of pesky humans. The oceans, then, could conceivably serve as the perfect hiding places for furtive, advanced aliens. There are plenty of reports, however, that implicate inland rivers as possible hangouts for out-of-this-world crafts, as well. Consider the following report that I received recently.

STURGEON RIVER USO

USOs seem to be able to navigate flowing rivers just as easily as they do lakes and seas. One Michigan couple had an unforgettable sighting near the Dickinson County village of Loretto late one night several decades ago. The husband, whom I'll call Ted, wasn't altogether surprised by the event, since he'd had a previous experience with something in the water in that very same spot. The seventy-eight-year-old wrote to me via my Weird Michigan Web site:

> In the spring of 1977 or perhaps 1978, I and my former wife were traveling at night on U.S. 2 West. Just after passing the village of Loretto we were approaching the Sturgeon River Bridge when I noticed a bright light that seemed to be reflected from the river. My wife was driving so I could watch this. As it approached the bridge it was getting brighter and appeared to be some light (located) above the river and reflecting off the water.
>
> It was approaching the bridge as we were approaching the bridge, when it must have seen my car headlamps and the light went dark. I looked downstream to see if I could see anything because that was the direction the light had been traveling, when in about four seconds the light went on again, above the river at the end of a rapids by an old railroad bridge foundation that I had once fished. There were three small lighted portholes in this object about fifty feet in the air, and a light beam showing down to the water as though it was searching for something; it may have been a helicopter. I could not see its shape.

Ted added that viewed from that distance, the portholes were about the size of an eraser on a wood pencil. He was able to see some type of movement inside the portholes but couldn't tell what it was (very similar to what the pilot reported seeing in Puerto Rico). He watched for what he estimated to be about eight seconds until the light blinked out again.

Ted may have had a little easier time than would the average passing driver in estimating where things were relative to the bridge, since this was a fishing spot he had visited frequently. He said that several years earlier, he and a fishing partner were drifting downstream in his twelve-foot boat in exactly the same spot when something huge in the water almost capsized them. His best guess at that time was that the giant mass was a school of very large fish.

"We startled these things," he said, "which in their hurry to escape our boat crashed into the boat. Until this day I still find this unexplainable and I would like to be able to search this river to see if this particular spot has something mysterious [that] attracted this craft and those fish (or whatever almost capsized the boat)."

Was it a helicopter? Helicopters are not generally equipped with portholes, and they usually keep their lights on at night. And would this Michigan river contain a school of fish big enough to nearly capsize a twelve-foot boat? Ted, a mature and experienced fisherman, tried to rationalize the baffling things he had seen and experienced at this spot, but what caused them is still a mystery. Ted's experience may not comprise the most galvanizing USO report ever made, but I believe it's typical of hundreds of incidents that lurk below the radar in this country each year.

CALIFORNIA COASTAL CREATURES

The southern Pacific coast of the United States not only boasts many sightings of unknown craft spotted entering or exiting the ocean, but also is the site of some reports that include close-up looks at the craft inhabitants. An article in the February 2006 issue of *FATE* magazine by MUFON (Mutual UFO Network) investigator Preston Dennett highlights an astonishing list of such sightings along California's seashore between Long Beach and Santa Barbara.[3] The sightings date back as far as 1947, the year of the famous alleged flying saucer crash in Roswell, New Mexico, and some include descriptions of humanoids.

One of these reports in the latter category occurred the morning of November 6, 1957, when the drivers of three automobiles cruising the beach highway at Playa del Rey all saw a large object set down on the sand. They had no choice but to stop, since something had stalled each car's mechanical system. They described the object as egg-shaped and partly obscured by bluish mist. Dennett wrote, "Witnesses Richard Kehoe, Ronald Burke, and Joe Thomas exit their cars and observe two strange-looking men disembarking from the object. The UFO occupants have 'yellowish green skin' and wear 'black leather pants, white belts and light colored jerseys.' They walk up to the witnesses and begin asking questions."[4]

The strange-looking "men" tried to communicate with the three astonished witnesses, but Kehoe, Burke, and Thomas were all unable to understand the language of the chartreuse people. Dennett adds that local officials received many other reports of metallic flying objects in that area the same day.

Skipping past more than a dozen other reports of strange craft in or over the ocean, fast-forward to July 28, 1962. This time it was a fishing-boat captain six miles south of Catalina Island who investigated what he had first taken to be the stern of a Russian submarine. Only its tail and an "odd aft-structure" were visible above the water, but inside, the captain and his crew members observed five male figures, "two in white garb, two in dark trousers and white shirts, and one in a sky-blue jumpsuit."[5]

Without warning, the captain had to make emergency evasive maneuvers as the submarine headed straight for them at a high rate of speed, making no noise and leaving no wake. The incident remained unexplained.

In 1967, in another incident near Catalina Island, two boys vacationing on their parents' boat discovered that they both lacked any memory whatsoever of a specific period of time one day. They were never able to explain this until, as an adult, one of the boys allowed himself to be hypnotized in hope of finding out what the pair had been doing during that episode of "missing time." What he "remembered" (hypnotic regression is an admittedly controversial technique) was not comforting. He was able to recall that somehow both boys were conducted to what he thought was some sort of round, underground room by creatures that looked like giant praying mantises, a particularly monstrous type of presumed ET that is described fairly often by UFO abductees.

Dennett noted that this recalled encounter was echoed by Malibu author Kim Carlsberg, whose book *Beyond My Wildest Dreams* recounted her own multiple abductions by praying mantis types and the even more common "grays" that have become our standard, go-to image of alien beings.

If all of these witnesses are to be believed, we are left with the sobering conclusion that more than one race or species of unknown humanoid may be entrenched beneath the waters off Southern California. There's another unsettling possibility here in the category of aquatic monsters; as mentioned at the beginning of this chapter, some researchers have suggested that the crafts *themselves* are living or sentient beings.

IN THE BELLIES OF THE BEASTS

A 2012 article in HuffPost Weird News asked, "Are some UFOs living space beings?" Dr. Franklin Ruehl has a name for the proposed beings: "zeroids." He speculates that they might have formed from prebiotic material found in massive gas clouds. He says, "Already dozens of organic compounds have been identified in space, including formaldehyde, prussic acid, and cellulose. In short, there is an abundance of basic building blocks out there to allow for the evolution of zeroids. Considering that our island universe is approximately 13.7 billion years old, it is conceivable that zeroids represent the earliest life forms in the cosmic backdrop, perhaps even existing for nearly that entire time!"[6]

Such creatures might be either simple or complex, says Ruehl, and his best guess for their dining habits is that they might consume intergalactic dust and gas—or one another, either of which is preferable to their consuming *us*. We may be safe on that score, however, since he also believes that even given their ability to propel themselves and to process information, they might find it difficult to enter our planet's atmosphere.

"Yet, some may have evolved a protective shield—either physical or electromagnetic in nature—that has enabled them to survive entry into our domain," he cautioned. "These would be the living UFOs!"

Ruehl also thinks that there may be several cases on record that support his theory. One case involved something that looked like a "living sphere of light" in Romania in 1976, and the other was a series of photographs shot in 1978 in British Columbia by a researcher named Dorothy Wilkinson. The phenomenon she captured resembled what Ruehl characterized as "space worms."[7]

"So," concluded Ruehl, "considering the vastness of both space and time, it is certainly within the realm of feasibility that at least some UFOs may actually be living space creatures!"[8]

At least one TV series, *Farscape*, based an eighty-eight-episode show on a similar idea with a band of escaped alien prisoners careening about the galaxy in a living ship named Moya. One of my personal sci-fi favorites, the Australian series ran from 1999 through 2003— well before Ruehl's article was published.

In present-day Washington State, there's a Native American narrative among the Chinook that is amazingly analogous to the idea of a spacecraft as an entity in its own. The story titled "The First Ship" is presented in *American Indian Myths and Legends* as retold by Richard Erdoes and Alfonzo Ortiz. It's about the first contact the Chinook had with Europeans: the sight of an oceangoing sailboat. While the book's authors do not relate the story to any specific known incident or date, they do say they believe it was based on an actual event. The old woman who sees it first describes it, in the words of Erdoes and Ortiz:

> At first she thought it was a whale. When she came nearer, she saw two spruce trees standing upright on it. "It's not a whale," she said to herself, "*it's a monster.*" [Emphasis mine.][9]
>
> When she came near the strange thing that lay at the edge of the water, she saw that its outside was covered with copper and that ropes were tied to the spruce trees, then a bear came out of the strange thing and stood on it. It looked like a bear, but the face was the face of a human being.[10]

She ran back to tell the villagers that the thing they had heard about from other people had come to them. She told him there were two bears that might be people who were standing on the strange thing. All the villagers ran to the water's edge and saw for themselves what the woman had described. The two strange creatures were holding copper kettles and indicated with sign language that they would like the kettles to be filled with water.

The story doesn't end well for the fur-faced people. A small delegation of villagers sneaked around behind the boat, boarded it, and found various trading objects made of iron, brass, and copper, which they removed and stashed onshore. Then they burned the strange large boat with its branchless spruce trees. Luckily the two bearded men were not still aboard. The story says that one of them was kept with the village chief and the other was sent to live at a more distant village. The heading of the story notes, "The Indians consider the *Wasichu*, the white men, as monstrous as any brokers or demons."[11]

Note that the villagers first described the ship, created with technology beyond anything they had witnessed, and then the white men, with their white skin and bearded faces, as monsters. The people's first reaction to this intrusion of the unknown was to destroy the unfamiliar craft and exploit the wonderful metals they found on board, while keeping the weird "bear people" for observation, study, or perhaps just as curiosities. Monsters, like beauty, are probably always in the eyes of the beholders.

Mermaids: People Acting Fishy

On May 26, 2013, Animal Planet premiered a documentary called *Mermaids: The New Evidence*, which the cable TV channel promised would change all that we knew about the ocean. More than three and a half million people tuned in that Sunday evening to learn whether aquatic humanoids inhabit our planet's oceans and waterways. As it turned out, viewers—including this writer—remained in the dark on the answer to this question because the documentary turned out to be a mostly fictional creation that used manufactured "videos" of the merpeople and hired actors to portray scientists.

I've learned not to expect TV shows about unexplained phenomena to be totally factual. This one was at least entertaining, with beautifully rendered, computer-generated images of handsome merpeople swimming in the ocean with dolphins and whales. The most amazing thing about this program, in my view, was not so much the enormous whopper it told, but the enormous viewership that it elicited. Evidently, a lot of people are more than mildly interested in the topic of mermaids. It may be worth a brief intercontinental detour to discuss the origins of this fascination.

THE TERRIBLE TRITON

It's possible that people today might not be so entranced by the idea of mermen and mermaids if they could hear their description by Greek writer Pausanias, penned in the second century CE. The ancient Greeks called these creatures Tritons, after a sea god of the same name. They were not pretty:

> The Tritons have green hair on their head, very fine and hard scales, breathing organs below their ears, a human nose, a broad mouth, with the teeth of animals, sea-green eyes, hands rough like the surface of a shell, and instead of feet, a tail like that of dolphins.[1]

Given the horrifying "teeth of animals" and stringy green hair, this ancient version of merbeings seems much more appropriate for a book on monsters than do modern Hollywood mermaids such as the beautiful sea siren played by actress Daryl Hannah in the 1984 movie *Splash* or the cute, animated Ariel of Disney's 1989 film *The Little*

Mermaid. Old-time, legendary mermaids also often acted more maliciously than do sweet Hollywood merfolk, as water beings of the past were known for playing tricks on sailors or luring people to watery graves.

Human Fish out of Water

Merpeople of various descriptions and behaviors have been spotted throughout Europe long after Pausanias's description, by sailors at sea and by residents of coastal countries. One alleged mermaid even became something of a fifteenth-century celebrity.

In the Netherlands in 1403, residents of Edam—a town today more famous for its cheese than for strange creatures—found a seaweed-covered female on the beach who they immediately took for a beached mermaid. The woman couldn't speak but otherwise appeared to be a normal human. She lived in the towns of Edam and Haarlem for fifteen years and eventually converted to Christianity by professing her faith through sign language so that she could be buried in a consecrated churchyard.

While she was certainly mysterious and was remembered for many centuries by a statue erected in Edam in her honor, the "mermaid" was no monster. Instead, she exemplified the more romantic side of European mermaid lore that sometimes even extended to governmental decree. In Denmark, for instance, in 1723, the king organized a special committee to examine all available evidence and decide once and for all whether mermaids existed as actual creatures. The committee decided in the affirmative and Denmark has since become well-known for its mermaids. Danish author Hans Christian Andersen wrote his famous fairy tale "The Little Mermaid" in 1845, and the mermaid statue in Copenhagen that commemorates his work is still one of the best-loved tourist sites in the world.

Mermaids and mermen still occupy a fairly high profile in the world of the unexplained, as a full range of Old World sightings that continue to the present day will attest. Writer and researcher Ulrich Magin says in a 2002 issue of *Strange Magazine*, "Mermen and mermaids are still regularly seen in the twentieth century, in salt as well as freshwater. Mainly ignored by cryptozoologists, the number of mermaid sightings could be as high as that of sea serpent observations."[2]

Magin believes that some cases of modern mermaids can be explained by people born with physical anomalies. He mentions a 1975 report of a "sirenoid" in Peru who was actually a child born with legs so closely attached that the lower body looked somewhat fish-shaped. The baby died shortly after birth and was preserved at a museum in Arequipa. Most contemporary mermaid sightings, however, cannot be explained by such rare and sad occurrences.

My favorite example of a modern sighting of a merperson comes from the Web site UFO Roundup and involves a creature some witnesses compared to the comic book character Aquaman. It showed up in the Caspian Sea off Iran in March and April 2005, said the Web site, citing an April 27, 2005, article in the Iranian newspaper *Zindagi*. The headline read, "'Merman' Spotted Again by a Fishing Boat on the Caspian."[3]

The article continued, "Gafar Gasanof, the captain of the M/V *Baku* (a trawler registered in Azerbaijan) told the Iranian newspaper *Zindagi* that 'the creature was swimming a parallel course near the boat for a long time. At the beginning, we thought it was a big fish, but then we spotted hair on the head of the monster and his fins looked pretty strange, the front part of his body was equipped with arms.'"

Eyewitnesses described the alleged merman as muscular and measuring about five and a half feet in length (not including its dark green hair), with a very prominent abdominal area. They also said that its fingers were webbed and that gills were visible on its neck.

In general, merbeings have historically been viewed as unusual or even magical versions of humans rather than as unknown fish or fearful monsters. Skeptics often explain them as misidentifications of dugongs or manatees—large marine mammals that hold their babies upright in the water in order to nurse them. This theory only holds water in reference to sightings made from a fairly great distance because these animals weigh many times as much as a human and resemble us very little when seen close-up. And Native Americans have their own beliefs about these creatures that predate the arrival of Europeans and their "ship monsters."

Native American Water People

Native American lore includes many types of mythic aquatic humanoids and monsters. Some types are widespread; many different indigenous peoples, for instance, believe in diminutive, humanoid water beings that live near bodies of water and cause everything from mischief to mayhem if they are not properly respected. Sometimes the beings are related to known animals, such as the seal maidens of the Pacific Northwest. These shape-shifting seals could become beautiful women in order to intermarry with humans, usually with tragic consequences.

There is also a tale from the Coos people of Oregon's coastal areas about a young woman who returned from her regular morning swim one day to find herself mysteriously pregnant. She had a son and eventually discovered that her unknown husband was a merman who lived with a whole village of others like himself on the ocean bottom. She was able to return to that magical place from time to time until eventually she turned into a scaly sea creature herself. But every year her merpeople left the land villagers two beached whales as gifts.[4]

The Kalapuyans of northwestern Oregon tell tales of the "frog people," amphibious beings who once commanded all known fresh water. No one could take so much as a container of drinking water without paying a fee of shells or other trade goods to the frog people, who kept constant watch on the shores of every lake and stream. Their downfall came when the universal Native American trickster, Coyote, finally managed to collapse one of the frog people's big dams so that all the earth's water freely redistributed itself.[5]

FROG-FACED ALIENS

The frog-like water-hoggers of the previous tale may seem bizarre, but they do have their contemporary counterparts. Many modern-day eyewitnesses of presumed extraterrestrials describe these creatures as resembling amphibians. Ulrich Magin says in his article on aquatic humanoids, "Any open-minded analysis into humanoid folklore will show that fish or frog-like extraterrestrials are far more numerous than the 'gray type' (of alien), a creature invented by ufologists and then forced into the percipient's minds via hypnotic regression."[6]

As an example in support of his opinion, he cites a case from an unnamed book on UFO abductees. Frog-like aliens abducted a cattle hand in the Sangre de Cristo Mountains of southern Colorado. They hauled the cowboy aboard their craft and he soon found himself in the usual spartan UFO examination room, where he had ample opportunity to observe the characteristics of his abductors. He said there were five of them, three males and two females. They had lizard-like arms and legs, hands that he described as greasy and "fish-like" (flipper or fin-like?), with humanoid torsos and private parts. The cattle hand endured the usual intrusive medical "exam" that is so often a part of alien abduction reports, but survived to tell the tale.

Magin believes this type of report is not so different from older, traditional tales of amphibious humanoids or mermen. He thinks that the ancient lore and modern sightings both serve some type of primal, poorly understood psychological mechanism in human beings that deserves scientific exploration.

I have a feeling that most abductees feel they've been explored quite enough, thank you, and yet the fantastical element of their experiences cannot be denied. I suspect there will continue to be a standoff between those who believe the abductions are tangible experiences and those who seek to explain them in some other way, unless and until we receive some breakthrough understanding of the forces at work in these encounters. But there is little doubt that many abductees have said their "hosts" appeared physically suited to life beneath the waves.

Not all water-creature encounters involve abductions, of course. Some types of aquatic humanoids have managed to terrify their witnesses in a completely hands-off way. Water-based mystery people tend to resemble very weird versions of similar, known creatures wherever they appear, and we will meet the amphibious frog people again in a land-based context.

Moving on from West Coast folklore to a modern-day, previously unpublished report from the southeastern United States, it seems only right that one Florida "water man" should somewhat resemble an alligator.

The Florida Gator Man

Part I: Gator Man

The eighteen-year-old man who sent me this report in 2012 is a volunteer at a Florida paleontology museum, working toward college degrees in paleontology and zoology. He affirmed to me that the following is a true and factual account of his experiences. It's a bit longer than I'd normally allow for the telling of an eyewitness encounter, but his interest, his area of study, and his familiarity with the environment and its flora and fauna make this case especially compelling—not to mention chilling. The fact that this particular area of Florida's eastern coastline is historically known for other sightings of river beasts lends an added dimension to his experiences, which began in 2010. He wrote:

Well, I can say flat out I only know one other person who's seen what I saw and she refuses to talk about it. There IS a local lore about a monster living in the [St. Johns] river but the description doesn't seem to match up fully with what was reported several decades ago. I would have thought I was hallucinating had it not been for the distinctiveness this memory for me has over dreams. There have been several [incidents] over the years and all seem to be the same type of being, or maybe even the same individual. I can safely say I have absolutely nothing to gain from any of this as you are the first and only person I've told who wasn't involved.

The first [incident] was three years ago [2010] in mid-March during spring break, but it wasn't as much what I saw as what likely was left by it. I live on a canal system that feeds directly into a large river system that spans most of the eastern side of Florida, called the St. Johns River delta. Wildlife that lives in the river frequently come up into the canals for a number of reasons, including fishing birds, dolphins, game fish, manatees, even bull sharks and alligators on occasion. It's brackish water due to the river meeting the ocean, fairly shallow (about five feet deep in most spots) but so full of silt and natural particles that it is nigh impossible to see through. People have seen the water so dark they've nicknamed it the "Black Tea River." Unless an object is less than three inches from the surface, it is impossible to see and if it's more than a foot under you can't even see the outline.

I was out on my dock rinsing off my family's small sailboat. It was a fairly good day, only a few thick clouds and a lot of sunshine. I had just finished off when I saw a manatee drift over, attracted to the sound of the water. They like to drink the hose water so I turned the setting down and slung the hose over the side of the dock to let it drink. It was moving a bit oddly but as soon as it rolled over on its back to drink I noticed its front flipper had several very deep bite marks on it in a U pattern.

Manatees have no natural predators due to their bulk and very tough hide so I'd never seen one with bite marks before, usually all scars or injuries are from boat propellers and the way this mark was set I know that was impossible as a cause. Because the tooth marks were conically shaped in a narrow row, I knew it couldn't have been a shark because when they bite they leave thin lines with dashes for each tooth. Alligators have peg-like teeth that are cone shaped, but barring an incredibly large bull gator (twelve to fifteen feet) they aren't bold enough or even big enough to attack a manatee, and large males simply don't even live in the brackish water—they prefer swamps and freshwater springs. The only alligators I'd seen in the river and canal were juveniles at maximum five feet long.

As I looked more, I could see something had attacked this manatee very recently as it was riddled with cuts and bites, with a chunk of its tail flipper having been torn off. Something big enough to attack a one-ton sea cow was in the river system. Hairs on the back of my neck were standing up at the thought.

Later that day when we took the boat out to the river for a ride, I kept getting this odd feeling like I was being watched but mostly blew it off on the grounds we'd see another boater every so often. Well, we docked on a small island where I usually saw a lot of pelicans and egrets nesting, but despite it being near nesting season I couldn't see a single bird in the mangroves. They were around, but on every shore and island except this one. I also kept finding recently broken and snapped-off branches up to my height and higher that cut through the island. It wouldn't make sense for it to be hunters because there were no game birds on the small island, and most tourists would avoid a spot like this because the mangroves were very dense and messy terrain to go through. Besides, entire colonies of birds wouldn't abandon raccoon- and possum-free habitat because of one or two people walking around.

I couldn't see any tracks because of how many fallen leaves there were, but on the far side of the island I did see slide marks that were too angular to be a boat on a patch of sand. That bad feeling like I was being watched and should go was back and, along with it getting dark out, I decided to head home.

Part II: The Figure in the Cypress

A year later, in early June I was out in River Lakes Conservation Park with my Boy Scout troop. It's a large cluster of swamp, lakes, savannah, and forest that borders along waterways that connect to the St. Johns River on the mainland side of the river (I live on the island side). It was about 7 p.m. and getting dark so I was heading back to camp after tramping around, but to get back I had to go around a patch of marsh. The sun was beginning to set but it was still fairly bright out sky-wise with a minimal overcast, though it was a bit darker since the forest was very thick in some places.

I can't recall much about the animals I'd seen around, but I noticed as soon as I got to the edge of the marsh all the birds and game either went silent or were completely absent from the area. Previously I had been seeing deer, a lot of song birds; and even heard a bobcat yowling, but there was none of that. I thought this was very unsettling because the marshes are usually rich with fauna.

I was circling around the marsh and crossing under a thicket of pine trees when I heard something in the water make a small splash. I thought it was a fish at first and brushed it off, but I started getting an unsettling feeling that made me nervous. I was about to pick up my pace when I heard something in the water shift, along with what I think was a small hiss. I looked over just in time to catch a glimpse of a blackish figure standing under some cypress trees duck down into the water. I couldn't make out much of its form, but it was standing in at least four feet of water and was several feet above the water line when I saw it. I think the water was maybe at its waist, but the outline just didn't look right for a human.

It had been about sixty feet away from me, and the way it dived underwater seemed like it was heading toward me. I nearly lost it and ran back to camp as soon as I could.

Over the next year or two I'd occasionally hear an odd sound, usually at night, if I was staying anywhere near the swamps, river bottoms, or dark woods. It was usually distant and far away, but I could at times make out bellows or hisses. They sounded like nothing I'd ever heard in my entire life, but given how many vocalizing species live in my area (bobcats, coyotes, several owl species, a lot of very vocal birds), I'd just attribute it to one of those making an unusual sound.

Part III: The Manatee's Warning

Last month [April 2013] I needed to go out and exercise as well as see some manatees, since they were just now coming out of their winter retreats and going back into the river and canals. It was a fairly clear day with some distant clouds. So I took my kayak and rowed out of the canals and into the river mouth, and paddled until I spotted a small inlet along the side of the river that wasn't developed. Usually the manatees in the area converged in spots like this due to the calm water and ample food, and I'd been to this spot numerous times with plenty of success.

After crossing the bend I reached the lagoon and I could see the kick marks of a sea cow a short distance ahead. (Since sea cows' flukes are so broad and they swim close to the surface, they displace so much water that they leave broad, round disturbances in the water surface called kick marks.) But it struck me as odd that it was about noon and they were already leaving the lagoon and at a speedy pace. Usually manatees stay in the lagoon and canals during the day and then move out between six and eight o'clock to the river in herds. I was watching the manatee depart and ignored it. Yes, there are normally patterns that they follow, but there always are the odd manatee out that will break the norm.

The lagoon was pleasant enough to look at and the woods around it were calm, and I rowed in. I was getting tired from all the rowing, so I set my oar down on my lap and pulled out my water to have a drink. In hindsight I probably should have noticed there were no birds present either, something very strange for the time of year. I was just finishing my drink when something bumped the bottom of my kayak.

Now I was stationary in the water, so I knew if something bumped me it had to be moving. I wasn't startled because I've been bumped by a lot of things before. Moving underwater logs, young bull sharks taking an exploratory bump (how they judge if it's food or not), large fish. Manatees frequently do this since they use boat bottoms as back scratchers; it could have been any of those. Considering this was a usually manatee-filled lagoon I immediately thought the latter and got excited. I looked over the edge and I did see a dark shape about the length of a sea cow; it swam away before I could ID it.

I glimpsed it turning around due to a disturbance it caused on the water surface and turn back around. I know the manatees in the river system and I knew several who make multiple passes for a scratch so I wasn't suspicious until I felt it bump the bottom a second time. The sound of the bump was all wrong. If it's a manatee, there's only a single, gentle bump and maybe a small sliding sound. This sounded more like something hard moving over an old washing board or running your knuckles over your ribs with a successive series of bumps.

NOW I was getting a bit spooked because I know my animals, and I know manatees, dolphins, and bull sharks can't do that. I could just barely see the outline that was at least as long as my kayak (fourteen feet long) and notably broader for the first two-thirds before tapering off. It moved out from under my kayak and I decided it was best to get out of the water as fast as I could. Since the shore was sandy and only about ten feet away, I seized the chance and rapidly rowed myself as fast as the boat could go onto shore, beached my kayak, jumped out, and ran back a short distance as I watched the shape head to another part of the shore approximately twenty feet away.

As it reached the shallower water that was partially see-through against the white sand, I could see it looked like an alligator with a scaly body and scutes down its back. That would explain the rapid series of bumps, since each scute has a bony lump in the center. That said, since it had to be a large male gator, I backed up about another three yards from shore since crocodilians can lunge several yards out of the water very quickly but not over a distance. (You can look at videos of Nile crocodiles attacking wildebeest and impala; they lunge out of the water to grab prey as the latter drink.)

But as I watched, something just seemed wrong. The alligator was the same color as normal (jet black with a tint of blue) but when it surfaced the head seemed off. Crocodilians have a very broad but very flat skull whereas this thing seemed to have a skull that was much taller vertically. It also reminded me of a rauisuchid (an extinct prehistoric group related to crocodilians and dinosaurs with skulls similar to a carnivorous dinosaur) but not to that extreme. The elbows also stuck out farther, even passing the top of the body in profile and that's not right because alligators have very short arms.

It was crawling ashore and the more it got out of the water the more un-gator-like it got. I could see the arms and they were MUCH larger than a normal crocodilian, with very obvious muscular tissue showing through the scales. The fingers were a bit longer than normal, but I couldn't tell what was claw and what was scale, so I didn't know where the digits ended. It did seem to have five fingers like a normal alligator but the fingers were held closer together and it was twenty feet away, so I might have miscounted. The legs were also much broader and thicker than the arms of an alligator and were held more like a mammal in that they were directly below the body rather than off to the sides like a reptile. When it lifted itself off the ground fully I could tell the limbs were definitely longer than normal, at least twice as much, though I think the hind legs were longer because they were curled up more.

It was almost like looking at a dragon. I have no idea how— maybe through scent or seeing me through its peripheral vision— but it swung its head around and looked right at me. I could feel the blood rushing out of my face because I could see this animal's build and I knew that it could probably run fast enough to catch me. It dug its forelimbs down like it was doing a push-up, and then it rose up on its hind legs as it forced its arms up. It then stood upright like a bear and glared right at me. I tried to scream but I couldn't even get it out of my throat. Reared up, this animal was at least six and a half to seven feet tall and very heavily built.

It was completely unlike anything I'd ever seen, either living or in the fossil record. The underbelly from the lower jaw to the base of the tail was a whitish-yellow color. I could see its pectoral bones and muscle through its chest, as well as where I think the ribs were, but no genitals (reptiles have them internally unless copulating). Its arms were hanging to its sides until its hips and I think the palms were facing downward. The tail looked like a normal alligator tail and was sticking out behind the body and slumped on the ground. There were no lips and the teeth were visible, but like an alligator's, only the top jaw's fangs were visible. No fur or feathers anywhere, just scales. I know when people think of upright walking animals they think human-like, but this reptile seemed built more like a bear or an ape (albeit with shorter arms) with a slightly hunched-over posture.

It raised its arms up at the elbows and let out a hiss that

sounded like a normal alligator but much deeper. It opened its mouth slightly and briefly, making a short snarl before rattling its throat and letting out a bellow so deep I swear I could feel it. Before I could turn and run it turned away from me and walked off into the woods. It took about ten steps before it dropped down to all fours and disappeared into the brush, but I could still hear it moving through the thicket for about a minute. I was still standing in shock for a bit before I roped my kayak to a tree, and ran to a nearby highway to follow it home. It might have taken longer, but I didn't want to risk getting in the water with that thing around. Later I drove back in my truck with a friend (and a machete) to get my kayak; I didn't tell her anything.

Part IV: How Strong Is That Porthole?

Later that day that same friend was staying over and since we had company, she and I vowed earlier that week when we planned the get-together (and before my encounter) to sleep in the sailboat since it has two wide mattress benches inside the cabin. I hid it the best I could but I was still absolutely reeling from getting near the water and the fact it was dark and raining only made it worse. We had a light rain shower blow through in bands but the clouds weren't very thick and since the moon was nearly full visibility was still good.

Well, after sealing the cabin door and turning out the lights at ten, my friend got drowsy and she was out in about ten minutes. I was still awake for another hour (I had brought my watch down), partly due to listening to the storm and partly due to still being shaken about what happened earlier that day.

It was about 3 a.m. when I suddenly awoke for no apparent reason. It was still raining outside, but it had lightened to more of a gentle drizzle, though I believe there was occasional thunder. There was no other sound on the canal aside from the storm as everyone was inside asleep and not holding any overnight get-togethers or parties. Since there wasn't anything loud, I felt at first maybe a flash of light from a house sensor light going off due to a passing raccoon or a flash of lightning had woken me up, so I looked out the portholes and Plexiglas doorway, but I couldn't see anything besides a distant street light obscured by a tree. Some minutes passed and I lay back down. That is when I heard a hissing sound and my mind flashed back to earlier that day.

Hoping and praying I wasn't right, I peered out the porthole facing the canal entrance and I could see a figure in the dim light on the distant side of the canal. The rain was pinging off its body so it was easy to make out the shape, and I nearly felt like I'd have a heart attack when I realized it was that "thing" from earlier and it was heading right for me. I can't explain how but the thought just warped into my mind—almost a feeling that it had followed me home from the river.

I was on the edge of screaming. The cabin has no weapons; I wasn't old enough to carry a firearm; the house was nearly one hundred feet as the crow flies from the boat; the creature was getting closer; and all that was between us and it was half an inch of Plexiglas, glass portholes, some old wood, and a latch. I quickly glanced out the porthole again, and I could see it was getting closer and closer, now about as far away as my neighbor's sailboat (which I later measured to be about fifty feet away).

By now my only thought was to try everything I could to get us away, so I turned and shook my friend awake. It took a moment, but as soon as her eyes were open and looked behind me she froze up and her eyes widened as far as I've ever seen, as I heard two thumps echo out through the deck. I looked back and saw the creature was right up to the edge of the boat, peering in through a glass porthole.

It was just staring in, and by the way its arms were positioned, I could tell the thumps earlier were made by it putting its arms up against the boat to hold itself away. Its head pointed downward to a good degree so its eyes, which were on the sides of its head more than forward facing, could look in. My friend and I were terrified and afraid to move unless it, too, moved; we were fearful of provoking it. All it would need to do was climb on to the lower portion of the boat, which is only about two feet out of the water, and break or remove the Plexiglas to be able to get to us. I just kept whispering to my friend over and over again to keep quiet and don't move.

We stayed like that for some time and all through it, while the sense of threat never faded, it seemed like it was looking us over more than it was looking over a meal and it never tried to break in. The breathing of this animal was very loud, but not in the sense it sounded labored, and it was only occasional, maybe once a minute. I don't know if it had some sort of bioluminescence or it was eye shine reflecting from the dim light, but the weirdest thing about it was this thing had amber- or bronze-colored eyes. I did a little digging, and I know that alligators have reddish-brown eyes, and when they give off eye shine, it's bright red.

It stayed still for about five more minutes before it let out this short grumble or snarl and backed away from the boat. At first I thought it was going to circle around and crawl onto the deck, but it just backed up, turned, lowered down into the water to where I could see only its back and the top of its head, and swam off into the storm. My friend and I were so scared that it was some sort of trap that we stayed in the boat until about nine and ran back up to the house. I used to go out on the river all the time, now I'm afraid to step foot on the dock. That water is so dark I would never see anything coming and that to me is just terrifying.

I asked the writer to keep me updated on any future developments, and he did write and call me at the end of December 2013 to say that he saw what he felt was the same creature lurking about his own dock a few nights previous. He surprised it with a spotlight after his two pit bull–Lab mix dogs came running from the dock as if terrified. It was close enough that he was able to confirm his previous estimates of its very large size, and he said it gave an aggressive-sounding bellow much like that of a mature alligator. He felt it had followed him home, and he was obviously disconcerted at the thought. The case seems to have the earmarks of an ongoing situation, unfortunately for him, and I do hope for his sake there is only one of these creatures hanging about in that river. He has since continued to stay in contact, and has signed a statement warranting that his story is factual.

OTHER CREATURES OF THE ST. JOHNS RIVER

I'm sure that the sight of a bipedal alligator would give even an experienced river man the shakes. But so would many other things found in these waters. Many different creatures from the St. Johns River area have terrified eyewitnesses over the years, especially during the 1950s, when its islands, marshes, and tributaries virtually swarmed with a highly diverse variety of water monsters. Some eyewitnesses saw only an unidentifiable creature's head and neck poking out of the water, while others spotted wholly emerged beasts foraging on nearby riverbanks. They have described the St. Johns water weirdies as resembling everything from dinosaurs to manatees to dragons. This potpourri of river beasts dates back at least as far as 1885.

PINKY

Some of the most frequent sightings were of an unknown pink aquatic creature that locals dubbed "Pinky." Some researchers point to the boto, or pink river dolphin, as Pinky's possible secret identity. This does make a lot of sense. The boto is the world's largest freshwater dolphin, weighing in at a hefty three hundred pounds and measuring around nine feet in length. Its usual home is in the Amazon rain forest, whose indigenous folks have long regarded the rosy cetacean as a magical, semidivine being.[1] They call it the *encantado*, or "enchanted one," and believe it can shape-shift to human form to intermingle socially or for reproductive purposes. That fact lends an interesting dimension to the idea of the boto accidentally doubling as a sea monster, but the pink river dolphin possesses several other features that further enhance the possibility.

The boto's pink hue, caused by blood capillaries close to the skin surface, combined with its extra-long snout and extremely flexible neck would make it a startling sight in places such as eastern Florida where it's relatively unknown. But could a boto manage to travel all the way from the Amazon to the southern parts of the United States? At least one pink dolphin may have done so. In 2008 and 2009, a bubble gum–pink dolphin was seen often in the brackish Lake Calcasieu in Louisiana, but photos in the United Kingdom's *Daily Mail* identi-

fied it as a different species—a bottlenose—by its short snout and pronounced dorsal fin.[2]

Pink river dolphins avoid seawater and so would have to find a
freshwater route to the United States, but perhaps that's possible. And
there is always the chance that humans could have transported a
boto to Florida in this day and age of rampant illegal trade in exotic
animals.

12

Serpents of the Sea

Water creatures that resemble mutated humans may be fascinating to ponder but, as the saying goes, it's not always about us. Many weird denizens of the deep look nothing like humans. And why should they? There are so many other animal kingdoms to emulate, and countless original forms of deep-sea life that remain unfamiliar to most people. Who among us could imagine a wonder such as the Dumbo octopus, with elephant-like ear flaps? Or the yeti crab, an eight-inch-long crustacean with appendages covered in white "fur"? The author of a *Smithsonian* magazine article calls these and other creatures such as the delightful Gorgon's head or the squarenose helmetfish "head-shakingly bizarre."[1]

But are they monsters? Probably not, technically, since they strike me as more fascinating than frightening. They do serve, however, to remind us just how vast and unknown are the reaches of our oceans, and how likely it is that other things that *would* frighten us may cavort in these depths, unseen. The Americas, in fact, do have a long history of sightings of giant water creatures unknown to science. The Eastern

Seaboard, for starters, was filled with great serpents in the first centuries of European exploration and settlement.

One of the first printed records of something that might be called a sea monster near American shores appeared in a 1674 publication by John Josselyn, *An Account of Two Voyages to New England*. Author Richard Ellis provides this partial description: "a sea-serpent or snake that lay coiled on a rock."[2] It had been spotted in 1639 near Cape Ann, Massachusetts, and resembled no other known animal. An illustration in the Hart Nautical collection at the MIT Museum shows a serpentine beast with a long head, great round eyes, and a classic row of humps breaking the water's surface at intervals behind it.

An astonishing list of similar appearances throughout the 1700s is provided by A. C. Oudemans in his 1892 book, *The Great Sea Serpent*.[3] To sum them up quickly, eyewitness sightings occurred in or near Broad Bay, Maine, in 1751 and 1780; off the "east coast of USA" in 1770, 1781, 1782, and 1787; Penobscot Bay, Maine, in 1777 or 1778, 1779, 1783, and 1785; "near Ash Point on Fox and Long Islands, Maine," in 1784, 1794, and 1799; and an observation made at sea, northeast of the Azores, in 1786.

Some of these listings included more than one sighting in the noted year. And the number of incidents seems even more amazing given the small size of population living along the coast in the 1700s to act as observers, compared to the densely inhabited cities of today.

The sea beasts undulated on into the nineteenth century, starting with one spotted in the Gulf of Maine in 1802 by a clergyman named Abraham Cummings. Cummings said the water creature's large head looked like that of an oversized serpent, and that its blue, snake-like body trailed over sixty feet behind it. Oudemans's list adds sightings near Newfoundland in 1805 and Cape Cod Bay, Massachusetts, in

1815. These reports all seemed to be taken seriously by the New England populace, perhaps since so many sightings came from sea captains and even the clergy. At the very least, the incidences primed local awareness of sea creatures and helped set the stage for what would today be considered a major flap, as absolute sea monster mania took over the Eastern Seaboard in 1817.

THE GLOUCESTER SEA SERPENT OF 1817

The amazing extent of the Massachusetts sea monster mystery—especially in an age before electronic forms of mass communication existed to quickly spread the news—is evident from the quick glimpse at Oudemans's sightings list. It's even more striking when we take a closer look at what went on within certain, relatively short time frames, such as the two dozen-plus sightings around Gloucester and Cape Ann Harbors and Long Island in the year 1817 alone.

The initial sightings of 1817 cropped up in early August. Something huge first surfaced in area waters on the 6th, when two women observed a huge snake-like "sea-monster" gliding into the harbor at Cape Ann. This was followed on the 10th by a report from a mariner named Amos Story who testified, "I saw a strange marine animal, that I believe to be a serpent, at the southward and eastward of Ten Pound Island, in the harbour of said Gloucester. It was between the hours of twelve and one o'clock when I first saw him, and he continued in sight for an hour and a half. I was setting on the shore, and was about twenty rods from him when he was the nearest to me. His head appeared shaped much like the head of a sea turtle, and he carried his head from ten to twelve inches above the surface of the water. His head at that distance appeared larger than the head of any dog I ever saw."[4]

Story estimated the length of that huge head to be between three and four feet, and added that he saw only ten or twelve feet of the mostly submerged, serpentine body, which he said moved in a straight line without exposing any "loops" above water.

A shipmaster named Solomon Allen saw quite a bit more of the monster on three consecutive days, August 12, 13, and 14. Allen estimated the length of its dark brown, scaly, jointed body at between eighty and ninety feet, and its width about equal to that of a half barrel. Its head was larger than that of a horse but serpent-shaped, and its body wiggled from side to side rather than vertically. Allen said that at least twenty other people were also on hand to observe the creature, and some of them questioned his claim that the creature swam with horizontal wiggles rather than vertical. But none of them disputed the sighting of the beast.

August 14 was evidently a busy day for the beast, as it was also seen in Gloucester Harbor by four other observers at separate times and places. Witnesses included William H. Foster; Gloucester justice of the peace Lonson Nash; Matthew Gaffney, who noticed it between 4 and 5 p.m.; and Epes Ellery plus another crew of fifteen to twenty people near sundown a few hours later.

Most witnesses reported slight variations in the creature's length and movements, but that seems only natural when the differing locations, distances from the creature, angles of sight, times of day, and effects of sun, clouds, and waves are factored in. Given all of that, in fact, the level of actual agreement in the eyewitness descriptions is actually quite remarkable. The general consensus was that the beast possessed a snake-like or turtle-shaped head that was larger than that of a horse, a very long, dark-colored serpentine body that sometimes displayed vertical humps above the surface of the water, and the ability to pass through the water very rapidly when it liked.

The fact that all these dozens of detailed reports still exist is also remarkable. We may thank three members of the Linnaean Society of New England—a naturalist, a judge, and a doctor—who were appointed to a committee dedicated to the documentation and scientific study of the creature. In addition, Lonson Nash, the justice of the peace who was himself an eyewitness, took officially sworn testimonies. The committee members conducted detailed interviews from every eyewitness they could find, and speculated at great length on the anomalous serpent's anatomy and appearance.

The public followed the committee's reports with great but sharply divided interest. As always occurs in any sightings flap of unknown or out-of-place creatures, some citizens declared the whole thing nonsense while others became fervent believers. A Mr. S. G. Perkins wrote a letter to an acquaintance in Paris describing the frenzied activity inspired by the serpent: "[T]he Country has been agitated with reports of the existence of the monster, and men of reputation and character have made known, that they have distinctly seen the animal. Many have gone off in search of him in boats, and muskets have been fired at him, without any other effect than alarming him and deterring him from suffering the approach of the boats."[5]

Some people noted that the creature's harbor visits seemed closely tied to the regular arrival of great shoals of herring and concluded the creature must be feeding on them. That sensible argument probably helped gain believers, but many others were dissuaded after eager monster hunters decided that a common black snake that happened to turn up on the beach around that time *must* be a juvenile specimen of the sea serpent. The three-foot-long "baby" serpent was duly dubbed *Scoliophis atlanticus*, a designation that had to be rescinded when a reptile specialist finally got a look at the supposed new species and quickly identified it.

Snake mistakes notwithstanding, no one has ever satisfactorily explained the Gloucester-area sightings. Theories, however, abounded at the time and continue to do so to this day. Oudemans was certain that the animal was some unknown type of giant seal, or other pinniped, while others offered suggestions that ranged from a row of porpoises swimming in a perfectly straight line to a whale. Author James B. Sweeney had yet another solution, which he put forth in *A Pictorial History of Sea Monsters and Other Dangerous Marine Life*:

> It might seem strange that no indication was given in regard to these sightings that what they saw was actually seaweed, for it was well known that in the area of certain sightings, there existed seaweed plants that grew to 1,000 feet in length and weighed hundreds of tons. If a cannonball were to be fired at any one of these enormous, cylindrical plants, and the sea savagely disrupted by the action, it is likely that they would bob, weave, and act much like a serpent in the act of making an escape.[6]

Few of the sightings, however, involved cannonballs being shot, and many of the eyewitness observations were made from shore with no boats in the immediate vicinity. Sweeney recounted one such incident, moreover, that involved a creature that suddenly surfaced only sixty feet off the bow of the schooner *Adamant* in May 1818. The ship's captain, Joseph Woodward, testified in a sworn statement also signed by two of his mates that his entire crew saw the beast break the water's surface and coil its body repeatedly to propel itself through the waves. This does not sound like drifting seaweed. The creature also possessed what all witnesses called a head, with eyes that seemed fixed upon the schooner.

On this occasion, Captain Woodward ordered his men to fire the cannon. If the target had been seaweed, the cannonball should have sunk the fronds in a tangle, or perhaps passed through them. Instead, it bounced off the creature's tough hide with a resounding thud, an action that caused the beast to head straight for them with mouth agape. The men were too frightened to fire again as the creature swam so close to the boat that they narrowly missed a collision. It dallied nearby for almost five hours as if to keep an eye on them, and gave captain and crew plenty of time to observe it at close range. I believe that rules out the seaweed hypothesis, especially in this one event where a cannonball was actually fired.

They estimated the creature's length at 130 feet long and six feet in diameter, including a twelve-foot head with indentions that they presumed were ear holes. Its color, they said, was very dark, almost black. It sounded much like the creature that had been so often reported in 1817. As also happened with the previous reports, not everyone believed the *Adamant*'s amazing encounter tale. But neither did anyone come up with a good reason as to why these seamen might have made up such a story. The captains and crews of these busy trade and passenger schooners surely wouldn't have thought news of a monster big enough to swamp large vessels would have been good for business!

KREATURE OF THE KEYS: FLORIDA 1905

Valhalla was the name of the grand hall of Norse mythology where the god Odin feasted with warriors slain in battle. It was also the name of the 1,700-ton yacht whose passengers enjoyed one of the most spectacular encounters with an unknown sea creature ever recorded.

This was no mere pleasure cruise. The yacht's owner, astronomer Lord James Lindsay, Earl of Crawford, had taken the vessel on a research voyage to cruise the Atlantic Ocean south of Florida on December 7, 1905, when one of the two other scientists aboard, Edmund

G. B. Meade-Waldo, spotted something large emerging from the ocean surface about one hundred feet from the yacht.

Meade-Waldo had nearly ideal viewing conditions. It was mid-morning on a clear day, so visibility was excellent, and he was equipped with a good pair of binoculars. He alerted Lord Lindsay and the other scientist, M. J. Nicoll, and the three men gasped as a dark brown, six-foot-long fin rose out of the water, followed by a turtle-head-shaped noggin and a neck that Meade-Waldo estimated to be the same width as a man's body. The head and neck swayed back and forth above the waves, but Meade-Waldo was still able to make out the creature's eyes through his binoculars.

The *Valhalla* had already been set on a rapid course aimed in the direction opposite the position of the animal, and they soon lost sight of it. It may have followed them, however, because later that day two of the ship's crewmen spied a huge animal that lay alongside the boat, visible just below the water. The ship's first mate recorded it in the official log, noting that it could not have been a whale because there was no blowhole.

The *Valhalla* sightings were corroborated by log entries made three days later within eighty miles of the *Valhalla*'s location by the large merchant vessel *Happy Warrior*, whose crew described the beast as a "sea snake of great magnitude."[7] They added that the long-necked creature was several times as long as their three-masted ship.

About seven days later, a third ship—one that happened to be entirely manned by deaf-mutes—reported its own glimpse of what seems to be exactly the same creature encountered by the *Valhalla* and *Happy Warrior*. This crew also described it as a serpent and compared its size to that of a large tree. They considered their sighting important enough to report it to a resident of Key West with a handwritten note when they later docked for supplies.

James Sweeney believes there were many other sightings in this region in the years prior to and during World War I that the military kept from the public. "During World War I," said Sweeney, "many records of sea monster sightings were lost when merchant ships, torpedoed by German U-boats, sank and carried their log books to the ocean floor."[8]

Sweeney cites several examples: a British freighter, the HMS *Hilary*, which encountered a sixty-foot snake-like beast in the north Atlantic on May 22, 1917, which it first mistook for a German submarine, and a report from a small British naval gunboat that saw a long-necked, horse-headed sea beast on April 17, 1917, in the same general area. The gunboat commander also first mistook the animal for a submarine.

At least one of those German submersibles reported to their superiors that they had seen a huge, snake-like creature. The commander, Admiral von Holtzendorff, was as suspicious of the creature as the Royal Navy officers had been of the monsters they saw; the German admiral believed the sea serpent must have been some sort of ingeniously engineered decoy intended to lure his submarine in for the kill.[9] It's hard to say which was stranger—the existence of an actual sea monster, or the idea of a complex Allied scheme to lure German subs with giant sea monster decoys!

I'd say the latter may just have been the less likely of the two options, since strange things were also swimming off the nation's Pacific shores in the first half of the twentieth century.

MONTEREY BAY'S BOBO, OLD MAN OF THE SEA, AND OTHER OCEANIC ODDITIES

It was baaack, announced the Lodi (California) *News-Sentinel* in a November 8, 1946, headline: "Bobo the Sea Monster Appears Again."[10]

The crew of the *Katrina F.*, a type of fishing vessel known as a purse seiner for its style of drawstring nets, had spotted the famed "gorilla-faced sea beast" between Monterey Bay and Santa Barbara as their boat headed northward at about six o'clock on the morning of November 7. All ten crew members saw the beast's enormous head surface and then remain about five feet above the water as the creature swam around the boat a few times before it dropped back into the deep, its curiosity evidently sated.

The crew probably knew they were looking at a living legend. "His snuffling, foreshortened snout has appeared in the waters near Monterey on an average of once a year for the last ten years," said the article.[11] But tales of Bobo and Monterey's Old Man of the Sea date back decades earlier than the *Katrina F.*'s encounter. Two of the earliest reports came from a fisherman named Sal Colletto, who claimed sightings of an odd creature in Monterey Bay in the early 1900s and whose reports are housed in the Museum of Monterey.

Staff reporters of the *Monterey County Weekly* retold the tale of Colletto's encounters in an article posted online October 25, 2007, and described his first glimpse of the creature as seen on a clear day from about one hundred feet: "He saw a creature with a head the size of a fifty-gallon barrel. It was tapered to where a duck-like bill protruded from the massive, bulging forehead."[12] There was no mention of body size or length.

Colletto had to wait sixteen years for his next encounter, but that time the beast was also witnessed by his crew and brother-in-law. Colletto pulled the forty-five-foot boat closer to the creature, which appeared to be floating on its back, eyes closed, as crew members argued over whether the creature's face looked more like that of a monkey or an old man. Its brown, wrinkled body was nearly as long as the boat, and it finally opened its huge, round, pink eyes to stare at the humans for a moment before dropping back under the waves.

Those human-like facial features earned it the nickname Old Man of the Sea, although some people also refer to the sea beast as Bobo, which is Spanish slang for "stupid" or "foolish." Just to throw in the usual bit of confusion that always seems to surround sightings of monstrous things, some researchers insist Bobo and the Old Man are separate, unique creatures.

The *News-Sentinel* speculated that Bobo was actually a sea elephant, or elephant seal, a huge marine mammal that can grow to a length of twenty feet, weigh over eight thousand pounds, and stay underwater for up to two hours at a time. Members of this species aren't always immediately recognizable as seals due to their weird, elongated snouts, so perhaps an elephant seal really can account for some of the sightings. There are still plenty of encounters left that cannot be explained in this way, however, to keep Bobo's legend alive and splashing.

CHESSIE OF CHESAPEAKE BAY

Back on the Eastern Seaboard, another Chesapeake Bay area creature showed up a bit south of the Gloucester serpent's domain—and in modern times. It caused a whole new sightings flap in the 1980s and may have been caught on a bit of video footage as well. It's known as Chessie, which rhymes happily with the über-famous Nessie of Loch Ness, Scotland. And like Nessie, Chessie also boasts a considerable history behind its modern-day sightings.

Reports of monstrous, serpent-like beasts in the Chesapeake area date back to at least 1846. A twentieth-century cluster occurred in the 1930s when two men fishing near Baltimore spied a black serpentine creature with a horse-like head raised twelve feet over the water. By implication, there was probably a much larger part of the beast still submerged to provide support for the huge neck and head. Other sightings were made by such reputable eyewitnesses as a helicopter pilot in 1963 and an employee of the CIA in the 1970s. The CIA employee and several neighbors actually saw four of the creatures, which they estimated as ranging between twenty-five and forty feet long.

A farmer with the lyrical name of Goodwin Muse observed a somewhat smaller creature in the Potomac River on June 14, 1980, along with five friends. Muse swore none of his companions were drinking and that the animal was nothing he'd ever seen in his fifty-nine years. According to researcher Mark Chorvinsky, the sighting of the creature just thirty yards offshore "was covered by the wire services and appeared nationally," as the *New York Times* heralded the "Return of Chessie."[13]

On June 22, 1980, the family of G. F. Green also spotted Chessie from their boat in the Potomac, from only about forty feet away. It looked just like the creature Muse described, except that the Green party also noticed humps on its back. Other sightings followed on July 3 and on into August, then again in the summer of 1981.

It was a computer salesman and wildlife management expert named Robert Frew, however, who made Chessie an overnight film sensation on Memorial Day of 1982 when he managed to capture several minutes' worth of video of the creature's serpentine motion from his Love Point home. His wife, Karen Frew, and several dinner guests also witnessed the dark brown or black creature slithering near a clueless knot of swimmers about fifty feet from shore, in water that was only three to five feet deep. They watched it dive and then resurface very close to the splashing young people.

Researcher Chorvinsky included Frew's thorough description in a 1995 article for *FATE* magazine. Frew estimated the creature's length at thirty feet and its thickness at about the size of a large human thigh, and added that it seemed to have humps on its back. "My mind says it's a snake," said Frew, "but its head was a little more round than a football."[14] Frew added that he and the other witnesses had observed the creature raise its head from the water several times, to heights that increased sequentially from four to twenty feet above the surface.

The film was subsequently studied by a group of scientists at the Smithsonian Institution. The study group would not confirm that the undulating form was indeed an unknown creature but went so far as to admit it was "animate."[15] They suggested that part of what appeared to be the creature's body was probably just its wake, but conceded that other usual sea monster explanations such as "a partially submerged log, a string of birds or marine animals, or an optical illusion seem inappropriate for the dark, elongated, animate object."[16] Further enhancements by Johns Hopkins Applied Physics Laboratory showed a much clearer image that included the "bumps" observed on its back by many witnesses, but again the experts would make no firm conclusion.

While the scientists may have considered the matter closed, however, the monster did not. It returned as if to flex its star-power muscles in the summer of 1982, revealing itself to a building contractor and his wife who agreed it was longer than their twenty-four-foot boat, and then upping the ante in 1984 when it startled, in turn, two fishermen and a retired business executive, according to bemused area newspaper reporters. The retired exec told a Maryland paper that he saw a giant snake's head pop up only twelve feet from his boat and regard him momentarily with "a big, black eye" before it dove back to the depths.[17]

It's said there have been other Chessie sightings since then, including one that occurred in September 1997, offshore at Maryland's Smallwood State Park near Pasadena, although I wasn't able to find any details of the incident. (Incidentally, that park is named for an ancestor of my paternal grandfather.) The most authoritative tally of sightings was probably that of Maryland journalist and sports columnist Bill Burton, who collected seventy-eight sightings of Chessie over several decades before his passing in 2009. The debate as to Chessie's true nature still rages, however; theories of its origin range from some sort of relict, prehistoric creature to a mutant sea worm to pure illusion.

Chorvinsky concluded in his article, ". . . the weight of the evidence mitigates strongly in favor of the existence of a strange marine creature in the Bay."[18] He noted that in light of the bay's connection to the ocean, Chessie had the option of returning to the open Atlantic whenever it seemed expedient, which would help explain the long stretches with no sightings. It seems to me that Chessie and its family could have been visiting the coastal area from the Chesapeake Bay to Gloucester as a preferred, seasonal feeding ground for centuries.

The dark brown, humpbacked great serpent may not be the only marine animal to forage those coastal waters, either. The name Chessie was repurposed for a manatee sighted in the bay during the 1990s. That creature was definitely a flesh-and-blood marine animal but gained attention for having ventured farther north than is normal for the species. Marine biologists speculated that it had somehow migrated from Florida.[19] A few would-be debunkers of the original Chessie have since tried to spin the sea monster stories as simple cases of confusion with the manatee, but the snake-like, dark brown creature did come first.

13

American Kraken:
Giant Squids of Humboldt Bay

"Release the Kraken!" Zeus, ruler of the Greek gods, uttered this bold command in the 2010 film remake of the 1981 movie *Clash of the Titans* and made it a household catchphrase. Despite the recent origin of this saying, though, the kraken is a sea monster with better historic chops than most. It struck terror into some of the earliest seafaring Europeans (and probably other early sailors as well) as far back as the sixteenth century: A Swede named Olaus Magnus wrote about it in 1523, and in 1752, Norwegian bishop Erik L. Pontoppidan called it "the largest sea monster in the world," describing it as so big that in one appearance it looked like several small islands—until the rest of it rose out of the water. Its arms, the adventurous bishop said, were as "high and large as the masts of middle-siz'd vessels."[1]

COLOSSAL SQUID

It may sound implausibly huge, but today's monster hunters and scientists alike are generally satisfied that the legendary kraken is an actual, known animal: the giant squid. Squids and their cousins, the octopuses, belong to the class of cephalopods, or "head-foot," since all there seems to be of them at first glance is an enormous head with a tangle of formidable, waving arms. Just because a creature is identifiable doesn't mean it's not scary.

Danish scientist Johan Steenstrup was the first to publish a paper on the giant squid that he named *Architeuthis* in 1857. Still, it took two decades until a suitably large, sixty-foot specimen turned up on a Newfoundland beach as proof. By 1880, a sixty-five-foot specimen (although the two tentacles and eight arms may have been stretched a bit during measurement) had washed up in New Zealand. The waters off the coast of this country must be fertile giant squid territory, since an example of another huge species, the colossal squid (*Mesonychoteuthis hamiltoni*), was taken there in 2007. It weighed almost one thousand pounds and was thirty-three feet long, and it had been caught in the act of stealing the catch of a commercial fishing vessel.

RED DEVIL MAYHEM

While the most spectacular squids seem to be found in other parts of the world, some species do show up in the Americas. The coastal waters of Southern California, South America, and Mexico are home to the Humboldt squid, a smaller variety that nonetheless can weigh over one hundred pounds and measure up to seven feet long. In Mexico it is called Diablo Roja, or "red devil," and a group of them encountered off California's San Onofre State Beach has generated headlines that recall sea monster stories of old.

"Huge Squid Cause Mayhem," read the *Orange County Register* on January 8, 2013. "The squid attacked the boat," said Jack Van Dyke, captain of the *Clemente*.[2] But the passengers were ready. His sixty-five-foot sport fishing boat was filled with thirty hopeful souls all wanting a chance to haul in a Humboldt, and they were granted their wish—in spades.

"For forty-five minutes it was like mayhem," said Van Dyke.[3]

The boat was entirely surrounded by the eerie, reddish phosphorescent light the creatures naturally emit, and the anglers were pulling in squid as fast as they could throw out their lines. They bagged a staggering eight hundred Humboldts, most of them weighing less than a monstrous five to ten pounds. Another four hundred of the squid, which had probably all come to the area to feast on krill, were taken by other boats the next day.

While in this case the mayhem was all produced by humans, there are incidents on record of Humboldts attacking people, especially skin divers. A 2007 article in the *Los Angeles Times* detailed an encounter that occurred around 1990.[4] Four divers in the Sea of Cortez had dropped into the water to record the activity as a fourteen-foot shark that a fifth man was attempting to land from their boat struggled and thrashed below. Several dozen squid, identifiable by their red-and-white phosphorescence, soon approached and homed in on the helpless shark, and the divers watched as the squids tore into it, biting and tearing off bits with their sharp beaks. Unfortunately, the Humboldts also began to investigate the dinner potential of one of the divers, who soon felt the unwelcome pull of tentacles around his neck, face, and chest.

The story had a happy ending when the creatures inexplicably let him go. Perhaps they didn't care for the taste of the diving suit. It's apparent in retrospect that the "red devils" were only sea animals taking advantage of a feeding opportunity, but I wouldn't have blamed that diver if he saw the Humboldts as something a bit more devilish.

Giant Octopus

There might well be other cephalopod contenders for the sea monster crown. It's logical to wonder whether an octopus, for instance, may ever be considered a kraken, since it's impossible to know whether some of the massive ocean beasts that inspired early legends were actually squid—or something else.

Some octopuses, such as the giant Pacific octopus, *Enteroctopus dofleini*, can come close to the giant squids in size. The largest of this species may weigh up to six hundred pounds, but most octopuses weigh far less. It's important to remember, however, that for all we know, there could be unbelievably larger examples of both squid and octopus in the deepest recesses of our oceans, and that the world's biggest example of either animal has probably not yet been found. All we can say for sure is that it would be terrifying to be clamped in the sharp, parrot-like beak or sucker-lined appendages of any oversized cephalopod, no matter its taxonomic classification.

I've bemoaned more than once the difficulty of classifying monsters of all types, but sorting sea creatures can be especially problematic, particularly in the case of those that wash up dead on beaches. Seawater, wave action, predators, and other natural processes tend to take their toll on tissue and flesh, leaving naturalists with a neverending source of bizarre zoological flotsam. And weird unidentified animal carcasses tend to be labeled monsters until proven otherwise. One alleged giant squid found in Florida in the late nineteenth century came to be one of the most studied and hotly debated unknown sea creatures ever put under a microscope.

14

The St. Augustine Monster and Other Gruesome Globsters

The year was 1896, less than a half century since the giant squid had been officially dubbed a new species. Even so, the idea that any type of mollusk could grow to such behemoth proportions was still highly controversial. So when DeWitt Webb, founder of the St. Augustine Historical Society and Institute of Science, learned of a truly massive but unidentified carcass discovered by two boys on the beach on Anastasia Island, he was understandably perplexed when certain features of the "thing" reminded him of a degraded giant octopus corpse. It was much larger than any octopus then known to science. And yet, two years later, a Yale professor concurred and named it *Octopus giganteus verrill* (after his own last name).

Because Webb sent preserved samples of the tough, rubbery tissue to the Smithsonian Institution, the question of the big blob's identity cropped up now and again. Every few decades someone else would study it with whatever new scientific method had become available and then declare it to be something different. Mary Markey wrote an admirably succinct summary of the labyrinthine twists and turns of the search for the St. Augustine Monster's identity for the *Smithsonian*'s August 2010 online newsletter.

The first big twist came when Dr. Addison Verrill, the professor who had named the supposed new octopus after himself, changed his mind and said the blob was part of a beached sperm whale. The samples then lay forgotten until 1971, when a structural analysis of the tissue led to a reversal and the creature was once again declared an octopus. Amino acid tests in 1986 confirmed this conclusion.

"However," wrote Markey, "in 1995, electron microscope and biochemical analysis indicated that the material was collagen from a warm-blooded mammal. In 2004, DNA tests applied to the St. Augustine sample along with other monster remnants from around the world identified all as the collagen matrix that holds together . . . whale blubber."[1]

Everyone had to admit that those two boys had been right in the first place. The final analysis did not disprove the existence of giant squids, however, especially since the giant squid had been acknowledged as an official, known animal ever since the first complete carcass was found in 1874 off Newfoundland. (The giant squid's existence received even stronger verification when Japanese scientists took the first photos of a living *Architeuthis* in autumn 2004, in the Pacific Ocean off the Ogasawara Islands. It was twenty-six feet long.) The DNA tests simply confirmed that this particular globster, as such tissue masses have come to be called ever since researcher and author Ivan T. Sanderson introduced the word in the early 1960s, was not a cephalopod. The puzzling nature of most amorphous beach carcasses, however, persists as they continue to pop up on beaches around the world.

Many of the most mysterious globsters—and therefore those also most likely to be tagged as sea monsters by the media—often turn out to be decomposed basking sharks. Researcher Mark Chorvinsky said in an article for *Strange Magazine*'s online edition, "It is one of those strange-but-true facts that when a basking shark decomposes, it begins to look a lot like a plesiosaur, the popular favorite for a living sea monster."[2] Chorvinsky also noted another fascinating tidbit about decrepit basking sharks: the fibers of their body tissues begin to separate into what looks like fine white hair, making the immediate identification of their carcasses a forensic nightmare.

Chorvinsky's roundup of beach blobs included a few in the Western Hemisphere. There was the 1925 Santa Cruz Sea Monster, for starters, whose grisly photo received front-page attention in newspapers across California. It was huge—between thirty and forty feet long—and possessed more of its bodily structures than do most globsters. Still discernible were its duckish, barrel-sized head and giant round eyes, and its thin twenty-foot neck and elephant-like legs. It was also said to have been covered with hair and feathers, which makes me think of those white filaments of decomposed tissue mentioned by Chorvinsky in his comments on the basking shark. Some scientists thought this was exactly what the blob must be, but other suggestions ranged from an actual plesiosaur recently thawed from a glacier to a type of whale so rare that almost no one had ever actually seen one. The Santa Cruz creature conundrum was never definitively solved.

Canada's Vancouver Island was the site of a 1947 beach blob, but that mass was quickly pronounced a basking shark and therefore caused little fuss. Not so in the case of the Tecoluta Sea Monster discovered in 1969 on a Mexican beach and hailed as a "prehistoric sea monster" in news releases worldwide.[3] That title didn't seem too farfetched for an unknown, thirty-five-ton beast with hardened skin jointed like armor and sporting a one-ton tusk, but some scientists still thought it might be a finback whale. The tip-off? The giant tusk, which was shown to match a certain part of a finback's huge skull.

But there are other types of monstrous carcasses in the water.

DROWNED-STERS: THE MONTAUK MONSTER

Akin to globsters are the decomposed but obviously nonaquatic corpses of mammalian quadrupeds that also sometimes turn up as grisly flotsam. "Drowned-sters" would be a more accurate name for this category. One of the best—and best-known—examples of mystery drowned-sters is the so-called Montauk Monster of Long Island, New York.

On July 30, 2008, *New York* magazine quoted a *Gawker* blog headline from the previous day that stated, "Monster Washes Ashore in Montauk."[4] According to *New York* magazine's accompanying article, the bloated animal of unknown origin—which both publications immediately branded with the "M" word—had washed up on Ditch Plains Beach near the Surfside Inn. A waiter at that restaurant spied it as he strolled near the water and said it "kind of looked like a dog, but it had this crazy-looking beak."[5]

The *Gawker* article read, "This is an actual monster, some sort of rodent-like creature with a dinosaur beak."[6]

It was only the size of a small- to medium-sized dog.

A passing woman took photos and passed them on to a friend who introduced them to the Web. Still, another woman, Jenna Hewitt, also took photos and told reporters that although East Hampton's animal control agency was called, no one ever came. Instead, an older man spirited the carcass away, telling bystanders he wanted to have it mounted. A local paper, the *Huntington Beach Independent*, wrote a story on the strange incident that incited further public interest.

Enough clear photos had been snapped, though, to allow zoologists and other wildlife experts to weigh in. Most of them identified the creepy critter as a raccoon that had undergone natural, but startling, changes during its dip in the drink. British scientist Darren Naish explained in his blog *Tetrapod Zoology*, "One of the first things that happens to bodies that roll around in the water is that their fur comes off and they look grotesque, hairless and bloated. The facial tissues then decompose, leaving a defleshed snout and eventually a totally defleshed skull. At the same time the flesh on the hands and feet is lost."[7]

The creature's identity was still far from clear, however. For one thing, the carcass had disappeared, preventing further examination. The man said to have snatched it from the beach melted into the scenery, and rumors swirled that men in uniform rather than the anonymous gent had removed the beast. A number of media outlets alleged that the whole thing had been hoaxed in hopes of promoting a movie, but others made counterstatements insisting the hoax claim was in itself a hoax.

Another popular theory posited that the creature was a mutant escapee from the nearby Plum Island Animal Disease Center, while amateur zoologists argued in forums all over the Web that the thing was merely some hitherto unguessed animal, perhaps a turtle, a capybara, or even a *chupacabras*.

The upshot is that years later, the Montauk Monster's true nature is still up for grabs. The Mashable Web site named it number one on its list of "Top 15 Web Hoaxes of All Time," but still noted, "Even today, no one really seems to know what it is."[8] Similarly eroded mammalian carcasses were discovered in Panama in 2011, near the Brooklyn Bridge in 2012, and in Wales, United Kingdom, in 2013, but none seemed to shed any light on the Montauk case. In addition, investigative TV shows *Ancient Aliens, MonsterQuest,* and Washington, D.C.'s

Fox 5 Morning News, among others, all failed to nail the animal's ID. The theory that it was a dead raccoon has probably retained the most traction of all the possibilities, however. And that has still not stopped people from referring to it as the Montauk Monster.

If globsters and drowned-sters do turn out to be dead, already-classified animals, does that prove that unknown sea monsters don't exist? Not at all. This only tells us which known animals are most likely to show up on beaches as gelatinous masses. Unfortunately, globsters have so far revealed nothing about actual sea monsters and have neither proven nor disproven their existence. They've instead become a little subcategory of monsters on their own.

Besides, of all the untold varieties and vast numbers of creatures cavorting through our oceans, only a small number make it to our populated shores as rotting carcasses. This select few can hardly be expected to be representative of every creature beneath the waves.

Globsters are even scarcer on the shores of inland freshwater lakes, where a host of creatures very similar to the most popular forms of sea serpents, snakes, and dragons have been seen by hundreds over the centuries. But lake boundaries are so much more restricted than those of, say, the Pacific Ocean, that lake monster witnesses tend to have better, closer looks at the creatures than do observers of sea beasts. Not that life in an underwater lake habitat is necessarily a bed of water lilies. . . .

15

Inland Lake Monsters

Monsters sighted in freshwater lakes have some inherent problems that oceangoing creatures need never bother about. Lake denizens are not only shut off from the great depths and vast reaches of the sea when they run low on food or want to hide from the pressures of encroaching humans or polluted water, but the size of the lake in which they're trapped determines how large they can grow and how big their family can be. These precise points are touted by skeptics who don't believe large prehistoric-looking creatures could overcome such obstacles to support breeding populations. But try telling that to the many people who have seen huge water beasts presently unknown to science gamboling in lakes from South America to Canada. One interesting and oft-disputed lake monster legend lies midway between these geographical extremes, in the heart of the American West.

THE BEAST OF BEAR LAKE

Utah is not a state most people associate with lake monsters. The state's second largest freshwater body, Bear Lake, covers 109 acres on the Utah-Idaho border and is probably more famous for its annual raspberry fest than for its resident lake monster, first allegedly observed in the 1800s. I say allegedly because many think the whole story was made up by Mormon colonist Joseph C. Rich for a story he wrote that appeared in the *Deseret News* in 1868.

If Rich did invent the story, he was a very thoughtful prevaricator. He included both native legends and details consistent with other sightings that were probably not as well-known in those times as they are in these days of rampant monster hunting. Moreover, Rich named names—at least the names of male witnesses—N. C. Davis and Allen Davis, Thomas Sleight, and James Collings—who along with six unnamed women, sighted the creature. Rich wrote of the group's encounter:

> Their attention was suddenly attracted to a peculiar motion of waves on the water about three miles distant. . . . Mr. Sleight says he distinctly saw the sides of a very large animal that he would suppose to be not less than ninety feet in length.[1]

That's a whopper of a lake beast, if not a whopper of a tale, as well. While many sources say Rich later retracted his story of secondhand sightings, there actually were some Bear Lake monster eyewitnesses of the same era who said they saw similar things and had pretty good credentials. A 1984 article in the *Spokesman-Review* asked Utah State University professor Ross Peterson about the legend of the monster. While joking that he thought many tales came from people who had had too much to drink (a standard debunking claim that seldom holds true for most people who report anomalous creatures), the historian added there were two reports he took more seriously.

"Wilford Woodruff and John Taylor, who later became presidents of the (Mormon) church, both recorded in their journals (in the 1870s) that they saw the monster silhouetted against the sunset," said Peterson.[2] It's hard to imagine that these two very religious men would have taken the time to write such a thing in their treasured personal diaries if their sightings were mere fish stories.

Glimpses of the Bear Lake monster have continued over the years, although a few have been judged suspect. In 2002, Brian Hirschi claimed to have seen a large, green-skinned, red-eyed creature with humps on its back come alongside his boat. Some wags have pointed out that Hirschi ran a tourist-oriented business and his sighting was made on Memorial Day, just in time for the start of the recreational season. On the other hand, most lake monster sightings do tend to occur during the summer, and the creature's return date may have been entirely coincidental.

More damning is the fact that descriptions of it are truly all over the zoological map, ranging from early Native American tales of a spirit-like "water devil" to a serpent-like creature with an unknown number of short legs. According to various witnesses, its body was brown or green; its head might be shaped like that of a walrus or elongated like an alligator's. As is true in the case of oceangoing creatures, some of this variation can be explained by things like lighting, distance, and the general problems inherent in viewing things in or on the water, but the Bear Lake beast is still tougher than most to pin down.

So why start this lake monster review with such a problematic specimen? Truth be told, I like this story because it's a good example of what the lake monster hunter is up against, in addition to the usual and, yes, sensible point that few lakes are large enough to support viable populations of huge creatures. The Bear Lake creature reminds us that much sorting may be required to organize widely varied reports from any lake into a profile that captures a comprehensible, single monster, and also provides a good example of the need to suss out commercial influences that may muddy the waters, so to speak.

And yet, despite the Bear Lake beast's modest credentials, it's become one of the country's best-known water monsters. Perhaps that's justified; it's hard to brush off the testimony of two Mormon church presidents. As for Mr. Rich's recanting of his story, I've seen a few contemporary eyewitnesses do the same thing after being ridiculed for coming forward. One Wisconsin man who had a very convincing encounter with an upright wolf-like creature told me he was taking the whole thing back because he was afraid his children would be teased. Who knows what may really have been in the mind of the Mormon colony leader? I'd still advise Bear Lake users to keep binoculars and a camera handy.

Utah is not the only western state with a water monster: Montana boasts an even better-known creature with a far deeper backstory and continuing sightings.

The Much-Featured Creature of Flathead Lake

With 188 square miles of open water, Montana's Flathead Lake is the largest natural freshwater lake contained in America's lower forty-eight. Surrounded by mountains and connected to a far-ranging river system, the lake measures 370 feet or more at its deepest point, having been part of a sea in ages past. It's unthinkable—to people interested in cryptids, at least—that such an impressive aquatic environment might not support its own lake monster. Happily, Flathead Lake doesn't disappoint in this regard. An oversized swimming thing, whose appearance has been compared to that of the Loch Ness monster, has been awing eyewitnesses around Flathead Lake since 1889, when a steamboat captain named James Kerr and an entire load of passengers plainly saw a large unknown animal churning its way toward them. Fearing the steamer would be rammed, one of the passengers shot at the creature as it neared the boat and scared it back down to the depths.

This daylight sighting, with its boatload of witnesses, made an understandably big splash in the press, and the creature has gained notoriety ever since. The late researcher and author John Keel called the Flathead Lake monster "the most authentic of American Lake Monsters," adding, "Whatever it is has been seen by a great many people over a long stretch of time."[3]

A better idea of what a "great many people" actually means may be found in the grand tally of 102 sightings and encounters as of 2013, in a sightings count updated for this book by Laney Hanzel, a former Montana Fisheries biologist. Hanzel tracked monster reports, which usually occur in the warmer months of the year, as he performed his other duties on the lake for thirty years. Space doesn't permit me to recount most of these sightings but the following samples will show that this is one robust and active beast. It may, in fact, be two or more robust and active beasts.

One notable incident involved a local couple and their four children in July 1949. The family saw a "fish" ten to twelve feet long that left a wake nearly a foot high. About six feet of its spine were visible,

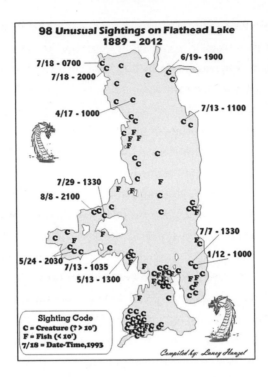

and they decided that judging from what they were able to see, it looked like a sturgeon.

The family may well have been correct. In 1955, a Flathead Lake angler did catch a seven-and-a-half-foot white sturgeon whose origins are still pondered by lake biologists. The fisherman had his trophy mounted and the gargantuan specimen now hangs in the Polson-Flathead Historical Museum. It weighed 181 pounds. And yet, the majority of Flathead Lake's monster descriptions just don't match up to that of this admittedly fierce, living fossil of a great fish. There's this example from two area residents, for instance.

"It was a horrible-looking thing," said Mrs. Gilbert Zigler of the gigantic black creature she and her husband saw scratching itself against their dock in September 1960.[4] They said that its head was the size of a horse's and that a foot of its neck showed above the water. It swam away before Gilbert Zigler could fetch his rifle, but it did not look nor behave like a sturgeon.

Another good year for sightings of the serpentine monster was 1963, with twelve eyewitnesses on June 15 and two on September 8. Those two witnesses on the 8th, Heather McLeod and Genevieve Parratt, were both schoolteachers. They described a ten-foot-long, dark gray beast undulating swiftly through the water, with three humps visible as it left a three-foot wake behind its wiggling posterior.

The blog *Cryptozoo-oscity* detailed a harrowing encounter back on the fish-like side just a year later, in summer 1964. Joyce Nelson's family was swimming offshore at Polson when several family members all felt something large brush their legs. "After much screaming and fuss," the site quoted Nelson, "we all got up on the dock. We were watching and a large creature similar to, but not quite a sturgeon was seen about one hundred feet from us."[5]

After about three decades of sporadic sightings, reports spiked once more in 1993 with thirteen known incidents. (An average year yields only two sightings, says Hanzel.) Also unusual was the fact that one of these thirteen sightings yielded the first observation of two creatures together. On May 24, in Big Arm Bay, witnesses saw both a larger and smaller version of the beast at the same time. The pair of beasts were first seen swimming together but then split, taking off across the lake on separate routes.

In July of that year, a vacationing bank officer from Seattle was able to capture a brief video that showed a dark but blurry figure he described as resembling an eel, and a policeman and his family saw a creature they likened to a plesiosaur, an extinct, long-necked marine animal often compared with the Loch Ness monster. They estimated its length at between fifteen and twenty feet and also noted the distinctive back humps often seen by other observers.

Despite the apparent divide between the two types of creatures, sturgeon-like or serpent-like, Hanzel says that witnesses present a fairly consistent description overall that leans statistically toward the serpent type: "The object most frequently (seventy percent) described is a large eel-shape creature that reaches in length from twenty to forty feet," says Hanzel. "It is round, brown to blue-black in color, and possesses very obvious steel-black eyes and undulating hips. Others identify it as a large-sized fish from six to ten feet in length."[6]

Hanzel also likes to emphasize the diversity of the witnesses, and notes that they include both visitors and lifelong residents. "Details of the creature have been described by mothers, doctors, lawyers, biologists, engineers, anglers, and policemen," he said in his article, adding that "the sighters were not drinking or on drugs and they hate to talk about it to anyone for fear of being identified as a 'weirdo' or worse."[7] He also said that he hadn't seen the creature himself but on more than one occasion has discovered big holes in fishing nets that had been made by something too large to explain by any known lake fauna.

Flathead Lake fishing guide Tim Shattuck said on the April 14, 2013, episode of Destination America's *Monsters and Mysteries in America* that he had personally seen the monster twice. "Once was on the surface of the lake and once in the depths," he told a Montana reporter who wrote about Shattuck's TV debut, "and I still believe it's a big old fish."[8]

Polson trial attorney James A. Manley and his wife, Julia Manley, also appeared on *Monsters and Mysteries*, but the horrific thing they described didn't sound like any known fish. Their encounter occurred on July 28, 2005, at Big Arm Bay on a weekday afternoon. The couple was enjoying a pleasant ride when their boat's motor died, and they moored their vessel while they waited for their daughter to come and assist them. While they sat near shore, their boat dead in the water, they began to hear the ominous sound of something very large slapping the lake's surface. Worse, the sound was coming directly toward them.

Julia said on the show that she felt total shock when she and James saw what was making all the noise. It was a serpent-like creature at least as long—and perhaps, they feared, longer—than their twenty-four-foot boat. Several back humps were visible just above the water. Just then, their daughter approached on another boat, and the monster slipped off without being seen or heard by anyone on the rescue vessel.

The sightings continue to the present, with several on record for 2013 by summer's end. One of the most recent eyewitnesses, Chris Thoman, wrote me about his sighting made at 1:30 p.m. on July 17, 2013.

He was camping at the West Shore Park at a site on a cliff overlooking the lake, Thoman said, and on that day was sitting in his camp chair, enjoying the view of the lake's calm inlet when he noticed a disturbance. He grabbed his binoculars and saw three large, porpoise-shaped objects moving slowly from east to west along the shore about one mile away, as he judged from his map. He said he stared for several long minutes, wondering if they could be whales or perhaps submarines, but soon discarded both ideas.

"They were a dark brownish color," he wrote, "not quite brown, not quite black. After a few minutes, I noticed the lead object was creating a wake of white water as it moved eastward. The lead object was longer than the other two, but they all seemed to have the same girth. It appeared that two were swimming in unison, with the other one swimming alongside those two. They never separated from each other and the two that were swimming in unison seemed to stay equidistant."

He noticed a few kayaks and boats in the same vicinity as the objects and used the known size of the vessels to estimate the length of each of the objects as about twenty feet. He didn't see anything above water that he could characterize as heads or tails. After the objects swam out of his sight, he tried searching Google on his phone to see if by some strange chance there really were whales in Flathead Lake, but of course found nothing to indicate that there were. Later that night Thoman told a camp ranger about his experience, and the ranger told him that he and his son had also seen Flathead Lake's creature years ago.

The "three objects" could be interpreted as parts of a single, large creature or three separate, smaller, unknown creatures, such as the giant sturgeons a few have reported. And who knows—it may well be there are two types of outsized aquatic beasts in this lake—it's certainly big enough for both.

There are myriad other lakes in nearly every state believed to harbor monsters. There's Champ of Lake Champlain, Indiana's Lake Manitou monster, British Columbia's Ogopogo of Lake Okanagan, and too many more to mention. Most of them have their own fans, researchers, and even associations dedicated to proving their creature's existence by whatever means possible, from sonar to submersible watercraft. Those who have seen the creatures usually affirm they don't need no stinkin' technology, they know what they saw. An encounter is always worth a thousand blurry videos—at least to the witness.

Native American Water Spirits

Before jumping into this next topic, I need to beg readers to bear with me for a moment while I insert a fast disclaimer: Native American tales of water monsters should not be viewed in exactly the same light as Western-style historical records. While some traditional legends may very well signify actual observed creatures, the creatures also embody their own cultural significance, which may vary widely from nation to nation—even when the monsters sound roughly similar in action and appearance.

Now that we have that straight, some of these monsters are, frankly, mythic, such as the water monster of several Eastern US tribes encountered by the culture hero Glooscap. This monster was gargantuan, with warts as big as mountains and "a mile-wide, grinning mouth going from ear to ear."[1] Glooscap must kill the great creature in order to release the water it carries in its body so that people may have use of it. The beast does sound like one of a kind, and it has occurred to me that it could be a metaphor for the memory of long-melted glaciers that once bound much of the continent's water into giant sheets of ice before melting into our lakes, rivers, and streams. The references to mountains and the mile-wide, grinning crack of a mouth make particular sense in this view.

The description can still be interpreted more literally, of course. Other native water monsters sound vaguely similar in terms of the giant size, shape, and saucer-like eyes, as do creatures that eyewitnesses sometimes observe to this day. And there are a lot of them. Almost every tribal culture of the Americas includes at least one or two aquatic terrors on its monster roster.

DEVILS LAKE

Delve into almost any lake with a long history of unknown creature sightings and you're likely to find an even older tradition of Native American lore attesting to the presence of lake monsters or other strange phenomena in that same body of water.

North Dakota's Devils Lake, with more than 130,000 acres situated near the United States–Canada border, is a perfect example. The Sioux and Chippewa people who lived there long before European settlement gave the lake various names that mostly meant, loosely translated, Spirit Water or Place of Mysteries. As often happened with any Native American place name that included the term "spirit," white settlers translated the indigenous terms into the darker sounding "Devils

Lake." Of course, in this North Dakota lake's case, the name might also have been partly due to the fact that spooked settlers claimed they often saw phantom boats and ghosts of drowned Native Americans floating eerily over its waters.

What's known for sure about the lake's history is that this place was long considered sacred ground. Both tribes believed their ancestors came from beneath the area's highest hill, known as Devil's Heart to settlers but by a phrase meaning Heart or Center of the Region to the Sioux and Chippewa. The Sioux also believed that in the late 1880s, their tribe's continued warfare against the Chippewa caused the Great Spirit to create a water monster to stop the bloody battles.

Authors Don Kaufman and Nan Belknap wrote of this hellish incarnation in a 2007 issue of *FATE* magazine: "Suddenly the earth trembled as the lake began to churn and boil. Out of the water rose a huge monster with short legs and saucer-like eyes that flashed like copper fire."[2]

The fiery-eyed creature killed most of the Sioux war party before committing another heinous act. According to legend, it used an underground river that snaked all the way to the Gulf of Mexico to drain the lake's fresh water and then fill it with brackish saltwater. This story may have been the Sioux's way of dealing with the fact that the lake levels did actually begin to drop around that same time as fish populations nosedived and the water quality changed. But in 1908, area tourists panicked after seeing a black twelve-foot, horned serpent rise high up out of the lake and then drop back down. A 2011 Prairie Public Broadcasting Web site article about the serpent's return to Devil's Lake quoted local 1908 newspaper headlines, one of which read, in part," "Probably the Same One that Indian(s) Saw."[3]

That same article also mentioned a Federal Writers' Project publication from the 1930s that had put forth the intriguing speculation that "the waters of the lake, under the right atmospheric conditions, could 'throw off a vapor through which birds swimming on the surface can be seen from a distance—highly magnified.'"[4] The 1930s article went on to propose that these oddly enlarged images might look like either phantom boats or sea monsters to excited viewers. The idea of a "vapor" clear enough and focused enough to maintain a lens-like configuration, however, sounds as unrealistic to me as the phenomena it is supposed to be explaining. But the passage does suggest that there must have been something very extraordinary happening on Devils Lake to have had people so anxiously racking their brains for a solution.

The *FATE* magazine article mentioned on the previous page added one later, monstrous factor to the Devils Lake puzzle: there was a flap of large black panther sightings that occurred in the 1980s. And the lake level has begun to rise again at a sometimes alarming rate. Perhaps the Great Spirit's lake monster has reopened his underground channel to the Gulf of Mexico, and he is on his way back along with the fresh water he's now so generously returning.

ALTAMAHA-HA: NO LAUGHING MATTER

Native American legends of huge serpent-like water monsters are often connected to rivers as well as lakes. Ancient traditions of Wisconsin's indigenous people, for instance, have long held that the twisty, turning Wisconsin River was created by a divine, giant serpent as it slithered across what would one day become the center of the state. Ohio boasts the ancient, enigmatic 1,348-foot-long effigy sculpture known as the Great Serpent Mound that hugs the Ohio Brush Creek, and in Georgia, sightings of the massive serpent guardian of the Altamaha River, known as Altamaha-ha (Ha-ha or Altie for short), span from ancient times to the present.

Author Jim Miles presents a very comprehensive look at Altie in *Weird Georgia: Close Encounters, Strange Creatures, and Unexplained Phenomena*. Despite the creature's comical, slightly demeaning nicknames, there's nothing cutesy about the beast itself. Miles calls it "the Loch Ness Monster of Georgia," and says that the Tama Indians have insisted since prehistoric times that a great river serpent that could hiss and make startling vocalizations lived in the Altamaha River and its tributaries along the state's southern coast.[5]

In the 1920s, loggers using the river to transport lumber began to tell of a monstrous snake swimming through the water traffic that sounded very much like the Tamas' ancient beast. Their reports died out along with the waning lumber industry, only to be replaced by sightings by hunters and Boy Scouts over the next few decades. In 1959, two vacationing state prison officials caught sight of a thirty-foot-long, snake-like creature as they crossed a bridge in Tattnall County.

The monster scene perked up again in the 1970s and 1980s. In 1970, said Miles, two brothers fishing from a houseboat at Clark's Bluff were shocked when a twelve-foot-long dark gray creature with a gator-like snout and a ridge along its back swam off with their line and destroyed it. In December 1980, two fishermen saw a giant creature suddenly dive down into Smith Lake. They estimated it was up to twenty feet long and said that it sported two back humps. Many other eyewitnesses have described very similar beasts in this river, says Miles, matching features right down to the two humps.

The last sighting reported by Miles was in 1989, but at least one more occurred in 2002 near Brunswick, by a boater who described a creature that was more than twenty feet long and six feet wide. There have probably been many other encounters that have gone unreported, as I've often surmised in my own experience in recording sightings of strange creatures.

As usual, speculation rages as to Altie's true nature. A few witnesses have said they could see the creature breathe out steam, and some researchers believe that this trait combined with Altie's up-and-down or vertical body movements may mean Altie is an aquatic mammal rather than a fish or reptile. Georgia resident Curt Holman interviewed a number of experts for an article he wrote for *Creative Loafing Atlanta*. One of them, author Dallas Tanner, thinks that Ha-ha may be "some kind of large, migratory seal ancestor that follows its food supply of fish."[6]

An ancestral seal that's been around for a while might explain the creature's prehistoric reputation, if not how the prehistoric animal survived to the present day. Several well-known researchers have suggested that a population of oversized, giant pinnipeds (seal-like mammals), as yet unknown to science, may explain both freshwater and saltwater monsters. But there are just too many creatures described as truly serpent-like for this to be a one-size-fits-all solution. The ancestral seal theory also fails to explain other aquatic creatures seen by modern witnesses, many of which were also described by Native Americans and portrayed in their art from antiquity.

WATER LYNX

One of North America's best-known rock paintings is that of Mishipeshu (variously spelled), the water lynx or water panther. Especially important to the Midwestern peoples, Mishipeshu jealously guarded the tribal copper mines of northern Michigan and lorded it over most lakes and rivers, as well. White sand left in a drowning victim's mouth always signified the involvement of a water lynx in the person's death. Mishipeshu is usually portrayed with an extremely long tail, great fangs, and curved horns. Many other tribes tell of "underwater cats" as well, of which an entry in the *Dictionary of Native American Mythology* says "may include lynxes, leopards, panthers or tigers, depending on the geographical region, that live under or near water."[7] It also tells a brief Cree story of how the city of Tulsa, Oklahoma, was started by a woman impregnated by a water tiger. The creature, whose name was Wi Katca, flooded the woman's town to prevent her relatives from killing the woman's hybrid children. Those who survived the torrent of water unleashed by Wi Katca rebuilt their homes, and the community eventually became known as Tulsa, which means "old town."

Horned Serpent

The water lynx is not to be confused with the horned water serpent known as Mishi Ginabig, Misikinipik, or, to the Lake Superior Ojibwe, as the Snake King. The Ojibwe tell a story of the culture hero Menaboju, who defeats the giant horned serpent the storyteller describes as around forty feet long and that is accompanied by a whole tribe of similar but smaller water monsters.[8] All of these water serpents were also believed to be powerful medicine men—shape-shifters, perhaps. They worked with the water lynxes to war against the Thunderbirds, or powers of the air.

Lake Guardians

The Hudson Bay Eskimo water monster is a giant hairy, faceless beast called Miqqiayuuq that tries to prevent people from taking drinking water from under the ice. The Navajo also take great care to avoid a water monster they call "the one who grabs in deep water."[9] This creature looks like a giant otter, but he brandishes a buffalo's horns on his forehead and has the power to cause great floods.

One of my favorite variations on Native American water beasts was a creature believed by Wisconsin's Ho-Chunk people to inhabit Lake Mendota, one of the four lakes of the state's capital city, Madison. These lakes, according to Ho-Chunk legend, were infested with water lynxes and horned serpents, both of which were portrayed in huge bas-relief earthworks called effigy mounds that lay carefully arranged all over the shores of these sacred waters.

Winnebozho, or Bozho, as modern Madisonians like to call him, was something quite different. Part human, part fish, and part sacred raccoon, Bozho was highly respected by the Ho-Chunk. By the 1800s, however, the area around the lakes had been settled by newcomers, European immigrants who knew little about these legends of antiquity. And in the 1860s, Bozho began to rear his divinely hybrid head as if checking out the new neighbors. First, a couple in a small boat was attacked by an unknown animal they first mistook for a floating log, and then a postman named Billy Dunn spotted a giant long-necked creature. He told so many people that it became known as Billy Dunn's Sea Serpent, even though it was seen in a lake rather than a sea.

In the 1890s, more than a dozen people reported seeing a huge eel-like creature whose hide was impervious to bullets. Its length was estimated at anywhere between twenty and sixty feet, and it was even said to have eaten a hapless dog that it snatched from the water. In 1899, two women said that its head was ten inches across and that it had "horns" on its tail! (Some ancient depictions of Mishipeshu also show great spikes on the end of its tail.)

A 1917 report claimed that the creature had large round, glowing or fiery eyes, and in another encounter that same year, perhaps the strangest lake creature incident ever, a great beast slithered up and licked the soles of the feet of a student sunbathing on her stomach next to the water. The monster seemed more playful than vicious, as its main mischief consisted of pranks such as overturning the occasional canoe or popping its head up harmlessly, and Bozho had all but disappeared from Lake Mendota by the 1920s.

Madison's lakes are far too busy these days for any water monsters to even try poking a horned head above the surface, and many of the magnificent effigy mounds that represented them have long since been razed to make way for the city. Who knows where the lake monsters go when that happens?

Seeking Aquatic Answers: From *Archelon* to *Zeuglodon*

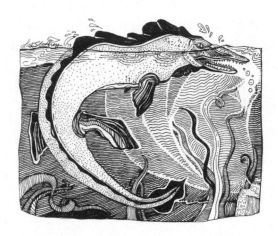

A s with any other collection of unknown creatures, most people are anxious to find mundane explanations for the sometimes hard-to-swallow sightings of water monsters. Seaweed clumps and floating logs are usually a skeptic's go-to rationale, and indeed could certainly explain a limited number of sightings. Living, contemporary creatures as yet unrecognized by science are another perfectly reasonable way to justify sightings of unknown marine animals. The discovery that there are truly giant squid in the ocean depths that fit centuries-old descriptions of krakens is a great example.

It's also tempting to go fishing in the murkier waters of the far-distant past, the days of dinosaurs, in the hope that a few relict specimens of some species long thought extinct might have survived to the present day. I do think that this scenario is far likelier to occur in oceans than in any other habitat, since our seas are vast, largely unknown, and probably much less disturbed by human activity than any other part of our planet. Also, such discoveries have actually happened.

Most people know the famous example of the coelacanth, a six-foot-long, two-hundred-pound fish scientists thought had died out sixty-five million years ago—until a very alive specimen turned up in 1938. Other live coelacanths have since been captured to prove that a breeding population of this prehistoric swimmer has somehow managed to hang on in mostly unchanged form for all those eons. But coelacanths aren't likely to be mistaken for monsters.

Titanic Turtles

One other creature that has been around in mostly original form for a very long time but that would be large and (under some conditions) odd enough to startle any unprepared observer is the giant leatherback sea turtle. Similar giant oceangoing turtles date back to the end of the Cretaceous period, the last era of the dinosaurs. One extinct genus, *Archelon*, could reach up to ten feet in length, and instead of a hard shell wore a leathery, ridged carapace on its back. Today's leatherback turtles are very like those forebears, often growing to seven feet or longer and weighing two thousand pounds or more. They also feature a ridged, leathery carapace that might in some cases look like the "humps" often described by aquatic monster eyewitnesses, and their head shape with its extra-long, overhanging beak could appear very unfamiliar while craning from atop the turtle's stretched-out neck.

The *Archelon* was very prevalent in the onetime oceanic area that in present day is better known as New York and New Jersey, and also in the oceanic seaway that covers present-day South Dakota and Kansas. That puts this species in the right place—although far from the right time—for many of today's "hot spot" areas of lake and sea monster sightings. And a full-grown *Archelon* would have been an imposing sight: Discovery Channel features an animated look at this creature on its Web site that makes it easy to see how a ten-foot specimen headed for a boat on the open water could be perceived as monstrous. No one expects to see a turtle that large or with such a long, beaked head.[1]

Modern leatherbacks are equally impressive and are widespread over the Americas and the rest of the world. An article in *Huffington Post* chronicling their successful return to beaches on the northern coasts of South America says, "With instincts honed over 100 million years, these mighty leatherbacks have migrated from cold North Atlantic waters in Canada and northern Europe to nest. The air-breathing reptiles can dive to ocean depths of more than 4,000 feet (1,200 meters) and remain underwater for an hour."[2] The article also quoted a Grand Riviere tour guide who called the leatherbacks "the world's last living dinosaurs." The crucial difference between the leatherbacks and the *Archelon*, of course, is that the leatherbacks show up in all the right places *and* in contemporary times.

More Monster Stand-ins

Even the most massive turtle, however, cannot account for those sightings where witnesses clearly observed serpent-like forms with slim, scaly bodies measuring dozens of feet long and undulating as no wide, leathery carapace could. Known animals of today that do come close to this type of description include twelve-foot-long giant eels and the ribbon-like oarfish, which can reach fifty feet in length and which have red dorsal fins fringed to resemble manes. I stress the words, "come close." If we're looking for exact matches, neither of these animals will fit most classic lake and sea monster accounts perfectly. Neither will giant, unknown pinnipeds, neatly lined-up dolphins, or alligator gars. These creatures, to paraphrase the famous quote often incorrectly attributed either to P. T. Barnum or Abraham Lincoln, may fool some of the eyewitnesses some of the time but not all of the eyewitnesses all of the time.

If only we could travel back in time, however, we could find many aqua-beasts that look like spot-on, bona fide sea monsters. It does seem unlikely that any of them would survive hundreds of millions of years to appear occasionally in our lakes and seas, but there's always that glimmer of hope held out to us by the resurrected coelacanth.

Ancient Sea Beasts

The best-known such creature is the plesiosaur, already mentioned as the spouting image of Loch Ness's Nessie and other lake monsters. Like the coelacanth, plesiosaurs were also supposed to have gone extinct sixty-five million years ago and included different species that had four flippers, long tails, and heads and necks of varying proportions. The largest measured fifty feet in length, and they survived for millions of years—a very respectable run for any type of beast.

Researchers also often zero in on mosasaurs, another genus of ancient water creatures that shared the seas with plesiosaurs, as potential extinction survivors. One particularly interesting mosasaur, *Tylosaurus*, lived in the same general area as Utah's Bear Lake. It was very closely related to snakes, with a long serpent-like body and jaws resembling those of an alligator.

The primitive, toothed whale, a *Zeuglodon,* is the final suspect I'll mention, although there are many other ancient animals known from the fossil record to resemble our modern-day notions of water monsters. Its official name, *Basilosaurus cetoides,* was based on early, mistaken identification of its fossils as reptilian. It lived between thirty-five and fifty-three million years ago and measured up to seventy-five feet in length, and was plentiful enough in North America that Alabama has named it their state fossil. It would certainly appear to be an unknown and scarily large creature if seen today, but alas, *Zeuglogon* represents another case of being in the right place at the wrong time. These creatures needed warm, shallow seas that were prevalent in their era but are far less widespread today. And they were many times larger than the long-enduring coelacanths, making it less likely that they could easily remain hidden in the shallower waters they prefer.

There are theoretical ways, however, of bridging those humongous time gaps. The possibility of creatures caught in time loops or being spit out of interdimensional portals is often raised by researchers not only to explain glimpses of out-of-time sea and lake creatures but, as we have seen in Part One, appearances of ancient flying things such as pterosaurs. We'll also see it mentioned in the next section in reference to unknown land-based creatures.

While there is as of yet no way to affirm that prehistoric animals (or our own perceptions) can time travel or that interdimensional creature transports could really happen, the continual advances of modern physics have taken these ideas from the realm of complete fairy tales to a place where they no longer seem completely inconceivable. To tackle any sort of explanation of these advances is beyond the scope of both my mastery of quantum theories and this book, but the very readable works of scientists like Brian Greene and Fred Alan Wolf are good places to further explore such ideas.

There are still more options. The idea that such creatures are phantom beings such as spirit entities, demons (as defined by various religions), or manifestations of human thought and emotion is widespread. So is the notion that people see these creatures only because one's mind is "playing tricks." But hallucinations are unlikely culprits in the case of water monsters, I think.

It's intriguing that eyewitnesses almost always see creatures that closely resemble animals that could once have been here and that look and behave appropriately for their given environments. No one reports seeing something that resembles, say, the giant marshmallow man from the movie *Ghostbusters* walking across the waves, as one might expect if sea monsters were appearing as willy-nilly products of individual imaginations. And there are many examples of multiple witnesses seeing the same thing at the same time.

Perhaps, though, we don't have to believe in spirit worlds or earn our doctorates in physics to ultimately learn the secrets of the sea serpents. There is real hope that our technology for exploring the deepest of the deep places will continue to improve and finally show us what's really lurking in the abyss. I secretly hope the lurkers turn out to look just like those things that appeared in Gloucester a couple of centuries ago.

PART THREE

MONSTERS BY LAND

If I could choose to encounter only one type of monster—as if anyone may *choose* to encounter large unknown creatures with any degree of reliability—I think I'd prefer to meet up with one that walks on terra firma like we do. Things that fly and swim have us grounded bipeds at a definite disadvantage.

Luckily for my hypothetical choice, there appears to be no shortage of land-based unknown beasts, and judging from prehistoric depictions of humanoid predators, snake gods, and upright lizards, it seems to have been that way for a long time. Skeptics may, in fact, suggest that instinctive, ancestral memories of giant cave bears, saber-toothed tigers, and other lethal megafauna still trigger people's visions of the upright wolves and massive apemen spotted in American woods, swamps, and fields today. Most contemporary eyewitnesses disagree. They believe these creatures are still here and that they are all too real.

While the prehistoric, humongous predators have largely (pun intended) disappeared from our landscape, more insidious things seem to have replaced them. But modern-day monsters are generally not the sort of animal that primitive hunters could surround and kill with a few good javelins and a supply of pointy rocks. They tend to escape our snares and trail cams, melting into the foliage at will. And even more eerily, many of them walk like us or look humanoid. If they are indeed echoes of the cave bear and the saber-tooth, then they must be anthropomorphized upgrades.

I'll begin with one that tends to be anthropomorphized even when it bears no recognizable human features. All a dog or wolf needs to do is take a few steps on its hind legs and suddenly people tag it with that ageless name some only dare whisper: werewolf.

Upright Canine Monsters

Canine creatures large, weird, and aggressive enough to be labeled monsters have one definite advantage over those limited to skulking upright around the countryside: They seem to be able to alternate between four legs or two. Dropped down into a normal, four-legged trot, an overly large canine isn't likely to attract much attention and can travel much more freely. Let it rise to a two-legged stance, however, and people will not only take notice but may also insist it's something from another realm. Although there's nothing supernatural about a dog or wolf walking on its hind legs, it often strikes people as frightening, because neither dogs nor wolves are known to prance bipedally unless trained by a human or motivated by, say, the loss of a forelimb.

It's shocking, then, to realize that people do see dogs, wolves, or wolf-dog hybrids sauntering, running, leaping, or lazily loitering on their hind legs far more often than logic would expect, since canid skeletons are not designed to work this way. Hundreds of credible eyewitnesses, however, have sent me first-person reports of canines committing random acts of bipedality over the past twenty years. And the creatures, moreover, seem to be able to change their stance at will: Sometimes they crouch on all fours before rising and running off on hind legs, and in other instances the reverse is true.

The creatures are usually described as extremely large even for a wolf (I think many may be wolf-dogs, based on paw shape and fur variations), averaging six to seven feet tall when standing. They glare at the witness with eyes that exhibit a yellow or yellow-green shine, and are usually reported to have tall pointed ears on top of their heads, long snouts, prominent fangs, slightly elongated paws with long claws, and standard canid limbs featuring heavier muscles than usual in the haunches and upper forelimbs. They are covered with fur usually described as shaggy and dark brown or black, but sometimes ranging to a light gray or tipped with silver, and they walk on their toe pads rather than flat-footed like primates or bears.

They do sometimes leave scant physical evidence such as wolf-like paw prints or deep scratches in the siding of a house or on a car's rear bumper, but I have yet to see a photo or video that definitively proves the upright wild canid called the manwolf, dogman, wolfman, or yes, sometimes werewolf, exists. The evidence is still mostly anecdotal, although there is an increasing amount of it. The eyewitnesses are surely seeing *some*thing. What most people really want to know, however, is whether these creatures are actually what most cultures worldwide call werewolves—humans who change physically into wolves and vice versa.

Let me state it again for the record: Based on twenty years of eyewitness reports, I don't believe that these contemporary eyewitnesses are seeing traditional, flesh-morphing werewolves. A very small percentage of upright canids do display appearances or behavior—glowing red eyes, bulletproof skin, and a tendency to fade into thin air—some might associate with supernatural phenomena, but most of the eyewitness reports include nothing that would rule out physical animals behaving oddly.

That fact begs the oft-asked question: If these creatures are "real" in the sense of belonging to our known, physical universe, why has no one ever shot or captured one? This same question is also frequently asked in regard to most unknown creatures and deserves some attention. Before I discuss anything to do with shooting or capturing, however, I'd like to be clear that any hunting I do personally is more akin to research and field observation. I do not advocate literally hunting down any unknown creature as if it were a game animal, especially with the intent of shooting it, for many good reasons. One of the best is that there is always a possibility that the "creature" in question may be a human hoaxer; this can and does happen.

In the case of the dogman's lack of proven mortal remains, I always need to point out that it's likely that some have indeed been shot or even hit by automobiles, but because most reports describe something that is fully canine, a dead one would merely look like a dead wolf, dog, or wolf-dog. In contrast, finding say, a dead gargoyle or Bigfoot would be entirely different—the finders would know they'd discovered something extraordinary. But upright canines probably don't look much different than quadrupedal canines when they are no longer upright.

The one obvious fact is that these creatures are elusive to a fault, although there are times when they seem to tease the eyewitnesses by showing themselves and then dashing out of sight. They also seem strangely bulletproof, as will be shown here in some notable incidents, and they exhibit a curious tendency to lurk near water and near the same types of landmarks frequented by anomalous animals worldwide: ancient sacred places, crossroads, churches, TV and telephone towers, military installations, and cemeteries. We'll start with a chiller in the latter category, sent to me by northern Illinois resident Anne Dakan.

McHenry Dogman

In 2002, I saw a dogman in McHenry, Illinois. We were on Route 31, southbound, returning to Elgin from Waukesha, Wisconsin, after the funeral of my mother-in-law, very late at night. The sighting was just south of the shopping area before the Route 31 dogleg, perpendicular to the cemetery on the west side of the road, somewhere around 2 a.m. on April 29, 2002. As we approached the residential area, south of the cemetery, I noticed glowing eyes and a dark shape off to my left.

Being fairly close to the Nippersink flowage, I always keep my eyes peeled for deer through there. I came to a complete stop as the dark shape rose out of the gully on the east side of the road, to my left. It went from all fours to two legs and as it crossed in front of the headlights, almost as if it was annoyed by our presence; it turned and looked at the truck, menacingly, curling its lip, briefly, in a snarling fashion. Then it finished crossing the road, and as it left the pavement, it returned to all fours, ran down into the gully, up the other side, and loped into the cemetery, where it was too dark to follow its progress.

My husband was sound asleep, understandably, as the previous two days had been exhausting for him, with his mom's funeral and all. I made a tiny attempt to wake him up, but since the phenomenon had already occurred, decided just to let him sleep.

The creature looked like an upright, walking wolf. Its forearms were held in a position not unlike the way a kangaroo holds its arms as it hops. The thighs were very powerful and strong-looking and it had an elongated nose and a long, bushy tail. It was walking on its back toes, as it crossed in front of me. It seemed to be a little over six feet in height. The top of my truck is almost six feet high, and it crossed so close to the front of the truck that I could judge its height quite well, and it seemed to be a bit taller than the top of my windshield.

The experience had a very surreal quality about it. As if the portion of the time it spent crossing the road was eerily slowed down a bit, making what could have only taken a few seconds seem about ten seconds longer. Needless to say it was weird, and, yes, no one believes me.

Dakan added in a later interview that its fur was medium gray, tipped with reddish brown, and that it had upright, pointed ears with tufts between a half inch and one inch long. Its eyes displayed a deep-yellow eye shine from the headlights. "I was looking more at its snarling mouth and its odd behavior of walking on its hind legs," she said.

This encounter was a fairly typical one, not just for its proximity to the cemetery but because so many sightings are made at night by passing motorists as a creature either crosses the road or lurks near the shoulder. Its description is a good standard for the upright canine nationwide, although dark brown is probably a more prevalent color. The long muzzle, forelimb position, and muscular thighs are all common characteristics. And finally, its behavior is classic: staring insolently at the eyewitness, snarling, as it proceeds on its hind legs to wherever it was headed.

All of these factors tend to ensure that encounters with manwolves, as I often call them in order to emphasize their upright stance while leaving out the baggage that comes with the word "werewolf," are engraved in the memories of most eyewitnesses. Many reports that I receive concern incidents already decades old, but the witnesses always say they remember their encounters as if they had just happened.

A Virginia woman who fits this category wrote me in 2008 about a sighting she and a female friend had in 1991 as they drove through North Carolina one night on their way to a Florida vacation. They'd been forced to take a detour from the freeway to a foggy, two-lane country road but were listening to music and chatting as they continued south. Suddenly, she said, "This large gray furry critter with glowing green eyes and eyeteeth showing ran across the road on its hind legs. I suspect the 'glowing' came from our headlights reflected, like hunters jacking deer, but it was creepy."

The creature was moving very fast through the fog and was around forty yards ahead of them, but they estimated it stood seven feet tall and "looked wolfish about the head." The body didn't look human, she wrote, but seemed to be more than simply pure wolf.

My friend and I both went silent for quite a while and I finally said, "Did you see that?" She responded with "What WAS that?" I said it looked like a werewolf and she agreed that it definitely looked like it could be one, although not really anything like some of the grotesque and distorted creatures you see in Hollywood. Just somehow looked like a cross between dog or wolf and human but not really describable.

We got the hell out of there and into the next truck stop diner that we could find, got back on the highway, and drove straight to Florida without any more detours, still talking about whatever that thing was . . . that memory creeps me out to this day.

Another trend I've noticed is that more reports come from west of the Mississippi lately, especially from Oklahoma and California. One sighting made by two young men in 1993 in Corona, California, at Ripchak Drive and Cresta Road demonstrates two other dogman characteristics I note time and again in reports: an amazing ability to leap and bound, and a willingness to use golf courses as areas of approach to suburban neighborhoods.

The men were high school students at the time and were walking from a car to one of their family homes at about 10 p.m. when they noticed an odd creature about three houses down the street in the wooded golf course area of multistory family homes. It was well lit by streetlights as it crouched on the home's roof. The man who reported it to me in December 2013 wrote:

A wolf-like creature with shaggy fur knelt on the rooftop apex, legs bent backward and crazy-like. At first I thought it was a dish for cable or something, but as I looked at it I thought it was a guy on the roof in a costume. My friend spotted it right after he noticed me observing it. He yelled out, "Hey, what the hell is that thing?"

It got scared or spooked by my friend yelling and it leapt from apex to apex across the rooftop away from us. The moment it moved I knew a human couldn't leap like that. I was running to my house and my buddy was right beside me running in terror.

The creature's eyes glowed yellow in the streetlight, he added, and the fur was brown or grayish brown.

This ability to leap from housetop to housetop would certainly seem beyond the ability of even the most gifted human athlete. It reminds me a little of the gargoyle sightings discussed in Part One of this book, but the witnesses didn't mention any sort of wings. Also, the description of the legs as "bent backward" is a very common phrase used by eyewitnesses who tell me they were seeing the creature walking on its toe pads, as canines normally do, rather than walking plantigrade or flat-footed like humans, bears, or great apes.

The yellow eye shine was also consistent with canines in general, whose eyes usually reflect a color somewhere in the yellow-green range.

This was also not the first report I've had of dogmen on a rooftop. Why it would choose to travel this way is anyone's guess, but there are far fewer people looking up at their roofs at night than at their sidewalks, and these beasts know it.

THE WOLFMAN OF CHESTNUT MOUNTAIN

Even when an upright canine doesn't perform any stunts that are obviously supernatural, sometimes its actions are so weird that eyewitnesses are still left with the uneasy feeling that what they saw was just not right. One such incident occurred about ten miles outside of the historic, picturesque Illinois town of Galena, an old mining town set into a hill not far from the Mississippi River in the state's northwestern corner. The encounter happened near the well-known Chestnut Mountain Resort area.

Rachel Gendreau, who has a PhD in behavioral psychology and who often treats people with cognitive disorders to help them distinguish between hallucinations and real-life events, witnessed something in October 2010 that she had never imagined she would see. She knew right away that this was no hallucination, however, because her fiancé, Chris, was driving and he saw it, too. Rachel wrote:

Around 10:30 p.m. or so, my fiancé and I were traveling back home from Galena, Illinois. We were at least eight miles out of Galena on a back road called Blackjack Road. When we got to a fairly curvy part in the road—this road is heavily wooded on both sides and there are not any homes where we were at that time—we noticed a large figure running out of the woods ahead of us. When we got closer, as we were driving fifty miles per hour, we distinctly saw a six- to seven-foot-tall wolf running on its hind legs.

It paused to look directly at us before leaping at great speed off the road and back into the woods. My fiancé and I looked at each other in pure shock, and he asked if we should turn around to go look for it. I, however, was so frightened I just wanted to get off that road quickly. We have never shared this story with anyone until just a couple weeks ago when another friend of ours shared their recent sighting with us.

Rachel said that the creature was not only illuminated by their headlights but by bright moonlight. As it paused and turned its head to stare at them, its eyes displayed a bright-white eye shine. "I felt it was looking right through me—as if it knew me," she said. Right after that, the creature resumed running across the road and leaped over a wire fence on the other side to disappear into the trees behind it. Rachel saw its legs clearly and said they were canine in structure and that it definitely had paws rather than hands and feet. She noticed that its dark gray fur was a bit sparser on its chest than on the rest of its body, and that it had a long snout.

This wasn't quite the end of the story, however. Rachel's fiancé, Chris, wrote me that, "Without question, my girlfriend and I encountered this on our drive from Galena, Illinois, to Savanna, Illinois, at night on a rural road. It was standing on its back legs in the road. . . . When we initially saw it, our brains couldn't quite process what it was fast enough. After we passed it I could see it just staring at us from the rearview mirror. Our hearts were pounding and we drove like hell. . . . We know what we saw."

In other words, after the creature ran across the road and cleared the fence, it quickly circled around and again entered the road behind the vehicle to watch it speed away. That seems odd, because if it merely wished to be sure that the car had indeed left the area, all it would have had to do was to remain inside the tree line and watch from a sheltered position.

The other sighting that Rachel mentioned occurred in 1999 when two coworkers at Chestnut Mountain encountered something similar just off State Highway 20 near Elizabeth, Illinois. In their case, however, the creature was first spotted in a crouching position and rose to its hind legs before running off bipedally.

With its bluffs and valleys, this part of Illinois is certainly an attractive habitat for any large creature. It's very close to a wonderful source of fresh water, the Mississippi River, and to several large wildlife areas: the Mississippi Palisades and the Apple River Canyon state parks. The Chestnut Mountain Resort sits on a lake fed by the Mississippi River, and the small community of Elizabeth is surrounded by a rich agricultural area. In the 1830s it was the site of an important battle in the Black Hawk War, an uprising by the Sauk and Fox Indians against the relocation policy of the United States.

Gendreau has often since pondered the irony, given her occupation, of an encounter with something that might not ordinarily be thought of as "real." The dogmen, however, don't seem to care about the occupation or other demographics of the people who manage to glimpse them. I've often noted that although creature characteristics reported by eyewitnesses remain fairly consistent, there is no such thing as a stereotypical manwolf witness. Witnesses from all walks of life report the same bizarre attributes, such as the eerie eye contact described by Gendreau. Below is another example of a creature seeming to "look through" the eyes of a witness.

Point Pleasant Beast

One of the most recent (at publication) sightings of upright canids occurred in that famous hotbed of cryptozoological wonders, Point Pleasant, West Virginia, in early January 2014. This beast bore no resemblance to Mothman, however, nor to the weird "sting ray" seen flying over a road between Point Pleasant and Huntington in 2004. Perhaps this sighting is as important to establishing the creature-rich environment of Point Pleasant as it is to adding to my upright canid files, but in any event it's another case where an unknown canine seemed to communicate via weird eye contact.

The report came to me in an e-mail from Robert Shaw, a Point Pleasant resident, and was told to him by a female acquaintance, "Glenda," who also lives in Point Pleasant and asked to remain anonymous. The young woman's neighborhood is bounded by railroad tracks, Oldtown Creek, and the eastern shore of the Ohio River, all attractive entry points to the city for a furtive predator.

Glenda was sitting on an enclosed front porch on a well-lit street at about 11 p.m., having a cigarette, Shaw said, with one porch window opened to help the smoke dissipate. She had noticed "strange noises" on previous nights, and on that night also heard more neighborhood dogs barking more frantically than was usual.

As she glanced up and down her street through the porch windows, a figure moving near the railroad tracks caught her eye—and held it. Her first impression was that it must be wearing a dark hooded sweatshirt, but as she continued to gaze she changed her mind. She could see it well, thanks to the streetlights, and realized that the "sweatshirt" was actually dark-colored fur. She described it as about six feet tall, walking on its hind legs, but with a head "almost exactly like a German shepherd's." About that time, a car came into view and at the first flash of headlights, the creature turned and ran in the opposite direction, still on its hind legs.

"She said the movement was impressive and scary, because it ran very fast," wrote Robert.

But as in Rachel Gendreau's case, perhaps the scariest part of the encounter was that the creature locked eyes with her as Glenda watched it. She told Shaw that she had a strange feeling that its eyes, reflecting the glow of the streetlights, were "drawing her in" and preventing her from noticing other details of its appearance. It's interesting to ponder, if the creature really did keep her from seeing all there was to see about it, what might have been revealed had she and the creature not made eye contact.

St. Cloud Creature

Another eloquently described report came from a state that I've always thought should produce many more dogman sightings than I've received, given its rampant wildlife, great tracts of forest, well-watered terrain, and nearness to the Great Lakes—all indicators of prime habitat for upright canids—or any large predator. The eyewitness wrote:

> I used to work in Princeton, Minnesota, from 2005 to 2006. I lived in St. Cloud, Minnesota, and commuted the forty minutes to work, taking State Highway 95 between St. Cloud and Princeton. In March of 2006 I hit a deer at night on the way home from work, so I was always more cautious and attentive when driving after that. The place where I struck the deer was the northern edge of the Sherburne National Wildlife Refuge, which butts up to the highway. Consequently I would slow down to about forty-five miles per hour when I would approach the refuge and drive holding down the high-beams switch; this allows me to drive with both high and low beams at the same time.
>
> In mid-April, about six weeks after I struck the deer, I was passing the refuge, driving slowly, looking for deer. I saw the reflection of eyes, like a deer or raccoon, near the south bank of the highway. I slowed down further and the animal bolted out twenty feet in front of my car. It crossed the road from south to north. I wish

I could tell you that it was another deer, but I'm convinced that it wasn't.

Whatever it was, it moved on TWO legs, not four. I only saw it for a few seconds and my adrenaline was pumping, thinking I was going to hit another animal, but I can see the flashes of what I saw in front of me in my mind's eye as clear as yesterday.

Its forward limbs did NOT touch the ground. This was bipedal, maybe six or seven feet tall. It was brown or maybe dark gray. The eyes were reflective, like a deer's. Its limbs were long and robust like a man's, not spindly like a deer's. I think that it was covered with hair or fur, accounting for the color. And the shape of its face was not flat like a man's, but prognathic to the point of having a snout, like a dog's. It ran north across the highway and I accelerated west toward St. Cloud.

Damnedest thing I ever saw. I have a degree in anthropology with a minor in biology, and a degree to teach social studies. I'm a teetotaler and have no serious religious convictions. The point is that I'm not prone to flights of fancy or wild imagination. I didn't see a deer or a black bear. And if it was a man in a suit he ran the risk of becoming roadkill.

This looked a lot like what folks have been describing as the "Michigan Dogman" or the so-called "Beast of Bray Road." I get the sense that it did have triangular ears. I can't be totally sure on that, though. I didn't see its feet; however, the walk seemed like there was a "spring" in its step. That makes me think that it wasn't walking flat-footed, but on the balls of its feet.

While I believe this eyewitness account leaves a smidgen of possibility that the creature was a Bigfoot due to the robust limbs and the fact that the witness didn't see its feet, its dog-like snout and the impression of triangular ears both smack of a dogman. It surely doesn't sound like it could have been a bear, considering the long limbs and springy step. Bears also have red eye shine, very different from that of a deer, and humans wearing fur suits don't have any. Whatever it was, the eyewitness was probably lucky that the creature kept on going.

New Mexico Walker

Not all sightings occur in the Midwest. A longtime contact who has collected several creature sightings from people she knows passed on the following encounter from a coworker in Farmington, New Mexico, near a Ute reservation. It happened in 1974 in early evening, while it was still light out, and a man named Mike was preparing for a small outdoor party on a low hill with several friends.

"About a half mile away," my contact wrote, "stood an abandoned adobe hut. Mike and his friends noticed what looked like a dog wandering around the hut, but they didn't pay it much attention. They hadn't been there for long (Mike assured me they had just started drinking and had not had enough to affect their faculties) when one of the guys noticed the dog was walking toward them. Mike said it was 'trotting' along on four legs.

"One of the guys yelled at it and that is when its attitude changed. It rose up on two legs and began running toward the group. Mike said he and his buddies ran for their cars and took off. He said it was light gray like a wolf and over six feet tall. He didn't get a good look at its head, but they thought it had looked like a dog from a distance."

Incidentally, people who camp or gather around campfires at night are often good candidates for dogman encounters, because so many sightings happen after dark (most of them between 10 p.m. and 5 a.m.)

and the creatures seem rather curious about humans who remain outside in the wee hours. I'm willing to bet that they are far more adept at observing us—especially on their own turf—than we are at observing them.

SHAPE-SHIFTERS: THE SHIFTY SIDE

While the great majority of sightings imply nothing more than some type of natural creature with an unaccountable ability to run around on two feet rather than all four, some encounters display an undeniably eerie side. The journal *The Gate to Strange Phenomena* reported one fearsome creature that a pair of Pennsylvania witnesses said looked like a traditional werewolf caught in the state of transformation. This truly weird encounter occurred on November 20, 2011, in Radford County near Troy. Researcher Stan Gordon investigated and recorded the incident.[1]

The man who reported the event to Gordon said that he and his girlfriend were driving at around 11 p.m. that evening on Mud Creek Road. As the two continued down the dark country lane, they saw something that appeared man-like moving on the road's left shoulder. Fearing it might be an injured person, they stopped and swiveled their car to aim their headlights at the thing now crouching only about ten to twelve yards away, and realized the thing was not human. At least, they said, it wasn't human at that present moment.

It sat up straight and held its forelimbs so that they could see long claws on each paw. The couple said it had a wolf-like head with tall pointed ears that reminded them of a bat's, and big sharp teeth. Its large black eyes did not reflect any color in the headlights, and its skin appeared wrinkly and black. They estimated its height while sitting at around five feet, and when it stood up briefly before dropping again to all fours, it rose to a height of between six and seven feet.

As soon as it resumed a four-legged stance, the creature turned its head to look at the couple with what they described as a panicked expression. They had the impression that it suddenly realized it had been seen, they said, and it immediately launched into a single, astounding leap that carried it over a seven-foot-high embankment and into some nearby woods. The witnesses estimated this leap to have been at least forty feet! It's hard to know how accurate that estimate was, given that the incident occurred at night in unfamiliar terrain, but it still sounds like a rather spectacular feat and one that couldn't be duplicated by a human.

As the creature bounded away, the couple had a good look at its legs. They described them as very thin and long. They also felt that during the twelve or so seconds of the encounter, the creature changed shape before their eyes. The woman told Gordon that by the end of the encounter, it had changed to a dark brown color with "a little back hair," and resembled what she called a "werewolf." The man likened it to "a gargoyle with no wings."[2]

One possible explanation for the "morphing" would be that the viewing conditions and position of the creature also changed during the encounter. The creature was first observed in a flattened, crawling position to the side of the headlights. As they watched the creature sit up, stand, and then drop to all fours again before taking that giant bound, the headlights were fully illuminating it. As it disappeared into the woods, it melted back into a darker environment and was probably much harder to see. This scenario takes nothing away from the extremely bizarre quality of the sighting, and it still sounds very much like a manwolf to me.

Not So Heavenly in Heavener

A more recent encounter I find even harder to try to explain occurred in April 2013, in the mountain-surrounded southeastern Oklahoma town of Heavener. The woman who wrote me, Arminda Morales, allowed me to publish her name despite the fact that she had already been ridiculed at her workplace after she shared her experience with coworkers. I believe she was genuinely terrified at what she saw, and I would have been, too. She asserted that she was not drinking or taking drugs of any kind on the night of her encounter. Arminda wrote:

> This past month on a full moon, in my neighborhood in the town where I live, I heard a weird howling and the neighborhood dogs fighting and growls from the top of the hill a few blocks away. . . . I thought, dang that sounds wolfy. Because I didn't recognize the new animal/dog making the howling sound, it kind of gave me chills. I thought, that sounds like how werewolves supposedly sound on TV and laughed. I went to bed around 12:30 or so. At around 3:18 a.m., I was awakened by my dogs growling—one sleeps with me, and one in my living room. Both are pit bulls. I made my old girl dog shush and put on my robe and walked into my living room.
>
> My husband works nights and had left early—around 9:30 or so. He had left the window shades up and my big living room window was only covered by (sheer) curtains. Through the curtains I could see what appeared to be the shadow of a dog-like thing with the body of a man—a big man—and its head was like a German shepherd's. I can't see good without my glasses; I am really nearsighted, so I went to my room and got my glasses because I thought, that's crazy as hell, must be a bush or a tree shadow. So with glasses

on, I peered from my hallway. It was the shape of a big dogman, and one hand—not paw—was rested up against the glass and one on the windowsill and he had his face up really close, looking in. I was so scared and shocked that I didn't know what to do.

I wanted to go to the window and look, yet I could not make myself go to it, and it was like this thing was beckoning me to come and raise up the window, like I could hear it in my mind communicating with me, saying that he was nice and don't be afraid . . . which really freaked me out. I couldn't see what color it was only a dark giant shadow. I was so terrified I just turned and ran into my bedroom and dove under the covers and was literally shaking in terror.

I have never felt like this ever in my life, but I have never seen a giant dog-thing either. It had the shoulders and body of a giant, muscled-up man with the head of a German shepherd with ears that were raised up. I couldn't see its legs because of my window. For it to be that tall on my window, whatever it was had to be around eight feet tall. I wanted to convince myself it was not real, and it took me around two hours, to about 5:30 a.m., before I could go look again, and it was gone. There was no shadow or anything.

The next day I went outside and looked and there were no prints, no nothing, no evidence. When it got dark that night, I left the blinds up and curtains down and looked again. No shadows were cast that looked like that [creature], nothing remotely the same, and the dogs were quiet. I told my two coworkers what I saw and my husband. My Mexican husband didn't dispute what I told him, he just never answered me, but my coworkers called me crazy. I am a grown woman and I know what I saw. I haven't heard a growling or howling like that since then, and I wonder if any dogs were hurt or missing, because they were clearly fighting with whatever was making that noise. The feeling I get is [it was] demonic, not of this earth.

Arminda added that, judging by where she heard the first calls emanating from in relation to her house, she thought the creature was advancing toward the town and her yard from the foothill of nearby Poteau Mountain, a city-run recreational area only about a mile away. She still wonders if anyone else may have seen it, given the great commotion of the neighboring dogs.

That mountain is worth a mention, as well. It is the home of an artifact carved with ancient runes that's known as the Heavener Runestone. This large stone with incised figures that look like ancient Nordic runes is thought by some to prove early Viking contact with the Americas, although that idea is still controversial. The Poteau area, however, was undisputedly once home to the mysterious Mound Builder people and features a wealth of architectural remnants from that civilization, including the well-known Spiro Mounds. There are also local legends that say the Mayan people visited this area in their own heyday. Arminda describes herself as a "full-blooded Cherokee" and she is acutely aware of these connections to ancient artifacts. She also noted that there have been many Sasquatch sightings in her area that date back at least to the early 1980s.

She's not the first person to report a dogman-like creature staring intently into a window. This behavior always strikes me as unlike that of most natural dogs or wolves, but not necessarily as a supernatural action. It's possible that the creature had detected the scent of Arminda's other pets (seven cats), and was checking to see if it could spot one inside.

What *is* definitely out of sync with most reports of upright canines, however, is that it possessed hands with fingers rather than paws with claws. That, along with the uncanny fear it provoked and her Native American heritage, makes me think of a skinwalker or some other type of spirit entity. Creatures exhibiting behavior and appearances beyond the norm for a natural animal are also frequently noted to have some human-like characteristics, as well. These might include broad shoulders, longer feet, a much more muscular build, and sometimes, like the one Arminda saw, hands rather than paws. This definite minority of upright, wolf-like creatures also often have red eyes, as mentioned earlier in this chapter.

"Skinwalker" is a term used by various tribes, but especially the Navajo, for a supernatural entity thought to be created or projected by a trained medicine person who has gone to the dark side. They are very much feared as a form of harmful black magic, as are the similar beings called "bearwalkers" by the Canadian Cree. As far as I know, Arminda never did discover whether any neighborhood dogs were hurt or killed that night. All we can assume is that they were very unhappy with something that entered their turf—almost as unhappy as our eyewitness.

British Columbia Baffler

One of the eeriest tales I've ever received, perhaps because it stands completely unique among all the reports sent to me over the past twenty-plus years, came from a forty-nine-year-old British Columbia man who has never forgotten an experience he had in the city of Victoria at the age of seventeen. It's one of the few reports that made me actually stop and consider whether this particular unknown might be a true, traditional werewolf—despite the fact that I tend not to believe in them.

The eyewitness is now a successful businessman in a highly technical field who wishes his name withheld, but the incident occurred in early fall of 1980 while he was attending a crowded house party in Victoria, British Columbia. He remembered that it had started as a small, private party that, as often happens, got out of hand. The house was next to a lake in a residential neighborhood. The teen was familiar with the house because about ten years earlier it had been occupied by an aunt and uncle whom he had visited upon occasion.

"The house was only approximately one thousand square feet," he wrote, "with over fifty teenagers inside. As the party started, I was not tipsy at all and the bathroom had ten-plus persons in line so I went outside as it was dark out."

He found an isolated spot in the shadows and was about to conduct his business when the door of a small camping trailer that was parked about twenty feet from where he stood suddenly popped open.

"Then out walked a person (?) approximately six feet tall, ninety-five to ninety-nine percent covered in long hair, walking with a bad hunch, grunting, not a human face. The cul-de-sac street lamp and the moonlight were good enough for me to see with my twenty/twenty vision, but this thing?"

The creature didn't appear to see the teen, who stood rooted "deathly still" to the spot, hidden in the darkened foliage. He observed the bizarre figure with shocked attention as it walked on two legs into some nearby brush. It remained hidden for several long minutes, during which the teen hardly dared to breathe or move, afraid it would lurch back out of the brush and find him. He had no idea what it was doing during that time; perhaps it had also sought a private place in which to relieve itself. When it finally emerged, it shambled straight back to the trailer, opened the door, ducked inside, and slammed the door shut, leaving the young man dumbfounded.

"My thought then and all these years," he wrote, "is werewolf. Needless to say I did not knock on that trailer door nor ever tell anyone. Oddly, I was anxiety ridden from the first moment [of the encounter] until it reentered the trailer, then I went back to the safety of fifty-plus people."

He did not go back outside that night, however, choosing the long waits for the indoor bathroom over another possible encounter with that creature. He added that he never met the actual owners of the house at the party but presumed that they must've been several "older" persons in their twenties. "This house's ongoing occupants had to know what was in that trailer," he wrote, "and that always made me equally as shocked as the 'thing.'"

He retains a vivid memory of the creature's appearance. He estimated that, walking with its head and neck hunched forward, it stood about five feet tall and that it would have been at least six feet or more in height if it stood up straight. "As for build, going by [entertainment media] werewolf pics and a standard male human," he said, "I would say it was halfway in between, so it had a very plain build with no noticeable muscle form. It had on no clothing of any sort and the hair/fur was a dark copper color. As for its feet and hands, I never looked down that far as I kept my focus on the head-down-to-the-waist part. My sports-playing days always told me to look at the chest of any player, as that tells you the next place an opponent will go. At that point I knew things could turn out very bad for me, so instinct kicked in."

As the teen focused on the creature's face, he came to the disturbing conclusion that it was not human.

"It was canine-like," he said, "like a werewolf's as per pics I have seen over the years. The nose/snout was not protruding, just slightly larger than a human snout. Same for the jawline, almost human-like. But it was very odd that it could open and close a door on the trailer (I never looked at the doorknob/handle assembly). The thing went in and out of that trailer like that was its living quarters ongoing; it knew how to open the door, where to go next, then come back, open the door/close it again, then silence. As it came and went, it made low-decibel grunt sounds that were evident to me."

The man said that he kept this frightening incident to himself for thirty-three years, until a chance viewing of a TV show led him to find my Web site and contact me. He included Google Earth links to the location, but of course the camper is no longer in view. The site of the incident, however, appears to be an extremely logical place for an inquisitive but secretive humanoid to lurk on the fringes of civilization. Victoria is a port city on the island of Vancouver in the Pacific Ocean, about sixty miles from Seattle by ferry. The dead-end street where the man's encounter took place abuts a densely wooded nature trail that runs past Swan Lake. There is plenty of vegetation in the area around the house, at least today, to make it possible that he could indeed have hidden from the creature and that the creature would've had its own separate wooded area in which to disappear.

The description of the creature, however, is a head-scratcher. Although it made the teen think of a werewolf, and he described the face as "canine," the human-like face and jaw do not sound canid at all. The type of werewolf he was picturing at the time was probably closer to the popular image in Hollywood films, which often depict werewolves with human faces augmented with a lot of fur, latex, and some sharp-fanged dental appliances. He doesn't mention eyes or ears, leading me to believe that neither of these features was very prominent. He did not see the lower part of the body so we can't tell whether the creature walked on toe pads as canine animals do or was flat-footed like a human or a Bigfoot.

And what about the fact that it was able to open and shut the camper door? I've seen some campers, especially older models, with very simple push-down handles that could conceivably be managed by a large, flexible paw. I've known people whose dogs could get into similarly equipped cupboards indoors. But I must say it seems likelier that a Bigfoot with its fingers and opposable thumbs would be the likelier candidate of the two candidates. Ditto on the human jaw and flat nose—unless, of course, it was an actual werewolf, shape-shifter, or other entity of supernatural origin. But what was a magical being doing in a tiny camper trailer, especially when it was only a couple of dozen feet away from a whole houseful of young, tender humans, many of whom were probably so inebriated that they would've been easy pickings?

The creature could possibly have been a Bigfoot. This was the Pacific Northwest, after all, home of the Sasquatch. I do have a report from an unrelated source in Delafield, Wisconsin, where a resident of a boys' camp observed a Bigfoot opening and closing each cabin unit's door in turn as it investigated the sleeping inhabitants. It's entirely possible that a Bigfoot snooping for food found some camping staples in that little trailer and stayed to devour the goodies in relative privacy. And I've had a slew of reports of both Bigfoots and dogmen seen peering into house windows, shed windows, and barn windows as if curious about who or what was inside. Such an inordinate and somewhat reckless interest in humans is unsettling to think about, but not beyond the realm of possible animal behavior. There's one other occasionally observed trait, however, that most woodsmen and hunters will admit is far beyond their ken.

BULLETPROOF BEASTS AND
THE INVINCIBILITY QUESTION

A possible clue to the puzzle of whether unknown upright canines are flesh and blood or something from other realms may be found in several eyewitness accounts in which the creatures were fired upon—sometimes by semiautomatic weapons—but appeared as bulletproof as Superman. There aren't many eyewitnesses who claim to have tested this characteristic, perhaps because only a small percentage of those who have encountered dogmen at close range in the wild were armed. And of that percentage, only a few of them had the time, opportunity, or inclination to shoot. But I continue to receive occasional reports of seemingly invincible, upright canids from credible witnesses.

One experience was fully described in *Real Wolfmen*, when an Alabama man fishing in the river shallows near Selma in 2007 fired multiple shots from his pistol after an upright wolfman began to wade toward him and appeared about to attack his pit bull. Although he was sure he had hit the creature, it merely turned and walked, still upright, back into the woods. It left no blood or other evidence of injury.[3] This imperviousness to injury occurs in shootings of all types of unknown creatures, especially Bigfoot. I don't know why it happens, and I'd never advise testing an unknown creature's hide to see if it's bullet-proof, but I invite readers to imagine the choices that faced eyewitnesses in the next sampling of such incidents.

MISSOURI MARAUDER

The Selma riverside creature described above sounds like one tough beast—almost as though it wore a Kevlar vest under its fur. But I recently received another report of a lead-defying wolfman, this time in Pulaski County, Missouri. It occurred in late spring 2013, when two experienced woodsmen who had set out to explore an area they believed was frequented by Bigfoots came upon something else one moonlit evening. The eyewitness who wrote furnished full identification but asked for anonymity. I'll call the pair Tom and Joe. Tom wrote:

Two months ago we witnessed what we have come to believe was a dogman or skinwalker that once it spotted us, in turn, started hunting us. Now what we saw was a little over six feet, skinny framed, and extremely aggressive; it had a long snout. As it approached I did shoot at it and I do know that I hit it. (I carry a weapon, as we do have cougar in this area.) I would never dream of shooting a Bigfoot, but both Joe and I felt we were prey at this point as it kept coming at us, even in direct light from my flashlight. What we smelled was a very strong odor of hay, like it had been holing up in remote barns. We did track it after I shot it and tracked it as far as we could possibly go without our being billy goats. We found where it fell down twice (and we did hear it fall ahead of us) and we found a very large, seven-and-one-half-inch canine track in the dirt.

Now, we are both intelligent enough to accept something that we both witnessed with our eyes and other senses, but what is very hard for me to swallow is that there was NO BLOOD trail! I spoke with a native couple I know—he is a Cherokee and she a Blackfoot—and both of them said, either skinwalker or (Native American) witch. We are both pretty shaken up about this, but it has seemed to go away from the area and things have gone back to "normal."

"Normal," in this case, would seem to be a relative term. But something very similar happened in that same neck of the United States only about a year earlier.

THE JEFFERSON PARISH PROWLER

A hunter wrote me that in November 2012, in Jefferson Parish in southeastern Louisiana, he had taken his dog to a field to look for deer and feral hogs. In the middle of the field sat some type of broadcasting tower (as noted earlier, all types of communications towers and stations are often associated with sightings of weird animals), and just as they reached the tower, his dog stopped short.

"The hairs on her back were sticking straight up," he wrote, "and she was trembling and growling. Then I heard a growl back."

He shined his handheld spotlight in the direction of the unknown growl and realized it was neither a deer nor a wild pig.

"Standing there at least seven feet tall," he wrote, "with bright-yellow shining eyes—on two legs—was what I would say was a werewolf. It looked like (the one) in that movie *The Howling*. It was covered in black fur with a few strips of a grayish color here and there."

The man began to slowly back away.

"My rifle was on my back," he continued, "but I also carry a pistol and I drew it immediately as I turned to walk away. Once the light was off him (I say him for obvious reasons—it had male genitals), I was still close to this creature, I would say thirty feet or less, when he squatted down and hit the woods on all fours. I immediately couldn't see him, so I started heading back to my truck, which was a few football-field lengths away. As I'm running on this levee, I can hear him tearing through the woods, and then he popped back out.

"I heard the growl he made, turned around, turned on the light I have on my pistol. This time we were close enough where I think he could have leaped at me, and I fired, hitting him in the chest area. He stumbled slightly, hit the woods, and went the other way and I ran to my truck and went straight home. I never spoke of this to my wife or any family members; they would think I was crazy.

"My grandpaw told me to stay away from that area. He said when he was seventeen, he had something follow him and make a howling noise he never heard before, but I thought he was just telling me that because shining at night for deer or pigs isn't legal."

That is probably one reason the hunter didn't give permission to use his name.

In all of these cases, the eyewitnesses only shot when they felt it was necessary for self-defense. And although it doesn't usually provoke a hail of gunfire, the dogman's aggressiveness is a fairly common observation among the reports I receive. I've had plenty of eyewitnesses say they've been menaced, stalked, chased, lunged at, growled at, and more. In all cases except one Canadian incident where a man was grazed on his hip and flank by the fang of a large, upright wolf-like creature as it lunged past him into the woods, the creatures have never caused any actual injury to the witnesses. One British Columbia man said the wolf-like creature he saw observing him from the edge of a wooded trail seemed unfazed when he pointed a gun at it, but it took off like a shot when he raised his camera to take a picture instead. It was gone before he could click the shutter.

I have seen enough mounted wolf carcasses to know that normal wolves do die from gunshot wounds, traps, and other human-inflicted injuries. So what is it that gives these upright canines their apparent powers of immunity? If my only example was that of the Selma fisherman, I'd start looking seriously at alternative explanations such as the native shape-shifter idea suggested by Tom's friends. The creature

Tom shot, however, did seem at least somewhat physically affected since it was staggering and falling, even if it didn't leave a blood trail.

If there are such things as supernaturally created skinwalkers, as many of my Native American friends believe, I'd have to say these bulletproof manwolves fill the paranormal bill better than most of the upright canids reported to me.

An explanation on the opposite end of the reality spectrum might involve a human in a reinforced wolf suit. If so, the perpetrators were very lucky not to have been hit in a vulnerable spot. The possibility should be even more sobering for the shooters, who in that case might have narrowly missed murdering some prankster. Most hoaxers, however, do their dirty work near roadsides or campgrounds where they are more likely to find someone on which to play tricks, and they keep a fair distance so that their fake appearance is less easily detected. This creature that menaced Tom and Joe was roaming a deep forest at night, and it aggressively advanced on two armed men in such a way that they feared for their lives. Few people in that situation would think about possible pranksters before firing at least a warning shot.

Here is one more example of someone who did exactly that, and found that the creature was not impressed.

THE SCORNFUL WOLFMAN

Canadian researcher Sean Viala sent me this account of a husband and wife's experience at Crowsnest Pass, Alberta, on December 1, 2012. It was around noon on a cold and overcast day. Viala interviewed the wife, a woman in her forties, who spoke on condition of anonymity. He wrote:

I received another report of a strange wolf-like creature. In this report a husband and wife were out cross-country skiing. They had just crossed a remote country road and were about to ski across a field. On the other side of this field they spotted an extremely large wolf standing just inside of the tree line.

The wolf was covered in black fur and was on all fours at that point, said Viala. The woman said its height in that position was between three and three and one-half feet tall, and she felt uncomfortable since the creature was staring right at them and following their movement. Her husband evidently felt wary as well as he slung his .22 from his back, loaded it, and fired in the beast's direction, aiming at the ground in hopes of scaring it off. This action did not achieve its intended effect.

Viala continued:

She said that the creature looked at the ground, then back at them, and began to growl. She said that the growl "went up and down in sound," and it was very deep and menacing. She said that her husband shouldered his rifle again but did not fire, but what really gave her the chills was the look on the creature's face. She felt that the creature knew that the rifle was small caliber and was not something that could kill it with one shot. Moments later her husband fired again, this time into a tree that was next to the creature. The creature didn't even flinch, but what it did next made both of them flee in terror.

About thirty seconds after the second shot, the creature stood up on two legs to rise to a height of between six and a half to seven feet tall. One of its front legs (arms?) was against the tree that her husband shot. The growling continued, but it had increased in volume by quite a bit and the creature was moving its jaws up and down, like it was gnashing its teeth. Her husband fired three shots directly at the creature, all three hitting it in the chest. The creature let out a drawn-out scream/howl and ran off into the forest on two legs; they fled the other way back toward their vehicle. As they were skiing back they had to pass through a small area of forest, and as they were passing through the forest they could hear something running toward them from a distance through the woods. They cleared the woods without anything happening, but when they broke out of the forest they estimated that whatever was chasing them was no more than thirty-five to forty yards behind them.

This next part of the tale may sound as strange as the wife's feeling that the creature was able to judge the rifle caliber as too small to hurt it, but what Viala is about to relate is actually fairly commonplace in reports of wolfman encounters:

She had her cell phone with her and was thinking about using it to take a picture of the creature. As she was thinking this she suddenly got a "feeling" that if she took a photograph, the creature would kill both of them. She said that the feeling was so strong that she immediately shoved the phone in her pocket. It wasn't as if the creature sent her a psychic message or anything, it was just a feeling.

She had actually been so scared that she lost control of her bladder, even though she always thought that was just something from the movies.

The sighting itself lasted only a little more than a minute, but I'm sure the run through the woods felt like an eternity. Sean added:

> I have interviewed a lot of witnesses of Sasquatch-related occurrences throughout the years, but this type of thing is waaaay beyond my scope of knowledge. After interviewing over five hundred witnesses over seventeen years, I have gotten used to picking the fakes out. This woman appears (to me) to be telling the truth; I am going by body language, eye contact, steadiness of voice and story, and other cues, such as: quavering of voice, tears, gasps, widening of eyes, etc. I have seen people fake fear; this woman was not pretending. She was still afraid.

Creature Communications

Readers will agree, I believe, that most wild animals would have reacted with more than a yawn and an implied response of "Really? That's all you got for me?" at the first rifle blast sent their way. And even if the husband's warning ground shot hadn't done the trick, the subsequent tree hit would have caused most critters to flee. But this strange lack of fear tallies very well with comments I've received from so many eyewitnesses over the years that also describe the creature's apparent sense of superiority, enhanced intelligence, and casual attitude toward the presence of humans, armed or not.

The woman's perception of the creature's scorn toward the modest rifle seems like an extension of this common report characteristic. What makes it so weird is that it's almost impossible to imagine having the same experience with, say, a black bear or even a normal timber wolf. Imputing the ability to judge a gun's firepower to these animals seems preposterous. And yet eyewitnesses "feel" this sort of thing time and again from upright canids (Bigfoot, too), and usually find it very disturbing.

If the creature's seeming dismissal of the .22 wasn't enough, there is that final "message" that the woman felt she received from the creature as she began to raise her phone, impressing her with great certainty that the creature would kill her and her husband if she didn't stop. This type of phenomenon does not occur in every sighting but happens enough that I can't dismiss it as less than a bona fide, if mysterious, component of some people's encounters.

There was the medical worker, for example, who saw a wolf-like creature pop up from a ditch on a Wisconsin-Illinois border road as she drove to work one morning in 2004. She said she felt it was "telling" her it would come and find her if she told anyone of her sighting.[4]

Other witnesses have said they felt the creature communicated that it could jump on their vehicles—or on the witnesses—if it so desired. Even more common is the feeling people get that the creature is "angry" at them for seeing it! Again, this is not something I believe most people experience when happening upon normal wildlife.

I addressed this question in *Real Wolfmen*, where I wondered whether these perceptions might come from our own inherent, subconscious ability to read a predator's body language. But the messages just seem too specific for that to always be the case.

I also explored one man's scientific studies on animal telepathy and quoted Rupert Sheldrake, author of *Dogs That Know When Their Owners Are Coming Home*, who said, "The study of animal telepathy is still in its infancy. . . . It may be of considerable survival value. If so, the capacity for telepathic communication must be subject to natural selection. Telepathy must have evolved."[5]

The ability of a dog to sense when its owner is on the way home, however, is a long way from a wild animal willfully impressing a random human with a detailed threat. And if these animals do somehow possess the ability to direct a telepathic message to a particular person, then that is scary, indeed. It reminds me of reports of encounters with the occupants of UFOs, who are described time and again by abductees or eyewitnesses as communicating telepathically with them.

Speaking of aliens, people do frequently ask me whether, indeed, there seem to be any connections between unknown, upright canids and UFOs. While I've never known an eyewitness to link the two phenomena directly, I did find a reference to something like that in Kevin Randle and Russ Estes's *Faces of the Visitors*. This rather well-known incident first reported by Andrew Collins in *Flying Saucer Review* serves to make at least one dogman-ET connection, weird and a bit tenuous though it may be.[6] Randle and Estes referred to the 1978 abduction of John and Elaine Avis from their family car while driving near Aveley near Essex, England, when they wrote, "The creatures described by both John and Elaine Avis do not fit into the classic gray category. In fact, both abductees reported that the work was done by a hairy little beast that is *more reminiscent of a werewolf* than of an alien from space [emphasis mine]."[7]

The Avises described the creatures as about four feet tall, which is a good deal shorter than the average dogman reported today, but the hairy little beasts otherwise looked very typically canid, with pointed ears and snouts. They even had four-digit rather than five-digit hands—with claws. They also sported white laboratory-style gowns and were directed in their medical exams of the couple by taller, more reptilian-looking beings. They did not communicate telepathically, although the reptilian beings did.

There is, I might add, a much larger body of reports of Bigfoot-like creatures appearing both in and near UFO craft. These humanoids also seem to play the role of helper rather than supervisor in most cases. But Bigfoot and dogmen are often sighted within howling range of one another even when no UFOs are present, and in their "normal" heights and sizes. The Missouri dogman that ran away after being shot, for instance, appeared in the very same area where multiple Bigfoots had also been observed.

MARKING DOGMAN TERRITORY

Two kinds of large, upright, unknown creatures occupying the same tract of land seems like an embarrassment of cryptid riches and begs the question of what might have attracted both Bigfoot and dogman to this same bit of woodland. The Missouri eyewitnesses speculated that the dogman may have been hunting a small Bigfoot they had observed on another occasion, which they had presumed to be a youngster.

This actually makes some sense to me, and although we will be sussing out Sasquatch later on, I'll take a moment to address this idea of more than one type of unknown creature sharing the same habitat. I have often felt that, based on maps I've made of sighting areas, dogmen and Bigfoots are in territorial competition with each other. Other large predators vie for the best hunting grounds, so why shouldn't cryptid animals do the same?

They seem to have many of the same tastes. Many eyewitnesses have reported seeing both Bigfoots and dogmen chasing deer or carrying off a nice haunch of venison, which indicates they are both dependent on large prey animals for protein (although there is much anecdotal evidence that Bigfoots eat a wide variety of vegetation as well). Both creatures prefer to stick close to rivers or lakes and seem to require forests or cornfields for cover and perhaps shelter. And there are numerous areas around my own home turf of southeast Wisconsin where witnesses have reported sightings and footprints of both unknown primates and upright canines.

There was even a recent sighting of what sounds like a possible Bigfoot on that most hallowed of dogman stomping grounds, Bray Road, the two-mile stretch outside Elkhorn, Wisconsin, where I reported the first dogman sightings flap in early 1992. Jay Bachochin, a southeast Wisconsin resident who is a member of a group called Wisconsin Paranormal Investigators, was cruising Bray Road one afternoon in April 2013 with his wife at the wheel when he spotted something large and dark orange-brown against the trees behind a field. He asked his wife to pull over and continued to observe the creature, which seemed aware it had been spotted. It had been standing stock-still, hunched over on all fours, but it slowly began to move back into the tree line.

"What was really strange was the way it moved," Bachochin wrote. "Very, very slow and then, just out of sight."

I've never had a report of a cinnamon-colored dogman, at least not in the midwestern United States and definitely not in Wisconsin, but I've had multiple sightings of reddish-haired Bigfoots in this part of the state. The creature was much larger than any known dog breed, he said, and it didn't resemble or move like a horse, steer, or bear. Ruling out these possibilities does not prove it a Bigfoot, of course, but I think given the many other Bigfoot sightings in the county dating back several decades, there is still at least a chance Bachochin saw the first 'Squatch of Bray Road. After all, upright canine sightings have been on the wane there for many years; perhaps other things have taken their chance to move on in. Perhaps they even take turns. But who really knows? Without tracking collars or identifiable populations, it's tough to declare anything about unknown animals with any certainty at all. I simply like to remain open to the possibilities.

There's one more point, however, that I feel does support the idea that the dogmen are territorial animals: their very consistent "bluff and run" response to those who encounter them. Even witnesses who've been chased on foot have felt that the creatures could easily have caught them, yet their pursuers veered off into the underbrush or woods at the last second. This behavior seems much more indicative of something defending its home base than it does of an opportunistic predator.

The need to establish their own territories would also probably rule out inter-species chumminess with other large predators, and I actually know of one example. This was a February 2014 case in Wisconsin wherein a rural landowner reported seeing an upright, shaggy-furred, wolf-like creature furiously chasing a coyote from an area that happened to contain a very munchable deer carcass.

It's probably just safest to conclude that large, unknown bipedal canines don't play well with others.

Native American Ice, Bone, and Cannibal Monsters

WINDIGO: ICE CANNIBAL OF THE NORTH

Sometimes I wonder if monsters are made more real by our telling of them, as some Native Americans have told me they believe.

Take the Windigo. Please. The Windigo is one of the scariest and most widespread monsters in the lore of North America's indigenous people. You can tell that right away by the great number of variations in spelling: Wendigo and Witiku are only two of many. It's also one of the most feared mythic creatures in Native American lore, probably because its main monster power is cannibalism. And it's a complex beast to digest, appearing in many different forms across the United States and Canada.

Johann Georg Kohl, one of my favorite early recorders of Native American beliefs and lore, says about these man-eaters in his 1860 book *Kitchi-gami,* "They give them the opprobrious name of 'Windigo,' which is nearly synonymous with our cannibal. And it is quite certain that if a man has ever had recourse to this last and most horrible method of saving his life, even when the circumstances are pressing and almost excusable, he is always regarded with terror and horror

by the Indians. They avoid him, and he lives among the savages like a timid head of game."[1]

The German-born Kohl was a geographer and ethnographer who spent part of the year 1855 living with the northern Wisconsin Ojibwe on the Lake Superior shores. He was also a fairly successful travel writer and had read widely on the New World and especially its native people. He found himself among the Ojibwe as part of a survey-writing expedition and set out to record everything that he could find out about their way of living and beliefs. He was extremely interested in all of their legendary creatures, even those that seemed obviously derived from certain mythologized human conditions—such as cannibalism.

But hold on, the intrepid reader may be objecting. How does an indigenous person who has succumbed to cannibalism in order to avoid starvation become known as a roaring monster? That depends.

Descriptions of the Windigo vary widely from tribe to tribe, its physical characteristics morphing to suit each particular legend. In some eastern tribes it is described as a beast akin to a werewolf, whereas in many others it is a gaunt, thirty- to eighty-foot-high ravening ice monster with sweeping antlers and only a bit of human left in its frozen heart. In this latter vein, Kohl continues:

> It is very natural that in a country [that] really produces isolated instances of such horrors, and with a nation so devoted to fancies and dreams, superstition should be mixed up in the matter, and that at last, through this superstition, wonderful stories of Windigos should be produced, as among us, in the Middle Ages, the belief in witches produced witches. . . . It is a universal tradition among the Indians that in the primitive ages there were anthropophagous giants, called Windigos. [I had to look up *anthropophagous*; it means, simply, "cannibalistic."][2]

Kohl's description of these people's beliefs as "superstitions" is typical of the popular religious bias of his time. Essentially, he is saying that the stories of legendary monsters evolved from ancient memories of starving wretches or psychopaths who were shunned by their people for cannibalism. He doesn't deny that there may have been some supernatural aspect to the powers of the Windigo, in the same way European medieval witches were believed to be users of magic. He noted, "Just as among us some people really did unusual things through electromagnetism and spiritualism, and performed incantations, the Native Americans known as Windigos used forces they believed to be natural, if poorly understood, sources of power to make themselves look otherworldly to their fellow human beings."[3]

He added that in his experience, Windigos were more often talked about than actually observed. "To this I may add," said Kohl, "that you hear more frequently of Windigos than you find or see them, and I may further remark that the word is much more frequently used with reference to the giant race of cannibals known by the name, than to the monsters now having their being among us."[4]

An even earlier writer, Anglo-Canadian fur trader George Nelson, lived among several northern Cree and Algonquian tribes at various times between 1802 and 1823, and kept copious journals on everything he was able to learn about their culture and spiritual beliefs. His journals were published in 1988 in the book *Orders of the Dreamed* and contained many tales of the Windigo.

Nelson believed the Algonquian tribes acknowledged three distinct forms of Windigo: a man-eating, skeletal giant; humans who became cannibalistic due to starvation; and finally, humans who dreamed of certain spirits known as Ice or the North.[5] In the last two forms, the person was believed possessed by the Windigo spirit.

Nelson also collected many ghastly stories of Windigo predation from among his Native American friends, many of whom said they knew of such people. Nelson knew one personally, too, he said, one who was afflicted with the Windigo "fever" between 1812 and 1813. The man lived with his daughter and her husband, said Nelson, and one cold December evening the man suddenly began to stare at his daughter strangely, declaring that he loved her so much that he could eat her.

The daughter and her husband were startled by this statement, and they were even more disturbed when the man began sleeping naked on the woodpile outside the tent every night and eating only raw flesh as if he were some kind of wild beast. Luckily, this situation turned out better than most Windigo stories.

"In the daytime he was more composed," wrote Nelson, "but his face bore the appearance of one possessed of the Devil. He recovered and became as usual, composed and good natured—I knew them all well."[6]

In a different story that didn't end so nicely, Nelson told of another young man who, several years earlier, had had recurring dreams of the North and Ice spirits. He asked his friends to kill him immediately if he began showing Windigo symptoms, before he could murder and eat anyone. He advised them to aim for his heart since that was the key spot for Windigo control. The man was a much-liked person and a good hunter and his friends were understandably reluctant to do him in, but they changed their minds as he began to grow strange and moody.

Eventually a group of his friends and his own brother laid an ambush for him, and his brother shot him in the heart with a rifle. The young man fell, but immediately got back up, laughing, without having shed a drop of blood. "The ball went through and through," wrote Nelson, quoting the teller of this story that had come to him secondhand, "but not a drop of blood was seen—his heart was already formed into Ice."[7]

The group could not let him escape; they chopped his body into pieces and burned the remains, but the heart remained whole and kept rolling out of the fire until they pulverized it with ice picks, at last removing the threat.

I'd like to interject an interesting thought that occurred to me when I read about the bullet hitting the heart with little to no effect—not even a drop of blood—on the Windigo. It sounds exactly like what happens in the case of the "invincible" dogmen described in the previous chapter, right down to the creature getting back up and running away after being shot by eyewitnesses. Some tribes believe that the Windigo can change forms—might it appear in the shape of a dogman? The only thing missing, in the case of our unknown, upright canines, is any evidence that they are eating humans.

Many Native Americans believe the Windigo legend continues to stalk the northern expanses of Canada, and newspapers did report one horrific case that occurred on a bus heading to Winnipeg from Edmonton in 2008 as having possible Windigo connections. Headlines in the *Toronto Sun* read, "Bus Beheading Similar to Windigo Phenomenon."[8]

On July 30, Vincent Weiguang Li killed a sleeping passenger, beheaded him, and then ate some of his body organs in front of the thirty-seven other, screaming passengers. Li later told authorities that he thought the victim, twenty-two-year-old Tim McLean, was an alien, and Li was eventually diagnosed as schizophrenic. But Edmonton ethnohistorian Nathan Carlson, a specialist in Windigo lore and legend, claimed in the *Toronto Sun* article that he saw many connections between Windigo tradition and the grisly bus incident. The article also noted that a week and a half before the killing, the *Sun* ran a story detailing Carlson's knowledge of the ancient lore. Li worked as a *Sun* newspaper carrier and would have delivered that issue to his customers.

The true nature of the Windigo, whether it is the result of mental illness, myth, a supernatural creature, or an actual being that still lurks in the northern forests in the shape of Bigfoot or a werewolf is still a matter of debate among cryptozoologists and ethnologists. The Native Americans I've talked to each seem to stick with his or her own tribal beliefs. I believe the Windigo endures as one of our most fascinating native monsters because even in its most monstrous, giant shape, it is so very close to human. It's never nice to look in the mirror and see something frightening staring back at you. And yet, Vincent Li didn't look at all like a monster, he just acted like one.

SKELETON MONSTERS

The Old Testament chapter of Ezekiel, named for a Jewish priest whose prophecies date back to the sixth century BCE, contains an account of dry bones—human bones—reassembling themselves in the desert to rise again. But while Ezekiel's valley of bones ultimately received flesh and breath to become a vast living army, Native American lore is rife with stories of skeletal monsters that also manage to clack around. One of the best-known is Pahkahk, or Pauguk. Henry Schoolcraft describes the horrible entity in his *Myth of Hiawatha*, originally published in 1856:

> Death, where the mythos of the condition of the human frame, deprived of even the semblance of blood, and muscle, and life, is represented by the word Pauguk. Pauguk is a horrible phantom of human bones, without bones, without muscular tissue or voice, the appearance of which presages speedy dissolution. Of all the myths of the Indians, this is the most gloomy and fearful. . . . To see him is indicative of death. Some accounts represent him as covered with a thin transparent skin, with the sockets of his eyes filled with balls of fire.[9]

Pauguk is also a hunter, but he hunts people rather than animals. He is totally silent and cannot shift into other forms. The North American hero Manabozho is the only warrior able to defeat the phantom skeleton.

A similar creature, Pakahk, of the plains and woodland Cree, is not a unique entity in his own right like Pauguk but (similar to many Windigo tales) comes into being from a person who died of starvation. Pakahk announces his presence with a chilling cackle and actually may benefit people by healing the sick or aiding the hunting powers of those who treat him right by offering his favorite food, an animal bladder filled with melted fat.

George Nelson's journals related a story about the skeleton monster he heard from a Cree acquaintance in the early 1800s. The man said he and his friend were camping outdoors one night after a successful day spent hunting beavers, when he awoke to see an elderly man sitting by the campfire in a pose that told the hunter this visitor was displeased.

"He had but skin and bone," wrote Nelson, "not the least particle of flesh, and this one had hair on his head."[10]

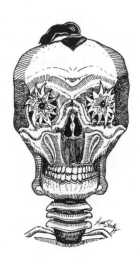

The hunter awakened his sleeping companion, and the pair fearfully decided to offer the skeletal visitor half of one of the beavers they had taken that day. The Pakahk refused the offering until they thought of cutting it into bite-size pieces and throwing the bits into the fire. The creature finally seemed satisfied and vanished into the night.

Bony beings were also part of the culture of indigenous people of the western states. "The Skeleton Who Fell Down Piece by Piece" is a Pueblo tale probably influenced by early Spanish folklore. A skeleton man appears one night to a boy and challenges the lad to a wrestling match. While not pretty to look at, this skeleton wasn't much of a monster, since the boy defeated it and thereby earned a pile of money for his village.

It's easy to see why societies that practiced excarnation, or the setting of corpses out in the open to allow vultures or other predators to strip the flesh from the body before burial, might settle upon bones as a symbol of death. The bones of their ancestors were a constant and familiar presence. Today, however, when common practice is to bury our dead in the ground to allow corpses to decompose, our mythic symbolism is more centered on vampires and zombies. Perhaps these modern-day monsters help us deal with that reality.

The immortal vampire, after all, is a sort of denial of the inevitable corruption of the flesh. The "undead" may rise from its coffin and live forever on the blood of those still breathing. The ragtag zombie, on the other hand, forces us to stare down the perfectly natural state of dissolution that is the human body when no longer needed—flesh rotting off bones and moldy clothing hanging in shreds. As my youngest son once sagely observed as we drove past a graveyard when he was about four years old, "Cemeteries are where we put dead people so we don't hafta look at them."

Perhaps an inner fear that *we* are the monsters explains our morbid fascination with creatures that look like nastier versions of ourselves. Author Barton Nunnelly appropriately calls them "inhumanoids" in his book by the same title. I share his belief that while many of these land-based monsters may look somewhat human in form, they are definitely not us.

Unholy Hybrids and Other Manimals

Anyone who has read Greek mythology is familiar with unholy hybrids—creatures composed of parts from multiple animals and, sometimes, humans. The ancient monsters and demigods include the likes of centaurs with human heads and torsos, sphinxes that are part human and part lion, and characters such as the Minotaur, which featured the head of a bull on the body of a muscular man. These creature combos actually go even further back in time, to the ancient Egyptians and before them, the Sumerians. Although it's fairly certain Mother Nature never intended such jumbled entities to exist, some researchers believe that these chimeras really did once live and breathe here, cooked up in laboratories by visiting extraterrestrials who used their greatly advanced genetic and medical capabilities to tinker with the local wildlife.

Author Jim Marrs cites a Sumerian clay tablet that depicts deities named Enki and Ninhursag in a setting he interprets as some sort of scientific workspace. He believes that these so-called deities were actually ETs, and that they "produced many mutated creatures, including animals, such as bulls and lions with human heads, winged animals and apes, and humanoids with the head and feet of goats. If true, it is obvious that these experiments may have been the source for the many legends of 'mythological' creatures and superhumans, such as Atlas, Goliath, Polyphemus, and Typhon."[1]

Of course, Mother Nature is no slouch and can produce a breathtaking diversity of animal life when she has a mind to. Think of the little platypus with its duck bill, webbed feet, and beaver tail. It's a mammal but it lays eggs. The first Western scientists confronted with a specimen of a platypus were certain it was some sort of a hoax. But a platypus is an obviously established species with the power to reproduce itself, and few people would mistake one for a monster.

The same cannot be said for a whole slew of weird creature mashups reported by witnesses in the Americas in recent times. Few people would hesitate to brand the impossible beasts in this chapter as full-on, flat-out monsters. We've already talked about flying things with bat wings and horse feet; it's time to move on to terrestrial terrors such as dogs with snake heads, dog-cats, and lizard men!

SNAKE-HEADED DOG

A reader and researcher wrote me about a report he'd received of an encounter with something I'm not sure even the ancient Sumerians could have invented. The creature popped up in Northern California in 1996, scaring a woman and her son, as well as an unrelated eyewitness. The researcher interviewed all three and noted that sightings of *chupacabras* were rampant at the time in other parts of California and southern states around the country. This creature, however, sounds like something entirely different than the goat sucker of Puerto Rico and the southwestern United States. Here's the reader's account, edited for clarity and brevity.

The middle-aged woman and her sixteen-year-old son were driving to the store in a new (to them) used convertible, winding through the foothills of the High Sierra at an elevation of about 2,500 feet. The only mountain road between their home and the nearest town drops off 1,800 feet into a canyon on one side, with a trail that tapers more gradually into another canyon to the west. On the road ahead of them, the woman suddenly saw what she called "the dog from hell." She described it as the ugliest and weirdest-looking dog she ever saw. It was black and the dog's neck was two feet long from its head to shoulders. I named it the Snake Dog. I reported this to Art Bell [a former late-night radio host of a show that dealt with mysterious phenomena]. At the time, I did not have any photographs, so it did not go any further.

She said as fast as it appeared, it had gone to the right of her car and disappeared. She estimated her speed at about thirty-five miles per hour as she swerved her car to the left to avoid hitting it. The car swung around and skidded backward toward the side of the road and then shot out over the canyon and flipped upside down. Luckily both the woman and her son had their seat belts buckled as the car flew out about one hundred feet and landed upside down about ninety feet down the sloping canyon wall.

The woman said that when the car hit the ground, they heard the car's windows breaking, but they were both alive, upside down, and the engine was still running. She turned off the engine and they both crawled out from under the car, unhurt except for a scratch on the son's hand. By that time help was arriving since the car behind them had witnessed this whole event—including the weird, long-necked canine.

I talked with the second driver, who confirmed the whole story. This driver had seen the Snake Dog also. By now it was gone and has not been seen again. To my knowledge there are no known dogs in existence with twenty-four-inch-long necks. This is a strange event. It was real. It happened fast. It was over just as fast as it began. This is another corroborated story for your collection. Have you ever heard of any creature that looked like this alleged snake dog?

To answer the researcher's question, I have! It was not from anywhere near the High Sierra, however. The encounter occurred in Hovedgård, Denmark, in late 2007. A young man wrote to tell me he was walking his pet dachshund at about 6:30 p.m. one evening on a tree-lined lane that leads to a school. They reached the end of the lane and turned to walk back, but he couldn't shake the feeling of being watched and added, "I also had an eerie unexplainable feeling that if I were to turn around, something terrible would happen."

The dachschund did just that, however, as it stopped and stared back down the path, its tail raised and its fur standing up. "I turned around," the young man wrote, "and saw something that still sends chills down my spine. It was a jet-black, big, roughly dog-shaped thing standing on all fours by the end of the path." Its muzzle was both long and broad, and he thought that the ears may have been very small or flattened against the head as they were not noticeable. He compared the length of the fur to that of a Saint Bernard, but said it was a deep, absorbent black with no sheen whatsoever. Its eyes reflected no light and appeared as black as the rest of it.

He estimated that the creature was tall enough on all fours to have reached up to his chest. Even weirder was that it had an unusually long neck, "almost as if it had the neck of a horse," he said, and it was busily sniffing the ground where he had just stood as his dog did its business. "I have told very few people about this," he wrote, "and I am prepared to swear on my name, life, and pride that what I saw is true."

If both these long-necked creatures really were canine, they sound like some sort of truly unusual hybrid. Mange, as we've noted earlier, is something that should always be considered in such cases since it can cause an animal's body parts to appear elongated due to a lack of fluffy fur, but mange causes noticeable patches of pink-gray skin and both these animals were all black. I've received many reports of very large canid creatures traveling on all fours (usually at great speed while crossing a road), but none of them sound like these specimens. Canines are not the only animals that sometimes pop up looking as if they have just escaped from some mad scientist's genetics lab, however.

PORCINE PEOPLE

In one of my favorite episodes of the TV show *Seinfeld*, the gang is visiting someone in a hospital when the comical hipster character, Kramer, accidentally walks into the wrong room and emerges screaming that he has seen a pigman. While this may sound more appropriate as a sitcom premise than a page lifted from real life, actual people do occasionally report encounters with pig-like humanoids. In a sighting documented on the Phantoms and Monsters Web site, a woman and her three children had a somewhat similar experience in the picturesque, historic village of Mariemont, Ohio, on July 26, 1974.[2] The incident occurred in the early afternoon, so viewing conditions were good.

The family lived in an area that had been temporarily evacuated due to a suspected gas leak and was killing time by driving around town. They were cruising southward on Homewood Avenue when all four of them noticed a most peculiar being mincing its way along the sidewalk in their direction.

The figure stood about five feet tall, said the mother in her report, and walked upright with its body tilted forward, arms swinging sideways rather than front to back. They couldn't see its face below the bald head, possibly because at least part of the face was covered with hair or fur. Its only clothing was what the family assumed to be dark-colored pants, which seemed to blend straight into little black hooves that they could hear tapping on the sidewalk as it went along. The mother swung their vehicle around and they all craned their necks for a second look but by the time they reached the spot where it had been, it was gone.

There's no mention in the report as to what color the visible skin might have been or whether the creature paid any attention to them at all. I presume that their impression that this creature was somehow related to a pig was mostly due to its hooves.

As bizarre as this story may sound, there is some historic precedent to the notion of porcine people. A collection of folktales from the Eastern Seaboard, *A Faraway Time and Place: Lore of the Eastern Shore* by George Gibson Carey, makes mention of werepigs, according to an article in a 1989 issue of *Strange Magazine*.[3]

In the spirit of equality of the sexes, there is also at least one known swine-headed female in American folklore, known as the Pigwoman of Cecil County, Maryland. The legend springs from the vicinity of Elkton and Rising Sun, where it was alleged a woman was so badly burned in a farmhouse fire that she took on the appearance of a hog and went feral, haunting the nearby woods and occasionally eating people. The legend evolved into the standard tropes of a monster attacking parked couples and screaming (or oinking) at midnight on a certain old wooden bridge. The Pigwoman's calling card is an array of hoof-shaped dents she stamps onto the automobiles of people who dare to come to her woods.

I've also found at least three separate examples of pigman tales in different spots around the state of Wisconsin. Brussels, a town in Door County that was originally a Belgian settlement, is home to the legend of a pigman curse, one that is reputed to have afflicted an early settler. The man was disappointed at failing to receive an inheritance and decided to express his anger by cursing the local priest. The curse reflected off the priest's crucifix, however, and bounced back onto the man. From that point on he was bedeviled by poltergeists throwing furniture around in his house and would find pigs with the faces of men following him wherever he went. He found relief only after he built a small prayer chapel as atonement.

Folklorist and author Dennis Boyer tells of another pigman he calls the Sprague Stumper Jumper in *Giants in the Land*.[4] This creature seemed to be a true pig-humanoid, clad in rags and scrounging unattended hunting cabins around the Juneau County community of Necedah for sustenance. It was said to have had a special fondness for women, especially widows, living alone and was also known to be a shape-shifter.

The third Wisconsin pigman—or, actually, a whole *clan* of pigmen—may be found living somewhere near Marshfield, Wisconsin, to this day. According to several citizens of that city (unrelated to one another) who all spoke to me soberly in 2005 while I was in Marshfield researching another book, their town was visited by pigmen, although none of them had seen one of the creatures. The porkish peeps liked to shop at a downtown thrift store, I was told, and had once left their hoofprints on the sidewalk in front of it after they stepped in some black paint. There were indeed roughly hoof-shaped, black paint marks in front of the store, but I'm pretty sure the Marshfield pigmen can safely be filed under the heading of urban legend. Urban legends are generally identifiable because they repeat themselves from location to location, allowing for certain local variations. There's another colony of animal-human hybrids that also shop at a Salvation Army store—a half continent away, in Connecticut. But if they left tracks, the prints would not be of tiny hooves but webbed flippers.

CONNECTICUT FROGFOLK

Amphibious humanoids tend to stand out in a crowd once they dare to leave the pond. That's probably why the frog people of Fairfield County, Connecticut, prefer to leave their secluded country compound only at night. And I doubt they are any relation to the famous Loveland Frogman, a frog-like humanoid seen around Loveland, Ohio, in the 1970s. *Weird U.S.* authors Mark Moran and Mark Sceurman quoted a 1998 *Fairfield County Weekly* article about the mysterious, living legends:

> For years, rumors of an inbred family of large-eyed freaks have been circulating through the town, even seeping into the gossip of neighboring burgs. It is said that this mysterious family lives together on a decrepit compound not far from Bethel's center, and that members of the clan have been observed milling about the place, spilling from open doors and windows and performing various bizarre, unspecified acts. They even venture into town from time to time, we hear, for the occasional shopping trip.[5]

Unlike the Marshfield, Wisconsin, pig people, however, Connecticut's froggy folk seem to have plenty of eyewitnesses. Moran and

Sceurman found at least one person who had been to their "decrepit compound" and described them in that same article quoted above from *Weird U.S.* as having "eyeballs on the sides of their heads, and crusty lips and white bollocks, and sunken noses with nostrils that were just thin slits."

They also had large heads, small bodies, and hair that tended to appear only in patches, all of which enhanced the amphibious look. The eyewitness went so far as to call one of them a monster, but the general local consensus seems to be that the frog people's grotesque features are caused by years of inbreeding. No one knows that for sure, however. The inbreeding explanation also fails to account for another, more widespread type of manimal, the goatman. I'm sure that it takes more than a few kissin' cousins to create a clan of people with horns, fur, hooves, and a penchant for tin cans.

Ghastly Goatmen

Maryland, Kentucky, and Wisconsin are just a few of the states with long-standing legends of creatures described as half goat, half man, known in classic literature as satyrs. They're normally bipedal and, like the pigman, give themselves away by their tiny, clacking hooves. Goatmen tend to be on the cranky side, often jealously guarding old roadways and even snacking on unwary travelers (goats, after all, are said to eat anything). In short, they do as much or more to earn their monster stripes as do the pig or frog people. Of course, goatmen already have a strike or two against them because of their resemblance to the Greek god Pan.

Maryland's Goatman of Prince George's County is one of the most famous of these upright billy goats gruff. It comes with several different origin stories, but the most widely known involves the Henry A.

Wallace Beltsville Agricultural Research Center, a former tobacco plantation northeast of Washington, D.C., that became a government center for genetic experimentation.

As the tale goes, a scientist at the center was carrying out genetic experiments on some goats back in the 1970s when one of the ornery critters attacked him, transferring saliva through a bite. A classic transformation scene ensued as the scientist grew horns, hooves, a tail, and brown fur. The trauma of his makeover caused him to go mad, and he hoofed it into the woods where he supposedly remains to this day, snapping the heads off stray pets and other animals when not hovering around the parked cars of teenage couples as these creatures seem wont to do. And according to *Weird Maryland*, some people claim to have seen the goatman tossing dogs off several overpasses on Interstate 495.

Kentucky's goatman has been seen all over the state, according to author and investigator Barton Nunnelly, who interviewed an eyewitness named Stapleton. Nunnelly says in *Mysterious Kentucky*, "Stapleton and his entire family, including his wife and parents, all claim to have seen the goatman on their farm in Smith Mills, Henderson County, in the late 1970s. They described it as having the familiar traits. It had long, shaggy hair falling down to its shoulders with two short horns growing from its forehead. It had a hairy chest and arms with the hair thinning out around the abdomen and entirely covering the creature from its narrow waist to its split-hoofed feet. Its eyes, according to the Stapletons, were a glowing yellow color."[6]

Stapleton and another male member of his party, perhaps feeling there was safety in numbers, walked cautiously up to the creature as it stood regarding them. They managed to get within several yards when it suddenly disappeared into thin air—a stunt that certainly casts a supernatural shadow over the family's experience.

Nunnelly cites another incident dating back to the 1840s in Livingston County. It occurred near an iron ore mine in an area pocked with entrance and extraction holes. Some of these holes were quite large and had filled with a combination of quicksand and water, which made them extremely dangerous. Stories grew up around one particularly large opening known as the Red Hole that was supposed to house a giant half-man, half-goat creature that emerged once year to gorge on any animals in its path. Sightings of the great beast continued into the 1900s, and today the area is known for appearances of a hornless, bipedal furry creature that sounds much more like Bigfoot than a goatman. Legends do tend to morph over time—or perhaps the creature merely evolved.

Wisconsin's goatman legend also harkens back to the mid-1800s. It springs from an area northwest of Milwaukee known today as Holy Hill for the magnificent twin-spired Roman Catholic shrine that overlooks the heavily forested river valley and part of the northern unit of the Kettle Moraine State Forest. Back in the Civil War era there was no shrine, but that hill had been held sacred by Native Americans for as long as they had lived there. As settlers began to establish small communities and farms, the newcomers began to whisper of an unknown, upright hairy creature that stalked the hills by night.

The creature's first victim, according to the legend, was a newly married young man who had been transporting his bride along one of the dirt roads in a covered wagon when it became stuck. He climbed out to see if there might be any help nearby, ordering his wife to stay in the wagon. She did, but her husband did not return. When she dared to peep through a hole in the wagon cover, she saw what she took for a goatman stomping and sniffing around the wagon. When daylight came she found the remains of her husband jammed into the fork of a tree branch. To this day, the creature is said to menace travelers in the wee hours of the night, trying to nudge their cars over the embankments of hillside roads.

As in the case of the second Kentucky goatman, this area is now well-known for sightings of both Bigfoot and large canines that walk upright. One sighting that has been presented on several national TV shows involves the creature I dubbed the Holy Hill Bearwolf.

A contractor for the Department of Natural Resources, Stephen Krueger, was making normal rounds in his pickup during the wee hours of the morning in October 2006, picking up carcasses of deer killed by automobiles, when he came across a dead doe that was not on his list. It lay almost directly across the road from the shrine. He had to fill out paperwork on the unexpected find, so he threw it in the rear of his truck and settled back into the cab with every one of the vehicle's lights shining. Suddenly, he felt something push down on the trailer bed. He glanced at the truck's big side-view mirror and beheld a reflection of the torso, head, and forearms of a huge, wolf-like creature reaching toward the deer carcass. An experienced outdoorsman who now publishes the hunting and fishing magazine *Outer Boundary*, Krueger felt terror as he realized that he couldn't identify the animal.

Although the creature looked wolf-like, its torso and arms were thicker, like those of a bear, and it stood about seven feet tall on its hind legs. Krueger instinctively stepped on the gas and heard both the deer and an aluminum ATV ramp that had lain under the carcass thump and clatter onto the road. Neither the deer nor the ramp was ever found. Other witnesses who had seen what sounded like the same creature in the general vicinity also came forth to corroborate Krueger's story.

My personal theory is that perhaps the creature that was once known as the goatman is actually the same being that Krueger identified as an unknown upright canine. People tend to interpret things that they don't understand in terms of something that is more familiar. In the mid-1800s, most people would have been very familiar with religious imagery depicting the devil as an upright goat-like creature and also with illustrations of satyrs in ancient mythology. It would have been very natural, then, to assume that something furry and upright with prominent ears and that walks on its toes rather than flat feet would be some type of supernatural goat or goatman. As a matter of fact, witnesses in other locations have occasionally told me that they saw a satyr, but when shown my composite sketch of a typical dogman description, they have exclaimed that this was exactly the creature they encountered.

I admit that this theory doesn't work as well regarding pigmen, frogmen, and other alleged faunazoids, but it might help explain a few areas that seem besieged by a motley crew of monsters. And while it's hardly comforting to accept that there is still some malicious unknown beast cavorting in any particular woods, paring it down to one or two makes it seem a bit more manageable.

Many have also asked whether I believe all creatures like these are the products of secret genetic experimentation going on at labs run by the government, the military, extraterrestrials, or rogue scientists. Many urban legends, like that of the aforementioned Maryland Goatman, do place the blame squarely on such covert operations. I must admit that as the science of genetics continuously progresses by huge leaps and bounds, it seems likely that more may go on behind some closed doors than we know. However, the legends of pigmen, goatmen, and such date back centuries, before the computers, genetics, and medical technology we have now were even imagined by the human race. So unless we're willing to believe some advanced unknown society physically created the manimal hybrids depicted in the art and stories of our most ancient civilizations, I don't think extreme, purposeful genetic modification is the answer.

That doesn't mean other natural explanations don't exist. There are many possible mundane factors that may have inspired belief in the existence of these weird beings, such as spontaneous mutation, birth deformity, and little-known diseases. Ichthyosis, which makes human skin resemble scales and has spawned many a sideshow "snake-man" is one good example of the latter. If none of those ideas will suffice, we may always take that leap to co-opt the same theories of supernatural origin—aliens, demonic entities, earth spirits, thought-forms manifested by certain esoteric practices—that could apply to most entries in this book, including a few more creatures that deserve their own chapters.

21

Reptoids, Cold-Blooded Conundrums

This chapter was another that presented challenges in deciding which beasts qualified for inclusion. Creatures that resemble humanoid reptiles are versatile; some examples of reptoids could well have appeared in the aquatic creature section, and one that did—the Florida Gator Man—would have fit equally well here. One or two may also have settled nicely into the section on flying things. Those chosen for this chapter were mostly land-based, according to the observers who reported them. But who knows where anomalous creatures really spend most of their time? Some researchers even believe that many of them hail from a galaxy far, far away. We've already discussed possible aquatic aliens and UFOs, but the reptilian types are as likely to be found on land as in the sea. We'll have a look here at some that seem not to fear to tread among us.

ALIEN REPTOIDS

Humanoid reptilians have left their three-toed prints all over today's popular culture, as aliens from outer space that resemble lizards, dinosaurs, and other reptiles play villains in science-fiction movies and books. One of the most classic examples might be the TV sci-fi drama *V* (1983 original and 2009 through 2011 remake) in which lizard-like aliens disguised themselves as humans in order to take over the planet and process humanity as a vast protein resource.

Author and lecturer David Icke has built a career on claims that many of our celebrities and world leaders are descended from a reptilian bloodline that dates back to the origins of human civilization. And he isn't alone. Internet surfers may easily find sites providing lists of suspected human-reptilians, from the satirical slideshow at TruTV .com that includes Queen Elizabeth, Kenny Rogers, and Lyle Lovett to the lengthy, alleged reptoid roster of US government lawmakers and officials at *The Watcher Files*.[1] That site claims reptilianism is an inherited condition, adding, "Being a reptilian is something that must be activated through drinking blood and ritual among those who possess the serpent DNA."[2] (Pause for shudder.)

Many hundreds of people from around the world insist that these entities are neither fiction nor mere Web hype, citing personal encounters—mostly unpleasant—with the several types of aliens collectively known as reptilians. They are mainly human-like in form, with heads like those of a lizard and scales instead of skin. Think Geico gecko meets Creature from Black Lagoon. Author Kevin Randles describes them in *Faces of the Visitors* as looking like "advanced predatory dinosaurs"[3] and adds:

> These aliens stand five to seven feet tall and are often said to have green skin and thick tails. They are not unlike the velociraptors from *Jurassic Park*. . . . They are also the most violent of the alien abductors. That is not a comforting thought, since not all reptoid sightings are linked to UFOs.

If other eyewitnesses are to be believed, we have plenty of our own homegrown reptoids lurking about, with no need to import any from other galaxies. Lanham, Maryland, for instance, has an old tradition of a half-man, half-snake creature called Boaman that was said to have "chewed up a little girl."[4] But there have been reptilian-human clashes in more recent times.

SOUTH CAROLINA LIZARD MAN

Probably the most famous example of a reptilian humanoid is the South Carolina Lizard Man, also known as the Scape Ore Swamp Monster. Its June 29, 1988, appearance near a swamp outside Bishopville sounds like a scene from a Hollywood monster movie. But for seventeen-year-old Chris Davis, the encounter was no cheap cinematic thrill.

As the well-known story documented in many newspapers, books, and investigative TV programs goes, one of Davis's tires went flat at about 2 a.m. as he drove home from a friend's house along a dark, deserted stretch of road surrounded by swampland. He was just putting the tire jack back in his trunk when he saw a large, upright figure with glowing red eyes running straight for him through the vegetation. He was barely able to get into his car and slam the door before the creature's three-fingered, clawed hand was on the glass of the partly open window. He could see that its skin was covered with green scales.

Davis stomped on the accelerator, but the creature had jumped atop his car and clung like a body surfer until the teen was able to shake it off by careering his vehicle wildly. His father returned to the site with him to investigate, but the creature was gone, leaving only a few claw marks on the car as evidence of Davis's wild ride.

Several other witnesses also claimed to see the same creature in the swamp during the following months, and two sheriff's deputies discovered several fourteen-inch-long, three-toed footprints in the sand near some forcefully demolished forty-gallon drums that appeared to have been scavenged from a nearby landfill. The officers made plaster casts of the strange tracks and displayed them in the sheriff's department building. Some researchers have since attempted to link the footprints to Bigfoot, even though each print is two digits short of a five-toed set.

Davis did come to a sad end—but not from any unknown creature. He was shot to death in mid-June 2009, at his Sumter home in what one article noted was a "drug-related" incident.[5] The article in *Cryptozoology News* quoted Liston Truesdale, the Lee County sheriff at the time of the monster sighting, in testimony to Davis's character:

In July 1988, Chris was the first witness interviewed as seeing the Lizard Man. And what impressed me was that he told the same story every time. And he had to tell the story over and over to the media and others. If you're lying, you can't tell the same story twice.[6]

REGIONAL REPTILIANS

Reptoids aren't confined to southern, swampy areas. Several of my books mention a few very odd sightings in Wisconsin. One was reported to me by a woman from La Crosse who wrote me to say that in 1993 or 1994, her ex-husband and his eighteen-year-old son were searching for their lost dog near the riverbank on the north side of town when they encountered something entirely non-canine. As they searched the slightly wooded area, their flashlights suddenly lit up a "mud-colored" creature standing next to a tree.

"The thing was taller than a man," she wrote me in 2007, "and it had scales and slitted yellow eyes. It stood and looked right at them until they ran away. He told me it was one of the weirdest things he had ever seen, and his son was traumatized. The reaction on both their parts and their reluctance to talk about it—that tells me there's something to it."

They did find their dog, and I can't help but wonder if the mud-colored creature may also have been on the pooch's trail. La Crosse is located at the confluence of the Mississippi and Black Rivers, and happens to also be the site of a decades-long string of unexplained drownings of young men. The Black River can be followed far to the northeast of La Crosse to Medford. There, only a year or two after the La Crosse sighting, a bipedal lizard man was spotted in separate incidents by a Wisconsin Department of Natural Resources game warden and then a truck filled with state highway employees on Highway 13 just south of

Medford. In both cases, the reptoid suddenly flicked a pair of bat-like wings attached to its back and soared away.

I have to mention again that La Crosse was also the site of the nighttime encounter I've dubbed the La Crosse Man Bat, covered in Part One. It's hard not to wonder whether all these phenomena might be related, especially the lizard man sightings.

Lizard men have also been spotted in the American West, where so many dinosaur fossils are still being discovered today.

"It was a *Jurassic Park* flashback," said eyewitness Shannon Ystesund in a 2002 article for *KSL TV Eyewitness News*.[7] Witnesses near Cortez, Colorado, were insisting they had seen a small, three- to five-foot-tall dinosaur-like creature near the Utah border. Reports were similar to that of Ystesund's, who said she and a friend both saw a "very big lizard, nearly vertical, running on its hind legs" dash across the road in front of her car. She added that she was so rattled by the sight that she immediately drove home and told her husband.[8]

Another witness in the story described what she saw as a miniature dinosaur. The article also noted that investigator Nick Sucik said that he had collected eight similar reports of something akin in the Four Corners area where Utah, Colorado, New Mexico, and Arizona meet, and that sightings have been reported for seven or eight decades. Suggested explanations have included the foot-long collared lizard or the monitor lizard. The latter seems a bit more likely since it can range from five to seven feet long and does stand up as if to "monitor" its surroundings, although it usually goes on all fours. It's also popular in the reptile pet trade, which might explain why this native of Africa and Indonesia is being found in the western United States, though it isn't designed to survive a Colorado winter.

A six-foot-long pet monitor named Dino did indeed escape in

Woodland Park, Colorado, in July 2012, causing a massive police search.[9] The city is close to Colorado Springs, however, quite a long crawl from the Four Corners, and Dino was found and returned to his owner in less than a week.

A four-foot pet monitor lizard also escaped but was shot and killed in Ledyard, Connecticut, on August 25, 2013, after a woman reported a large reptile was attacking her chickens. Monitor lizards are not legal as pets in that state.[10] There had been other sightings in the area for months, and I think it interesting that no one reported it as a reptile man or dinosaur. Known animals are generally recognized by those who see them.

I think it can be safely assumed that whether the large bipedal reptiles seen crossing roadways or invading chicken coops are aliens, relict dinosaurs, or supersized natural species of lizards that can sometimes stand or walk upright, they are not really part human. And it's only natural we would see them as monsters. Movies like *Jurassic Park*, *Godzilla*, and *Snakes on a Plane* aside, mammals seem to have an instinctive healthy respect for large reptiles, an instinct that has served us well over the millennia. It's probably one we should continue to obey.

Freakish Felines and Odd Dogs

A letter to my blog asked why there should be werewolves but not werecats. After all, great cats such as lions and tigers can certainly be as frightening as large canines, and cats sometimes just seem inherently spookier. The truth is, were-tigers, were-lions, and were-jaguars have existed for millennia in the lore of geographic regions where they are the top predators. The ancient Egyptians worshipped a cat-headed or lion-headed goddess, Bastet, along with at least two other lion-associated deities, and they also made a rather famous, giant sculpture of a human-headed lion called the Sphinx.

The idea of human-animal combinations wasn't limited to the gods. Priests or shamans who shape-shift into animal form are part of most nature-based religions, old and new. The ancient Olmecs of early Mesoamerica associated their shaman kings with jaguars, believed to be bringers of rain and fertility. Olmec artwork depicts these leaders as supernatural were-jaguars, clad in pelts to help effect their transformations.[1]

THE WAMPUS CAT

Were-cats and other freakish felines are still alleged to inhabit the Americas alongside all the wolfmen, pigmen, apemen, goatmen, and other seeming hybrids. The southern states have their own name for the feline-related monster: Wampus Cat.

It's a folksy name that hardly sounds as if it should refer to a monster. Cryptozoologist Loren Coleman has said in a Cryptomundo.com article that the name was used in old newspapers of the southern states to refer to "an unknown monster cat as well as other mystery animals," including Bigfoot.[2]

The name also has a Native American backstory. In southern Cherokee legend, a woman who wanted to see what her tribe's all-male medicine circle was up to hid in the darkness to listen as they conducted business around a campfire. They eventually discovered the curious woman and decided to punish her for spying by turning her into a creature that was part human, part great cat.

The idea of the Wampus has since evolved into the general notion of a fierce bipedal creature with a humanoid body and a head resembling that of a cougar or lynx, although that's only a loose guideline. A few years ago, I did receive a report of something that closely fit the description, but this beast was in Southern California rather than America's southeast.

DOBERMAN-LYNX

I first told the complete story of these California creatures in *Real Wolfmen* but will recap briefly to start things out. Outdoor adventurer Lee Ehrlich had several encounters in 1988 with upright animals he said look like some kind of feline-canine hybrid. The first sighting happened as Ehrlich rode a bicycle on the Mount Wilson Toll Road, which leads up a hill to the Mount Wilson Observatory in Los Angeles County. He had just turned a corner when he almost ran into a weird, devilish figure:

"It was standing there upright with pointy ears, a wolf-like snout, and hinged legs," Ehrlich told me in a phone interview. "It looked like a lynx but was the size of a Doberman. It held its front legs like a *Tyrannosaurus rex*, had short hair like a hyena, and was grayish-brown with a black frill running down the back of its head to its tail. It went to all fours, took a bounding leap, and disappeared."

Ehrlich saw the same type of creature a few months later in Malibu Creek State Park, standing upright at a Dumpster in a raiding position. Other than its dark, reddish fur color it looked just like the first one, he said. He added that park rangers told him he was not the only person to see the upright creatures and that they believed the animals were some type of lynx, even though lynxes don't generally reach the size of a Doberman—or walk upright.

I've received other reports of strange creatures with feline features in California: in Orange County's Modjeska Canyon in 2008 and in the Santa Ana Mountains in 2010. But they also occur widely around the United States. One man wrote me about a sighting he had at the age of ten in the early 1990s, which occurred in his hometown of Whitefield, New Hampshire. Jessop Hunt wrote:

> I was in my backyard and a friend and I had snuck out of my house. While we were out, my father had locked the front door so we were trying to get in through the basement. While my friend was trying to open the door, I noticed something running around the backyard. The moon was shining through the trees creating a striped pattern of light and dark on the lawn. I could see a creature as it ran between shadow and light.
>
> It ran on all fours but appeared to be able to also walk bipedally like a primate. It appeared to have short black fur and in the moonlight you could make out muscle definition. It was probably two feet tall when on all fours, leading me to think that it was probably about three feet tall [I presume he means when upright]. Its upper body looked thick and muscular, while its legs looked proportionately short. Its head looked rather cat-like: short muzzle/snout with upright, pointy, triangular-shaped ears. We got a rather good look at it because it ran right up to us as if it were heading in our direction but didn't see us or act as if it were going to attack us.

I must note that if the creature was two feet high on all fours, it must have stood closer to four or more feet when upright, based on most other four-legged mammals. And if the story had ended there, I might not have included it. But four years after that incident, when Jessop was fourteen, three other friends of his saw a group or pack of exactly the same creature in a cemetery in the same city. Jessop and the first friend had never told them of their experience.

He went to the cemetery the next day with one of the boys and they found numerous small round, hoof-like prints in the snow. One of the boys' grandmothers then told them there were old legends of black-furred demons haunting that cemetery. It's hard to say whether there really was such a legend or if she was merely trying to keep the boys from hanging out in the cemetery at night, as teens often like to do, but that combined with the weirdly hoof-shaped footprints make me start thinking of other famous, anomalous critters.

THE BEAST OF BLADENBORO

These muscular dog-cats just described have some historical prece-dence. The March 25, 1824, edition of Quebec's *British Colonist* con-tained a short item about such a creature seen in Trenton, New Jersey. The brown-furred animal was said to be the size of a large, long-tailed dog but with a head like a cat's and footprints unrecognizable as those of any known species. The alleged sheep killer was so fast that even horses couldn't run it down.

Another, more publicized creature in the American South became known as North Carolina's Beast of Bladenboro. This mystery mon-ster terrorized a whole town in January 1954 after it was blamed for the horrific killings of some local dogs and livestock.

The creature left large, cat-like prints in the snow rather than hoof-shaped tracks, but otherwise it sounded much like Jessop Hunt's "black demon." Most eyewitnesses described it as having dark fur, weighing in at about one hundred-plus pounds, and endowed with a cat-like face set onto a sturdy, muscular body. Estimates of its height on all fours ranged from two to four feet, with a length of five feet.

The predations started in early January when three dogs were killed in one night, their heads flattened like griddle cakes and bodies drained of blood. (Many have compared it to the *chupacabras* based on that detail.) Other dogs, a pig, and a small cow also succumbed to the same brutal treatment. The beast wasn't thought to have killed any humans, but it did approach a woman on her front porch in a way she viewed as threatening. Nervous residents began carrying guns every time they went out and were joined by hundreds of eager monster hunters excited by the creature's widespread news coverage.

"At the height of the hunt, according to newspaper accounts, 1,000 men armed with pistols, shotguns and rifles divided into posses and combed about 400 acres of swamp," wrote Amy Hotz for the *Wilmington Star*.[3]

It sounds more like some type of large wild cat than anything else, especially since no one ever claimed to have seen it standing upright. The depredations did cease right after two different wild cats met their ends. On January 13, an area farmer trapped and shot a bobcat, and another man who was either a visitor to the city or a professional hunter (newspaper reports are unclear) killed some sort of large, spotted feline that weighed between seventy-five and ninety pounds. Even though the mayor had the bobcat's hide displayed on the town flagpole, no one knew for sure that either of these cats was the culprit, and some even blamed a large hybrid dog for the mayhem. As with many localized monsters, the beast lives on in the form of a Beast of Bladenboro festival around Halloween every year.

SOUTH OF THE MASON-DIXON LION

Sightings of feline beasts still seem most frequent in the southern states. A man camping near the Pea River in Ariton, Alabama, saw a creature outside his RV in April 2010 that he called a dog-cat in his report. He described it as a large, black-furred animal larger than a standard poodle and resembling a collie-Labrador mix, except that its tail was exactly like a cougar's. I expanded upon this incident in *Real Wolfmen*.

In a more frightening but undated encounter described in the June 2008 issue of *FATE* magazine, a woman from Watertown, Tennessee, wrote the magazine to say that she was awakened in the night to the screams of her own pet cat. She assumed it must be under attack by some animal and rushed outside with her flashlight, shouting for the unknown beast to let her cat go. She was amazed when her flashlight illuminated an unrecognizable animal standing upright, the unhappy cat squeezed tightly in its forelimbs. The animal was about five feet tall, she said, and while it reminded her of a raccoon, she knew that it wasn't.

She began to pelt it with rocks and landed a blow on its head that she figured should have knocked it out, but the animal seemed only slightly fazed and did not release its grip on the squealing pet. She screamed at it again, and this time it let the cat go, growled "like a bobcat," and headed for her![4] She did the only thing she could think of and directed her flashlight into its eyes. At that it yowled and walked off into the darkness, presumably still upright.

The cat revived and had no scratches or other marks. The woman was left to wonder what the creature was, whether there were more of them, and if it would return. At least she had learned it did not like light.

"There Ain't Nothing Right About That Thing"

I found another example of a southern creature of unknown ancestry in an article by Tal H. Branco in the January 10, 2006, *Charleston Express*. It recounted reports of a pair of very creepy critters in western Arkansas near Ozark that were seen by more than a half-dozen witnesses on different occasions. Branco learned of them, he told me, while in the area investigating reports of Bigfoot, his main area of study. He gave me permission to discuss them at some length here.

One eyewitness was a local newspaper columnist named Lucille Elders, whose encounter occurred in 2004. Another, a farmer named Harley Edgin, had multiple sightings during the 1990s as he drove the roads and trails of his property with several different companions. He said that the creatures stood about three feet tall at the shoulder on all fours, were colored like a bobcat, and had oversized heads and faces that looked canine.

It gets weirder. "According to Mr. Edgin," wrote Branco, "the most noticeable feature on the head was the animals' ears. He stated the ears were unusually large for the size of the head. The ears were reportedly mule-like, about six inches long, with tufts of hair growing from their tips. He noted that the neck was also thick and muscular. He stated the animals had tails that were cat-like, but longer than a bobcat's and shorter than a cougar's. He particularly noted the tails were rounded on the ends, and not pointed like a dog's."

The animals were estimated to weigh 250 pounds and boasted beefy chests and powerful limbs that allowed them to spring about rather than running in the manner of most quadrupeds. As one of Edgin's companion eyewitnesses said, "There ain't nothing right about that thing."[5]

The first thing I thought of, especially given the ears, was kangaroos or wallabies, but Edgin reported the creatures left cat-like tracks with smaller *hind* paws—most un-'roo-like. These things didn't act like wallabies, either, as another witness found out.

Geraldine Wyers had taken a semiautomatic rifle and some tools with her one summer day in the mid-1990s to deal with an unwanted beaver dam built near Edgin's property. She had disposed of the dam and was returning with her rifle to dispatch the beavers, when she heard weird moans coming from a nearby area. She cautiously approached the area but suddenly found herself only thirty feet away from one of the same animals described by Edgin. Its head was turned in her direction, displaying prominent, bloody fangs. She felt it was about to charge her and decided to back slowly toward her truck about twenty yards behind her. She took her eyes off the animal only to slam the open door of her truck once she was inside, and in a split second felt the impact of the creature's body on the outside of the door. It left a huge dent.

Branco wrote that there was yet another encounter in the area that occurred in Johnson County when one of the creatures prowled around a truck driven by a businessman who had stopped at an intersection. The man was close enough to see huge fangs protruding from its closed, powerful-looking jaws. Branco also said in the article that similar creatures were also seen in Montgomery County, Arkansas, and in LeFlore and McCurtain Counties, Oklahoma.

They remind me again of those black "demon dogs" of New Hampshire but seem to be a hardy and aggressive breed. The canine face and feline tail do not match, however, and if not for those tails, I might wonder if they are the same breed or species as Phylis Canion's Texas Blue Dogs, as described earlier in the chapter on *chupacabras*. I *will* say that they don't display any overtly supernatural characteristics.

I've also seen some Internet speculation that perhaps they were relict survivors of the American scimitar cat, *Homotherium serum*, named for its protruding upper fangs shaped like short, curved swords. It once roamed from Alaska to Florida, although that was between two million and ten thousand years ago, and it was about the size of a lion. Its hind feet were long and slender, however, and not a match for the smaller, round, cat-like prints found by Edgin.

SHUNKA WARAK'IN AND WAHEELA

Branco has another theory. He told me in an e-mail that he believes these creatures were relict survivors of the fearsome, hyena-like animal called *shunka warak'in* by the Ioway (Iowa) Nation. The name means "carrying off dogs." I covered the *shunka* in *The Beast of Bray Road* and *Real Wolfmen* as a possible explanation for dogmen, but since there was no evidence the "carrying off dogs" walked upright, I think they are much more plausible in this case than those describing bipedal beasts.

Another possibility is the *waheela*, a name given by Native Americans to a large, canine creature that resembled a burly, muscular wolf with jaws powerful enough to crunch bones. The late biologist and paranormal and cryptozoological researcher Ivan Sanderson thought the *waheela* might be a remnant population of ancient, bear-like wolves called *Amphicyonidae*. He noted in a 1974 *Pursuit* article that Canada's Nahanni Valley, a place where *waheela* were said to still roam, was also known as Headless Valley after various campers were found decapitated by some large predator.[6]

Both the *shunka warak'in* and the *waheela* also sound like possible culprits in the next tale, if these creatures do in fact still exist in relict populations in the American South. And actually, there is a mounted carcass of something that looks very like descriptions of both beasts a few states to the northwest in the Madison Valley History Museum of Ennis, Montana. The powerful-looking beast, locally called a ringdocus, was shot on an area ranch in 1886—not so long ago in terms of wild animal populations. It also resembles Phylis Canion's Texas Blue Dogs in many ways. It's not inconceivable that there could still be a few of them around!

EAR-EATER OF JASPER COUNTY

Sometimes the most frightening monsters are the ones you do not see. But when there's an infestation of unknown predatory canines in a neighborhood, there are usually a few hints that something's amiss. Pets and small farm animals may begin to vanish, or something might bite the head off a farmer's penned hog.

That was precisely the scenario in late January 1977 in Jasper County, Mississippi. *The Jasper County News* reported, "A dog and an animal that could possibly be a young timber wolf have been killed within a mile of Calvin Martin's hog pen where his three hundred pound sow had her ears ripped out Sunday afternoon of last week, but it is still apparent that the 'ear-eating monster,' which has been the terror of the Nazarene and Blue Ridge communities for some three weeks, is still at large . . . and hungrier than ever. The monster 'graduated' to the whole head at Oneal Ducksworth's hog pen Thursday night to disprove that the dog Calvin Martin shot Wednesday morning, after it was tracked to six different hog pens in the snow, was 'it.'"[7]

The creature left canine tracks that measured at least four inches across—larger than prints of most dog breeds—and were accompanied by smaller tracks that may have been either pack members or pups. But according to the paper, sheriff's deputy Dorsett Hendry said, "That was a dog that made those tracks, he was a real monster."

One of the two animals shot before the largest creature snapped the head off the hog was a young wolf-like animal, which the paper speculated may have been the "monster's" pup. Deputy Hendry shot it after it attacked a calf and a duck. All told, the unknown canines attacked at least nine hog pens in a three-week period. There were no more depredations after Ducksworth found his fifty-pound hog minus its head.

"It [the head] was gone bones and all, and if there wasn't nothing left but the skin. The skin is still there, but the head is gone out of it," said a member of the Ducksworth family in the article. The family added that the attack occurred at about 1:30 a.m., after all the hogs and chickens began to squeal and make a ruckus. Strangely, the farm dogs did not bark at this time. The family elected not to go out into the dark barnyard, and by the next morning, the monster was gone and had taken the head along with it.

The implications of what kind of creature could possibly have done this are sobering. It had to be something that not only had jaws large, sharp, and strong enough to take the head off a fifty-pound animal, but then also had the capacity to tote the whole skull away, minus the skin that should hold it together. Of course, since the family politely left it alone to its meal, it did have time to devour the head on the spot. If that's the case, though, why wouldn't it have also eaten at least part of the remaining carcass or even taken it along for later?

The case remained a mystery as the creature evidently moved on to fresh hunting grounds minus its two sidekicks but nourished by nutrient-rich hog brains. It seemed from the article that the community felt the beast was an extremely large wolf, although no one ever actually saw it. There is little doubt, however, that they considered it a monster.

Might any of the monsterish creatures in this chapter be the legendary upright, lion-headed Wampus Cat? None of them fit the folktale version perfectly, and most seem as much dog or other unknown mammal as cat, but of such are legends born. Accepting that these skull crushers, car smashers, and chargers of gun-toting humans may at least have had a cat-like part or two will have to suffice . . . and that is strange enough.

23

Watch for the Sasquatch

If nine-foot-tall humanoid primates are truly natural animals indigenous to North America, it's unthinkable that they would have gone unnoticed by the many Native American peoples who have lived in intimate harmony with this land for millennia. The fact that there are plenty of native names for such creatures in native lore bears this idea out, although today the creatures are most often called Bigfoot or Sasquatch. Either of those monikers conjures instant images of something between a human and a gorilla, massive in size and highly elusive. Popular culture pokes constant fun at the mystery beast, using its size and anthropomorphic qualities to great effect in selling things like beef jerky and snack chips. But they are not always treated so lightly in other places.

Far beyond North America, most cultures in other parts of the globe also have ancient legends about hairy man-monsters often endowed with supernatural powers or amazing strength. Sometimes they are feared as man-eaters, and in other circumstances are merely left alone as much as possible. Occasionally, these hairy ones have a place in tribal culture stories as heroes. In Native American lore, they often command a special respect and are thought of as a different kind of people rather than as animals.

LITTLE-MAN-WITH-HAIR-ALL-OVER

One of my favorite bits of lore about the hairy man as culture hero is the tale of Little-Man-with-Hair-All-Over, a specimen from the eastern United States and Canada. Although he lacks the usual huge Bigfoot stature, this descriptively named humanoid was intelligent, good-humored, a great warrior, and a shape-shifter to boot. He could take the form of a woodpecker, a wasp, or a worm, and thereby legendarily defeated not only a water monster but a four-headed human giant as well. Like Bigfoot, he smelled terrible and was completely covered with hair that even grew out of his nostrils and between his buttocks. Nonetheless, he was very popular with the ladies and in one version of his adventures ended up with four wives.[1]

Could this legend be based upon an actual—if unusual—human being? What first comes to mind is a person with hypertrichosis, a condition in which thick hair grows all over a person's body. I've addressed this disorder in several of my books as a possible explanation for some reports of upright, dog-like creatures, but it could apply equally well to some sightings of the much more human-like Bigfoot.

Hypertrichosis is a very rare condition, but one large, extended family in Mexico, the Ramos-Gomez clan, proudly claims quite a few members who exhibit this trait. Two athletic young men of this family have created a circus act and call themselves the Wolf Brothers or Gomez Brothers. Another living example is found in China: a young man with rock star aspirations named Yu Zhenhuan, who calls himself Hair Boy. Like the legendary Little-Man-with-Hair-All-Over, his nostril and ear hair grew so thick that he became nearly deaf and needed surgery to remove the excess.

The problem with assuming such folks would be mistaken for either werewolves or Bigfoot is that people with hypertrichosis are obviously fully human in every other way. Their limbs are in proportion to those of other humans, and they have normal intelligence and aptitude for language and tools. They wear clothing and use smart phones. Indeed, their only difference is that their gene for complete hair coverage has somehow been switched on. I think, however, an isolated case or two of hypertrichosis just may have inspired a tale like that of Little-Man-with-Hair-All-Over, who was considered human enough to intermarry with tribal maidens.

Such individuals also may have been mistaken for a young Bigfoot upon occasion in more modern times, but they are too small, rare, and human to account for all the sightings of nine-foot hairy giants. On the other hand, not all of the hairy "giants" are nine feet tall. There are a variety of reports of shorter Bigfoots from various far-flung locales.

I also think that confusing an individual with hypertrichosis with an unknown animal is a mistake that was much more likely in the past, when superstition often caused babies with birth defects to be

cast out to fend for themselves. It may even be the basis for the endur-
ing belief most northern European countries have in their own "wild
man of the woods" or *wodewose*, a character whose image may still be
seen carved in stone on many medieval-era European cathedrals and
public buildings alongside the more horrific gargoyles. But again,
there are simply too many sightings and legends around the globe for
hypertrichosis to explain them all.

Ivan Sanderson listed four major categories of Bigfoot-like creatures in his book *Abominable Snowmen*, a title that he explains is misleading since they aren't necessarily associated with snow. Sanderson
says, "There are now some hundred separate and isolated areas in the
world where or from which ABSMs [abominable snowmen] have been
reported—and this is apart from myth, legend, and folklore. The creatures described vary considerably but, with a few notable exceptions,
they appear to fall very clearly into four main types—a large (or giant,
to us), a medium or man-sized, a small or pygmy, and an excessively
bestial creature known as the *Meh-teh*."[2]

Sanderson noted that there is considerable variation within and
between these four patterns or types of creatures. "However, they
would each seem to form a fairly well-defined animal form, having
certain particulars, characters, characteristics, and other perquisites
all their own," he added.[3]

Let's start with a few of the smaller creatures and work our way up
the fur chain.

The Chickcharney

The native people of Andros Island, the largest isle in the Bahamas,
have a long-standing tradition of small, hairy "pixie" people called the
Chickcharney. Some have suggested the tale was brought to these is-

lands by Seminoles migrating southward in the early 1880s. But present-day tourist guidebooks still include this local lore in their brief history of the Bahamas:

> One of the legends of Andros Island is that aborigines live in the interior. These were thought to be a lost tribe of native Arawaks— remnants of the archipelago's original inhabitants, who were exterminated by the Spanish centuries ago. However, low-flying planes, looking for evidence of human settlements, have not turned up any indication to support this far-fetched assertion.[4]

This terse introduction to the Chickcharney in a Frommer's Shortcuts book, *Bimini, the Berry Islands and Andros, Bahamas*, obviously puts little credence in the story. Frommer's, in fact, believes the best explanation is that these creatures were no more than misidentified giant barn owls, of a species called *Tyto pollens*. That's a fairly logical deduction, since the usual present-day descriptions of the Chickcharnies paint them as green, hairy-feathered, red-eyed, three-toed tree nesters, which does sound roughly owlish. But what if these beasties were neither owls nor native Arawaks but something—in terms of wildness, anyway—in between?

I came across another, rather different description of the creatures by someone who had visited Andros Island on a zoological expedition in the late 1960s. It was in a letter written by Terry Cullen of Milwaukee, Wisconsin, to the aforementioned pioneer of modern cryptozoology, Ivan T. Sanderson. Thanks to Michigan investigator William Kingsley, I happen to have a photocopy of the December 10, 1968, letter that had been typed on the "Cullen Vivarium" letterhead Cullen used for business correspondence—Cullen was a known reptile collector and budding showman at the time.

The opening description I'm about to share was only a minor section in the main document, whose main point was to alert Sanderson about an unusual exhibit of a hairy creature entombed in a block of ice, which would later become known as the Minnesota Iceman. (I'll delve more deeply into that important entity later.) But Cullen's introduction interested me more than the rest of the letter. It read:

> During the course of my work with the land iguanas of Andros Island (*Cyclura baelopha*), I was repeatedly warned by the local [population] to stay out of the mangrove swamps. It seems that the people have great fear of "hairy pixies," which make their homes in the branches of the trees. To gaze at one of these pixies is said to bring extreme misfortune, according to the local legends. I put absolutely no stock in these stories until my guide and I ran across a small hominid footprint in sandy mud, about five miles west of Fresh Creek. My guide informed me that the track was supposed to be made by one of the so-called pixies. Due to a rainstorm I was unable to take the print with me.
>
> I do not pretend to be an authority on primate tracks, however, the print seemed to be that of a human who had never worn shoes. The length of the print was not more than six inches. Very few people venture into the interior of Andros, thus allowing for the possibility that the print was made by some other type of primate (i.e., other than man). Another unusual feature is the fact that I could find no more than two persons in Fresh Creek who even knew of the existence of the iguanas, yet, everyone was familiar with the pixie tale.

Arboreal, tree-dwelling hominids? That is what the so-called pixies sound like to me, especially if the human-like footprint did come from one of these elusive creatures. Cullen didn't say whether the main population wore shoes habitually, but whether they did or not, the prints may have been made by an ordinary human child. If a human child could somehow be ruled out as the print maker, however, this factor coupled with the description of hairiness sounds less and less like an owl.

Other sources for these legendary creatures mention another anomaly associated with the Chickcharney that will sound familiar to any Bigfoot researcher. The Chickcharnies are said to mark their territory by binding slim trees into an arc shape and will tangle the upper branches of two or more trees to create a structure that supports and camouflages them. Many who study the North American Bigfoot in the field think the tree arcs are used as a territorial or trail marker by the creature, while the intertwined branches commonly called stick structures (often found along deer trails) may be used either as hunting blinds or resting areas. I have never heard of any sort of owl that binds or breaks whole trees or large branches to create arc shapes or hiding places. Bowerbirds do, but they live in Australia and New Guinea and have body lengths ranging only from eight to sixteen inches, with correspondingly sized "bowers" much too small to hide a Bigfoot.

This paragraph in Cullen's letter isn't definite proof that the Chickcharney may be a hominoid rather than a big bird or pixie, and Cullen surely didn't mean it to be. It seems to me that it was included only to add context or background for the Minnesota Iceman—a human-like, hairy creature a little over five feet tall—as it implies that creatures similar to the still-controversial Iceman might exist in the Bahamas. But there are other centuries-old traditions indicating that other sizes of furry hominoids have existed—and may still exist—alongside humans in the New World.

Karl Shuker cited ancient tales of Hawaii in a November 1993 issue of *FATE* magazine that described an almost forgotten race called the *nawao*. Though now vanished from those islands, they once lived in the forests and were "a tall, hairy, wildman-like race."[5] Perhaps they and the Chickcharney were just opposite ends of the height spectrum of some widespread Bigfoot-like species.

THE MATLOG

Consider another early account of some larger unknown primates—this time in the Pacific Northwest, as told to Spanish explorers in 1792 by inhabitants of what is present-day Oregon and Washington. Bilingual author Scott Corrales translated the original Spanish journal notation found in a document called *Noticias de Nutka*, or *News from Nootka*, written by a naturalist commissioned to study and record the people, flora, and fauna of the coastal region. The naturalist never personally witnessed the creature that the indigenous people called the matlog but noted that just speaking of it filled local inhabitants with "unspeakable dread."[6] It was certainly very real to them.

The matlog was of giant size with black bristly fur and a head like a human's, only bigger. That description sounds consistent with today's usual notion of Bigfoot, as does the writer's additional mention of very long arms. The passage also details, however, long, curved claws; fangs larger than those of a bear; and screams loud enough to knock people off their feet. The modern Bigfoot is usually said to have blunt nails, teeth more suited to an omnivore's diet, and screams that might hurt eardrums but don't usually blast people to the ground, although I've heard anecdotal exceptions.

Those features sound a bit over the top, but they don't mean that the creature did not exist. Mythic elements in indigenous narrative are very familiar to contemporary researchers, who might take those fearsome fangs, claws, and howls as examples of the normal exaggeration that occurs in the retelling of a story. Besides, we know today, centuries after that Spanish naturalist's scientific journey, that the Pacific Northwest carries a reputation as one of the most active areas on earth for reports of Sasquatch sightings and activity. That implies a healthy population of the creatures, and healthy populations of any animal are not built overnight.

So, what happened to the matlog? Since most of the sightings in those Pacific states are of the type Sanderson would've called the giant variety, perhaps they are still there but are known by a different name.

FROM HAIRY GIANTS TO SASQUATCH

The well-known term for these creatures, "Sasquatch," was derived from similar indigenous words or phrases recorded by a teacher named J. W. Burns, who worked on the Chehalis Indian reservation in British Columbia in the 1920s. Burns is well-known for his article titled "Introducing B.C.'s Hairy Giants," which he wrote for the April 1, 1929, *Maclean's* magazine. And no, the story was not intended as an April Fools' joke.

"In fact," wrote Marian T. Place in *On the Track of Bigfoot*, "he [Burns] was credited with noting the various Indian names . . . *Soss q'atl, Sokqueatl, Sami soq qia'm, Sasq'atl* and others . . . and coining the English version, Sasquatch, by which the creature has been known to white Canadians ever since."[7]

Burns's article included several anecdotes that suggested the creatures had been seen in those parts for some time. One elderly woman told him that one of these "wild men of the woods," as her people called them, had taken her from her family as a child and kept her prisoner in a rock shelter with its own clan for an entire year before returning her. This tale is very similar to that of Canadian Albert Ostman, who claimed a Bigfoot family kidnapped him in his sleeping bag in 1924 and held him in their lair until he was able to escape a week later.

A second, much more informative anecdote came from a lumberman named Mike King in 1901. King was working on Vancouver Island when he found his timber plans stymied because the indigenous people he hired to work there were too afraid of Sasquatch to get the logging done. King set out to prove that the creature was nothing more than a bear. Instead, he spotted a Sasquatch busily rinsing some type of roots in a creek and then arranging them neatly in stacks. When King shouted at the creature, it jumped up and ran into the forest on two legs, displaying long arms and a natural, loping bipedal gait very unlike the gait of the shorter-legged bear. As confirmation, King spied very large but human-looking footprints in the mud near where it had been working with the roots. King had to eat a large helping of crow and then agreed with his unsurprised workers that they had better leave that area alone.

By the 1800s, human-sized or giant hairy creatures seemed to have infiltrated most regions of the United States. Historian and folklorist Michael Shoemaker chronicled his investigations of a roundup of early sightings gathered by authors Colin and Janet Bord in their 1982 book, *The Bigfoot Casebook,* for the January 1990 issue of *Strange Magazine.* The reports range geographically from Maine to California and from 1818 up to the turn of the twentieth century.

And even though some of the early reports occurred long before *King Kong* hit the silver screen or Bigfoot was hijacked to star in beef jerky commercials, Shoemaker still insisted that other things may have tainted people's imaginations and caused them to think that they saw human-ape creatures. He mentioned as examples the 1841 Edgar Allan Poe story, "The Murders in the Rue Morgue," which featured a murderous orangutan, and the 1857 news that anthropologists had found evidence of the extinct human cousins we called the Neanderthals. (At that time, Neanderthals were thought of as brutish and subhuman, rather than as the close relations we now know them to have been.)

Among the reports that Shoemaker found most likely to be true were those that reported a minibeast, or perhaps a baby beast. The man who claimed to have found it near Waldoboro, Maine, in 1855 said it looked like a miniature human being covered with black fur and that it was not a monkey. The eyewitness, J. W. McHenrie, added that when he chased it, the eighteen-inch-high creature ran from him rather than leap up into a tree as a monkey would do.[8]

Fourteen years later, in 1869, there seemed to be a flurry of unrelated Sasquatch sightings across the continent. That year, a Bigfoot-like creature inadvertently revealed itself to an astonished hunter on the far western side of the country. Shoemaker mentioned this episode, and the man's eyewitness testimony was also recounted in *Alien Animals*.[9] According to the report, the hunter had several times found evidence of some sort of animal visitor in his camp on Orestimba Peak in Northern California. Finally he hid and watched to see what might venture into his apparently deserted camp.

Expecting to encounter a bear, he was thoroughly shocked when a five-foot-tall humanoid creature covered in cinnamon-brown hair wandered into his camp on two legs rather than four. He noted that the creature had very long arms in comparison to its legs and body, making it unlikely that this was some type of hairy human. The creature alternately whistled and played with a lit stick from the hunter's campfire for around a quarter of an hour until it eventually seemed to tire of the game. Another creature that the hunter described as "a female, unmistakably"[10] appeared and escorted the first creature back into the woods.

The hunter had written his account in a letter that appeared in the California newspaper the *Antioch Ledger* some months later in October 1870.

Moving eastward: in January 1869, a Bigfoot-like creature grabbed a man out of a horse-drawn carriage traveling near Gallipolis, Ohio, according to an article in the Michigan newspaper *The Hillsdale Standard*. Gallipolis, I remind readers, lies just across the river from Point Pleasant, West Virginia, site of the Mothman encounters almost one hundred years later. Evidently the woods in that area were already harboring something very strange. The paper noted that the creature "goes naked, is covered with hair, is gigantic in height, and his eyes 'start from their sockets.'"[11]

In this case the story had a happy ending. The man's daughter, who was riding with him, managed to bash the creature on the head with a rock. It let her father go, then ran back into the woods.

Shoemaker also mentioned 1869 incidents in Kansas and Iowa. While the Kansas kerfuffle was based on a letter to a newspaper that was probably political satire, the Iowa report was from a hunter who saw a figure that was almost certainly a "wild boy" dining on raw fish from a river. There seemed to be a lot of feral people out in the woods in the mid-1800s, but in those times it was not so uncommon for the very poor, the mentally ill, unwanted children, and other outcasts of society to run off to uninhabited spots where they could try to live off the land. There was also a lot more wilderness and undeveloped land to try to live upon in the nineteenth century.

Another tale from those days before Bigfoot became famous was that of the Mount St. Helens Apes from 1924. A reporter for the

Longview Times in Washington told of a man who told wardens at the Spirit Lake Ranger Station that he had shot the "mountain devil."[12] The man was one of a group of miners who said they had encountered four 7-foot-tall, 400-pound, erect-walking creatures and that the body of the one he shot toppled over a cliff. (Very convenient disposal, I feel bound to note.) Something or someone attacked their cabin with rocks that night, scaring the group down off the mountain in the belief it was the creatures taking revenge for the death of their friend.

The article described the creatures as having "the appearance of large gorillas . . . covered with long black hair." The men also said they found thirteen- to fourteen-inch-long prints that showed four toes.

Like many of these old tales, it's hard to separate legend from real events. Others later came forward and claimed to have hoaxed the prints and the hail of rocks, but I have to wonder where the idea to do these particular things originated. How would anyone know about big footprints or the alleged fondness Sasquatches have for chucking rocks at people and buildings unless someone, somewhere, had first observed these things? Sometimes where there's a lot of smoke, there only need be a lick of fire.

TRUTH OR BLUFF ON BLUFF CREEK?

Public usage of the term "Bigfoot" dates back to only the 1950s, and it is thought to have first appeared in print in a 1958 article in California's *The Humboldt Times*. Written by reporter Andrew Genzoli, the article was sparked partly by a report from a road construction crewman, appropriately named Jerry Crew.

Crew claimed to have seen large, unexplainable but human-like footprints around his bulldozer near Bluff Creek in Humboldt County in the northwestern part of the state. He even had proof in the form of plaster casts he had made of the prints on-site. According to Crew and several others who had also written letters to the newspaper about seeing fourteen- to sixteen-inch tracks in the area, the mysterious, apparently massive maker of the prints had a long-standing, local nickname: Bigfoot (then spelled Big Foot). In other words, it had been stomping around those parts for some time.

The public responded to the newspaper articles with great interest and curiosity, although many readers suspected a hoax. Crew's employers, construction contractors Ray and Wilbur Wallace, were not indifferent to the hoopla. The brothers added their own fuel to the fire when they said that a year earlier, in 1957, other bizarre events had occurred at their work site when someone—or something—with very strong arms had picked up and tossed metal oil drums around the camp as if they were toys.

Not every part of this saga pointed to the existence of a true monster. According to Loren Coleman's *Bigfoot!: The True Story of Apes in America*, "hoax tracks" were found nearby, in the area of the Mad River, at another work site of the Wallace brothers.[13] But members of the local Hoopa tribe told reporter Betty Allen that their people had known about the creature similar to the one now being called Bigfoot for many years, countering ideas that the entire sighting had been a prank. Moreover, they said, some of their people had seen one or more of the hairy giants at various sites around the creeks and on steep mountain slopes on the reservation. Marian Place quoted their reply to Allen's inquiry:

"We call him *Oh-Mah*," they replied. The name meant something like "man-wild creature," but Place said her informants also inferred that *Oh-Mah* was a spirit being. "Only a Hoopa," said Place, "could appreciate the full meaning of the name. . . . An older man revealed that his grandfather had told him there were many such creatures until white men, prospecting for gold along the Klamath, Trinity, and Salmon Rivers in the 1850s, drove them away."[14]

The older man also obliged Allen with a description of the Oh-Mah, said Place. He told her that the creature stood seven to eight feet tall and had a dark face, big teeth, and was fully covered with hair rather than fur. He noted that the creatures had a strong odor, to put it mildly, and made howling or whistling sounds and that their offspring resembled giant puppies.[15]

Place did an exemplary job of describing other sightings reported by Allen and laid out the continuing events around Bluff Creek that would eventually lead to one of the most famous pieces of crypto-zoological film footage ever made, which is usually referred to as the Patterson-Gimlin film. So much has been written about that short length of film, which shows what looks like a full-breasted female Big-foot running from human onlookers, that I could never do the whole story justice in my limited space here.

Suffice it to say that the film, made by rodeo rider and Bigfoot fan Roger Patterson and his outdoorsman friend Bob Gimlin on October 20, 1967, is still hotly contested. Accusations that there was a person inside a fur suit, fake footprints in the mud, and possible deathbed confessions have people still asking what actually transpired on that crisp fall day. Is the film a fabulous fake, or is it the best proof to date that Bigfoot exists? I believe neither side has made its case with absolute certainty, but I like to think the creature on that film was real.

THE MINNESOTA ICEMAN

As promised earlier, there was more to that letter written by Terry Cullen to Ivan Sanderson than the description of small, hairy human-oids in the mangrove swamps of the Bahamas. Cullen was excited about what looked like a once-living creature preserved in ice that was then being shown at shopping malls and state fairs around the Midwest. The frozen carcass wasn't easily identifiable as any known species—and despite its hair, it looked too similar to a human for viewers to be certain it was a mere animal. Sanderson had achieved a reputation for taking mysteries seriously, and Cullen wanted Sanderson to see it and give his opinion as to whether it was a real unknown creature. He described the creature he'd seen fifteen months earlier for Sanderson:

> The public is allowed to see the ventral side, and a restricted lateral view. The creature is about 6'-6'3" tall [Cullen later said the number six was a typo and that he meant five feet to five feet, three inches tall]—possibly taller, as it is somewhat sprawled. The body is covered with a dark brown, straight hair though the palms of the hands, soles of the feet, and portions of the face are naked. The creature is a male as shown by the external genitalia. It is barrel chested, and seemingly well-muscled. The hands and feet are remarkably human, with no opposed great toe. It has a quite conspicuous navel.

Cullen added that the head seemed to have a sagittal crest, which many Bigfoot witnesses have described as well, and that its skull had been cracked open from the back, with blood still visible in the ice. "The face has a rather broad nose, the eyes are closed, the mouth is position [sic] of a painful grimace, the teeth are rather large, canines seem to be entirely absent, and on the whole the head and facial area is more hominid than pongid."

Sanderson did take Cullen seriously enough to inspect the exhibit firsthand in Minnesota. After talking to Cullen during a phone call on

December 9, 1968, Sanderson wrote some notes, of which I also have a copy, that read, "An American is now touring local fairs with the body of an alleged ABSM frozen in a block of ice. This is reported to have been obtained from the Red Chinese, who stole it from the Russians. The American got it from the Red Chinese, in Hong Kong harbor. It was apparently found by a Russian fishing trawler which thought it was a seal frozen in the ice. As the ice melted somewhat a monkeylike form became visible."

Cullen later said the Russian ship was Japanese, and eventually the man displaying the exhibit, Frank Hansen, gave an entirely different explanation of how he procured the curious thing, saying that he shot it in the woods of Minnesota. But in 1968, the exotic tale of the Russian fishing trawler and Hong Kong harbor was conveniently difficult to verify, and this remained the premise under which Sanderson and Dr. Bernard Heuvelmans agreed to examine the specimen.

The exhibit's custodian, Frank Hansen, gave Sanderson and Heuvelmans several hours to examine the creature privately as best they could, obscured as it was in ice. After a very close inspection, Sanderson seemed to think the strange animal was worth further study.

The owner then stopped exhibiting the original frozen specimen and had at least two copies made of it to use as sideshow attractions. The original, whatever it was, disappeared into never-ending controversy. In summer 2013, one of the copies was acquired for exhibition by the Museum of the Weird in Austin, Texas. Allegations that the whole thing was a clever hoax continue to this day. But even if the original Minnesota Iceman is ever conclusively proven to have been faked, no act of trickery can negate the countless reports of sightings of very tall, hairy, human-like primates continuing to this day.

The following examples of such incidents from around the country can only hint at the sheer volume of reports turned in to various research organizations yearly regarding these creatures. Moreover, the reports are probably just a small percentage of the actual sightings. I firmly believe most encounters are never told to investigators.

Here are some that, luckily for us, were.

BIGFOOT WITH DEAD DOG

It always helps the belief factor in any cryptid story when there are two witnesses, if only to show that it wasn't a case of individual hallucination. That's especially important when a case is as unusual as this one. This is also a sighting that gives such a melancholy tug to the heartstrings that it stands out among most of the Bigfoot reports I've received.

The area where it occurred—near Holy Hill, north of Milwaukee—will be familiar to readers of my wolfman books. This was where Wisconsin Department of Natural Resources (DNR) contractor Stephen Krueger, whose story was told earlier, saw an upright, wolf-headed creature grab a deer carcass out of the back of his pickup. There have also been numerous other dogman sightings in the hilly, wooded region, and many Bigfoot sightings in the nearby northern unit of the Kettle Moraine State Forest. Again as noted earlier, the site has traditions of a goatman that date back to the Civil War, and it is close to an area known for high incidences of UFO sightings.

In the late 1980s, then-thirtysomething plumber Ross Tamms did not know about any of these creatures as he and his girlfriend at the time, "Beth," drove the scenic winding roads on their way to her parents' house. On a warm spring day at 11 a.m., they were on a street whose name he couldn't recall.

"We were coming up to a farmhouse," he wrote, "which I was admiring due to its position alongside of a hill to its west and the large amount of huge evergreens to its north. . . . As I am looking at the house, I notice a brown clump at the edge of the driveway, where the driveway meets the street. . . . The closer we got, the slower I drove. As we drove by it, I was so alarmed by what I was seeing I just about drove us off the road. I finally regained my composure and asked Beth what that was. She didn't respond, so I asked again, this time turning toward her. She had her hands tightly grasping the dash, probably from my going off the road, and her face was frozen and white."

Tamms asked Beth what the thing was, and if she thought "that thing" was kneeling and holding out its massive arms. "She said yes," said Tamms, "to which I told her, 'We are the only species that kneels.' Both of them were certain by that time that the brown creature wasn't human, however.

"She asked if I noticed what was in its arms and I said that I thought it had something, but I was busy running off the road, and it seemed to be staring at me with black, very human-like eyes." Tamms also told me in a recent, follow-up phone interview that he remembers clearly seeing the whites, or sclera, of its eyes as the dark irises tracked him when he slowly passed by. Beth then said it had a little dog in its arms.

"I asked if it was black and white," said Tamms, "and she said yes, and that it looked sad. I asked if she meant the dog looked sad and she said, 'No, the thing! The dog was dead!' I asked her if she was kidding me because that dog was probably its next meal. Beth got mad at that comment and insisted the thing looked like it just lost its best friend."

The couple had a very good look at the creature, since it was in broad daylight and unobscured by trees or brush. It was also very close to them as it kneeled next to the driveway. "This thing was huge," said Tamms. "I was working in plumbing back then and I had a very good eye for measurements because I worked with them daily. It definitely had humanistic qualities. It had very broad shoulders and not much of a neck—at least it seemed so because of its hair. The hair was three to four inches long all over its body, seemingly uniform, and it was definitely reddish brown. The face was black, almost mask-like, something like that of a great ape. The eyes were remarkably human. It almost looked surprised, like it got caught with its hand in the cookie jar.

"As we passed it, because our windows were partly open, an incredible odor entered the car. It was so foul, I asked Beth if she had passed gas. The stench was so bad that both of us literally felt as if we were going to get sick. Beth still wanted to turn around and go back to confirm what we just saw. I must admit it was me who said, 'Over my dead body, as far as I'm concerned the faster we can get away from that damned thing the better.'"

The creature had held the dog with its arms outstretched and palms skyward in its kneeling position, said Tamms, and the sight was etched in his memory. The other thing he vividly recalls was something he shared in his phone interview.

"It gave me a look," he said. "This sounds crazy, but I felt like it was trying to get into my mind. I looked away."

Tamms added that he had read about sightings of Bigfoot, and this creature definitely fit the description. "I know what I saw, and I am not ashamed or embarrassed to admit it," he wrote.

While it's not unusual for people to report seeing Bigfoot and also wolfmen holding or running off with roadkill, deer haunches, and even live cats or chickens, the sight of a sad-faced Sasquatch holding a small dead dog not like prey but in a beseeching manner is very unusual. It's impossible to know whether the creature considered the dog a playmate or dinner, but it's a memorable image.

It's also not unusual for witnesses of upright hairy bipeds to report the feeling that the creature was "in their head," sending them a mental message, or some similar indication of psychic intrusion as discussed earlier in Chapter Eighteen, on dogmen. What's really happening in these cases is also unknown, although many who experience it feel it's an intimidation ploy on the part of the creature or, in some instances, an attempt to initiate friendly communication.

I can't help but wish Tamms and Beth had gone back for a second look, but I can't say I blame them for not doing so.

THE BLUE RIDGE BOUNDER

Georgia is a state with mountains and wooded terrain aplenty, so it's not at all surprising that I should have received a Bigfoot report from that state. A man who lives in the Blue Ridge foothills forty-five minutes north of Atlanta wrote to tell me about something he saw one night in 1984.

About 10:30 at night, I was riding along one of our back roads (very rural area) with my girlfriend at the time. We came to an area of the road that had an embankment on the left and a house with a white, split-wood fence on the right. All of a sudden a big, brown, hairy "something" jumped off the embankment down onto the road in front of my car. I stomped the brakes so I wouldn't hit the thing. The embankment was a good five feet high, and when the thing hit the road it never even slowed down.

It looked over at the car while never missing a step. It took about three steps and was all the way across the road. It leaped over this fence that was around four to four and one-half feet tall like it wasn't even there! It ran down into the yard but I couldn't see where it went from there. Scared us both half to death. Haven't seen anything like it since, although one of our local papers printed an article once of a big, brown, hairy creature that was in one particular spot of the river. Each time it was spotted there it was reported to be eating a fish it had caught.

The eyewitness was seventeen at the time of the incident, although he was in his mid-forties when he wrote to me. He added that the creature's whole body was covered in fur, it was on two legs, and that "it could jump like nothing I'd seen before." He could see that it had a mouth but no snout and said he still remembers the reflection in its eyes as it turned its head to look at the car.

He continued on, answering my interview questions:

> Height . . . tall enough to jump over a fence. Looked well over six feet. Not sure if muscular is the right word, but it was big.
>
> I've lived in rural Georgia all my life. I've seen a lot of wild animals. I've seen bears on two legs, deer jump over bushes and logs, etc. Even though this thing matched the commonly accepted descriptions of a Bigfoot, I still think it was some sort of natural animal species. Just not one we normally encounter.
>
> I swear I didn't make this up. And I'm certainly not crazy. I saw something that was real. My girlfriend saw it too. It freaked us both out. Whatever these things are, I know for a fact that they're here in Georgia. Maybe soon somebody will finally make the discovery.

Sasquatch of the Swamps

Floridians have a name for things that look and act like Bigfoot: the skunk ape. Maybe it's the state's swamp water combined with heat and high humidity that intensifies the scent, but the creature gets its name from the ultra-pungent aroma that often announces its presence or lingers in the air after a sighting. This Bigfoot-like creature is also known as the swamp ape. Whatever anyone chooses to call it, reports are numerous in the Sunshine State. Writer and investigator Charlie Carlson says in *Weird Florida*, "In response to thousands of sightings, the state legislature in April 1977 introduced a bill (H.B. 1664) to protect the elusive man-ape."[16] The bill was never passed, but the mere attempt shows a lot of people take their skunk apes very seriously.

One woman's encounter in the Lakeland area near the center of the state made the *Orlando Sentinel* in 2004. It happened in August of that year, a week after Hurricane Charley, as she drove with her two sleeping daughters along a rural road near sundown. The first thing Jennifer Ward noticed was something crouching in a ditch. As she focused on the creature, it became aware of her, too, and rose to a standing position. She told the *Sentinel*'s Linda Florea, "When he saw me, he was as surprised as I was. I slowed down to a stop; I didn't stop because I was scared. It was almost dark, but I could see it and get a good look."[17]

Ward said that she estimated its standing height at between six and eight feet, and it was covered with fur that hid its ears and nose. It stood with hands "drawn up next to its body," and she could see its full lips, which reminded her of the texture of a dog's paw pad. It featured a whitish coloration around its eyes, which is an often-observed trait of the Florida creature. She kept the sighting to herself at first, afraid people would make fun of her.

Before the news story broke, however, Ward was interviewed by Florida writer and cryptozoologist Scott Marlowe, who wrote a more detailed account of her story in his book *The Cryptid Creatures of Florida*.[18] It gives a better picture of the woman's initial trauma, her impulse to fill sketchbooks and even one wall of her kitchen with drawings of the creature, and reveals that she did later find footprints similar to that of a cast that had been made in 1983 in Ocala National Forest. Much media attention and multiple interactions with various Bigfoot research organizations ensued, and her story became one of the best-known skunk ape encounters in recent times.

PENNSYLVANIA BIGFOOT

An article by Jason Van Hoose from the UFOINFO Web site details a sighting in western Mercer County, Pennsylvania, in early June 2005.[19] The witness was a young teenager visiting his friend at the friend's rural home. The sighting occurred as the boys were walking through a field, when the witness suddenly noticed the creature pop out of the grass only an estimated twenty-five feet away. He described it as about five and one-half feet tall, covered in dull white fur, and humanoid. Its facial features weren't visible—perhaps hidden by hair—and it had a gangly, lanky build.

The creature took off running on two legs toward a nearby wooded area, which was separated from the field by a barbed wire fence. It pried its way through some dense shrubbery on the other side of the fence and then hid in some tall brush, shaking the vegetation vigorously at the two teens. After the bushes stopped shaking, the boys waited about ten minutes and then cautiously approached the area where the creature had disappeared into the woods. They found nothing at the time but explored a little more after fetching a .22 rifle. They discovered some footprints that the report described only as unusual, without giving any specific description.

A scary and possibly related incident occurred the next day in the afternoon when the eighteen-year-old girlfriend of the second witness's brother encountered a small deer that approached her from the field. She watched it for a few minutes and then went back in the house. When she went outside a short time later, the deer was lying bloody and mutilated in the yard. Frightened, she ran for her boyfriend, and when the two of them returned, the carcass was completely gone but there were flattened areas of grass that appear to have been made when the deer was dragged away. That would certainly be consistent with other reported Bigfoot behavior and may explain why that whitish, gaunt biped was hanging about the property.

BIGFOOT BODY ART?

This truly unique sighting occurred in 1977 in Michigan, east of Ludington, the same region of the huge Manistee National Forest, which is also prime dogman territory. The man who sent me the report is middle-aged now but was in his late twenties at the time. The sighting occurred as he and his brother were riding Honda trail bikes on state land as they took a break from helping their father put up a house addition. It was around noon on a clear, sunny, warm day and viewing conditions were excellent, even in the woods.

The man had stopped on the trail to wipe dust off his face when he had the feeling of being watched, and then about seven feet off the ground he saw a face looking at him from behind a tree. They made eye contact and then the creature ran away on its thick hind legs. It was entirely covered with very black fur and was muscular, with arms longer than a human's, and, the man said, "had no dog-like features at all." He added that he didn't see any "features" that indicated whether it was male or female, but there was one extremely strange thing about it.

The witness's brother had ridden on ahead and was unaware of the creature, but the witness chased the beast for a short way on his trail bike, keeping a distance of about twenty yards and watching it jump over fallen trees as it ran away from him. He said he saw very clearly that each of the creature's big ankles ("ankles the size of tree stumps") was encircled by a band of dark, red-colored fur that stood in obvious contrast to the black fur on the rest of its body. I suppose it could be a mutant fur variation since many Bigfoots with reddish hair have been reported, but seems like unusual color distribution for a great ape.

The second possibility I thought of was something like bloody rope burn, but it's hard to imagine a scenario that would entail a Sasquatch having both its ankles bound that tightly by anything. If it had been caught in some sort of man-made trap, however, that would explain its eagerness to run away.

Paint? Who would paint a Bigfoot's ankles? Native Americans once made extensive use of red ochre for ceremonial purposes. Could some First Nation people have been conducting shape-shifting rituals near Ludington in 1977? Or might a Bigfoot simply adorn itself with something like red clay?

A more mundane proposition: Did the Bigfoot suffer an infestation of mites or chigger bites around the ankles so irritating that it scratched itself bloody? Whatever the solution, I feel this sighting provides a fascinating mystery that may show us something more about the Bigfoot's biological or social traits, if anyone can ever figure it out.

The witness felt the creature meant him no harm. He also felt that it wanted him to see it, and in fact he was so affected by the experience that he said he has neither hunted nor killed any animal since then. He noted he had not had any other type of unusual experience before that or since, and added, "When I watch these so-called experts on TV about Bigfoot I just laugh because I know it's true."

Many other eyewitnesses have said the very same thing.

WASHINGTON WILDLING

The heavily forested state of Washington, together with Northern California, has long been considered Bigfoot Central and is still a leading provider of encounter reports. As Yakima-area reporter Scott Sandsberry said in a 2012 *Sports Yakima* online article, "It would take a shelf of books to chronicle the recollections of the thousands of people who are convinced they've had a personal encounter with Bigfoot."[20] He then offered several of his top picks from around Yakima. Interestingly, they all involved eyewitnesses with guns, some of which were fired at the creatures, with similar results to the "invincible dogman" incidents discussed earlier.

My favorite was titled "Music Man and the Monster," and occurred in 1977 when professional trumpet player Dean Dewees, whose career included stints with the Four Tops and Lawrence Welk, heard his dogs start a ruckus outside his cabin one night. He and his nephew Dave armed themselves and discovered an eight- to nine-foot-tall, upright creature methodically arranging the five chickens it had just killed in Dewees's coop into a neat line.

Dave had a shotgun, so he fired first and hit the creature's rear end. It acted as if nothing had happened and almost casually walked away toward the nearby Hansel Creek, leaving the chickens behind. The men followed it, and Dewees unloaded birdshot in its direction from his pistol, only to watch it cross the creek in a single fifteen-foot bound and enter the woods. The men, thinking that at least it hadn't made away with the dead birds, went back at that point. Only one chicken carcass still lay there. Something, perhaps a hunting accomplice, had sneaked in as the men chased the creature to the creek.

Dewees described the Sasquatch—for he had no doubt that's what it was—as covered in grayish-white fur that hung longer over its shoulders and down to its back. (Note that this is the second Bigfoot described here with whitish fur, something most people wouldn't normally think of in connection with these creatures.) "You've got to see these things to really believe it," Dewees told Sandsberry. "I saw it and I have no doubt in my mind of what I saw."[21]

The Sightings Explosion

There are growing numbers of Bigfoot hot spots around the United States and Canada. British Columbia is one, the Farmington, New Mexico, area near the Four Corners is another. I've mentioned Florida and its skunk ape. California and Washington have the highest numbers of reports, according to the running total kept by the Bigfoot Field Researchers Organization (BFRO) Web site, bfro.net. As of September 1, 2013, California had reported 428 sightings to BFRO, and Washington a whopping 567. Ohio had a surprising 239; its Salt Fork State Park alone has had dozens of sightings over the years, with three new ones in May 2013, says Doug Waller, director of the Southeastern Ohio Society for Bigfoot Investigation (SOSBI).

Waller recently published a book focused just on southeastern Ohio sightings, *Standing in the Shadows*, and is starting another. There are many other Midwestern sightings on record, as well. I've personally collected about two dozen very credible reports within just several southeastern Wisconsin counties dating back to the 1960s, with many more around the rest of the state. I could go on, but it's clear this is a widespread phenomenon. It's easier than ever to find many good published books and comprehensive Web sites about Bigfoot sightings in nearly every part of the country, and I'll leave it at that.

Skeptics, however, still like to blame most of the sightings on hoaxes and misidentifications of bears or other animals. There are definitely hoaxers out there. A Montana man wearing a ghillie suit was hit by two cars and killed south of Kalispell in August 2012 as he tried to fool motorists into thinking he was Bigfoot. But as with other cryptids, there are too many incidents witnessed by sober, credible people for hoaxes and misidentified animals to account for a significant portion of them.

It also may be that the numbers don't necessarily reflect growing numbers of Bigfoots so much as they do a higher public awareness of this creature, combined with a greater human population density that leads to increased hiking and poking around in formerly secluded areas.

DNA testing also seems to be an ongoing process and may yield something truly conclusive one of these days. With the new Google Glass computer mounted on eyeglass frames and plans by researchers to glide silently over forests in blimps, perhaps that long-awaited proof is just around a river bend. As for me, I've witnessed a few things myself that tell me there is something to these and other creatures, and in the next chapter I will go to this place of personal revelation that so many researchers fear to tread.

24

Author Encounters

After twenty-some years of looking for and writing about un-known, upright canines, one of the questions people ask me most often is whether I have actually seen one of these creatures and if not, whether I'd *like* to have a face-to-face with a slavering, wolf-like beast. I've always answered that I would definitely like to see one—hopefully from a safe observation place—but that such a sighting might seem suspiciously self-serving given the subject matter of most of my books.

I do claim a partial sighting of something seven feet tall and cov-ered with gray fur in Michigan in 2006. I was on a late-night stakeout on a remote gravel road with several witnesses and a *MonsterQuest* cameraman. We had a spotlight trained in one direction down the road and had been seeing pairs of yellow eyes in the bushes and at one time heard something large shake the water out of its fur (it was a hot, humid night with rumbles of thunderstorms) within very close range, so we were all on high alert. Whatever it was had to have been larger than a raccoon and did not want us to see it.

Suddenly, for no obvious reason other than perhaps the fact that it could, something ran across the road at the edge of the lit area. Just for an instant, I saw what appeared to be the spine of an animal from about the waist up. It was covered in gray fur that just caught the outside of the spotlight, and it was moving in an upright position. It quickly dissolved into the darkness as it continued across the road and then momentarily blotted out a reflective sign on the road's opposite shoulder. A quick measurement of the sign revealed the creature had to have been at least seven feet tall on its hind legs. One of the eyewitnesses saw the same shadowy spectacle that I did. Since he had previously reported seeing a tall wolf-like creature covered in gray fur (as well as a shorter brown beast at the same location), he became extremely nervous and insisted we leave right away.

This incident was covered in more detail in *The Michigan Dog Man: Werewolves and Other Unknown Canines Across the U.S.A.*, but not without a few misgivings. I had the same philosophical problem including the partial, possible dogman sighting in that book that I do in sharing the next episode I'm about to relate: whether reporting my own personal experiences takes away from my objectivity as a reporter and researcher. This question became more critical after I had an encounter in July 2012 with what I believe—based on my experience, physical evidence, and eyewitness testimony of another person—was a Bigfoot, and I cannot deny that it happened.

Like many eyewitnesses of cryptids, I wondered if I would be made fun of and disbelieved, especially since I write about these things for publication. I finally decided to add it to this book for one important reason: I have spent two decades trying to convince people that it is not only okay to report a sighting of an anomalous creature but crucial to the cause of cryptozoology. Every credible report adds to our database of knowledge about dogmen, Bigfoot, big birds, and other skulking beasts that show themselves only rarely.

Moreover, each new report also affirms the fact that many sane and ordinary people have had these experiences with anomalous creatures and lets previous witnesses know that they are not alone—and, in fact, are in very good company. How could I continue to urge eyewitnesses to continue coming forward unless I was willing to do the same? If not, I might as well throw in my binoculars. Here's my experience, then, and readers are welcome to accept or reject it as with any other witness account. As so many others have said, I know what I saw.

THE RANDOM BEGINNING

On Sunday, July 8, 2012, at about 7:30 p.m., I decided to take a short hike in a little area of southern Wisconsin's Kettle Moraine region, an area that I've walked regularly for about nineteen years without incident. While strolling along next to a deep kettle, a huge bowl-shaped depression left by the last glacier, I noticed three young saplings had been bent over by someone or something to form a perfect, rainbow-styled triple arc. I know this sort of formation can happen naturally, but this one looked too perfect. Some people believe Bigfoot creates these sorts of tree sculptures to serve as game trail markers or perhaps simple navigational aids. I've never been sure of that, but seeing this example where there had been no recent windstorms made me start wondering if this particular kettle area could be a good habitat for a Sasquatch. I knew they had been seen in other parts of the Kettle Moraine area, both in and near the official Kettle Moraine State Forest.

As I thought about it, the basic requirements were all here: abundant deer and turkey, trees with dense foliage growing amid steep drop-offs where one could hide and move surreptitiously, a nearby lake, and a history of many credible sightings within about a thirty-mile radius.

Just for fun, I decided to pick up a stout stick and bang on a tree located about ten feet off my trail. I've often wondered about the effectiveness or wisdom of a crowd of Bigfoot hunters pounding trees en masse, but I think a furtive woodland creature might be likelier to respond if only one or two people try it in an attempt to communicate. Of course, we still can't be sure what such knocks might mean to a 'Squatch. Although many researchers believe they are used for long-distance communication, we don't know their tree-knock code. That could be dangerous. For all we know, two knocks on a tree might mean something like, "Yes, do throw a rock at me."

I knocked three times. Nothing. I tried again and then suddenly heard a return knock from down in the kettle. That was unexpected, and it was very close! I knocked again and received a response. I felt a growing excitement. While there are homes dotted around this area of the Kettle Moraine, there was absolutely no one else around right then, and the kettle was on private land too overgrown for even die-hard hikers. The slopes of many kettles are also very steep and treacherous for humans to navigate, so it was highly unlikely some jokester was down there. If there was, however, I wanted to know. I was standing on a ridge that separated two kettles and was sure I would be able to see anyone or anything trying to climb out and run away.

Then I heard something very large crashing through the underbrush. I couldn't see anything in the dense foliage except for some branches moving unaccountably.

At that point, I probably should have run, but I was in a state of rather shocked denial that it could be anything dangerous, so I whacked the tree again. I heard another crashing charge. Again—idiotically—I hit the tree because I wanted so much to see what was moving through the foliage. Did I mention that because I had intended only to take a short walk in familiar territory, I had neither camera nor an audio recorder with me, only a cheap phone with no photo capabilities?

There was a period of silence accompanied by muted scuffling and another knock from the kettle. I answered and this time heard a loud crack that sounded like wood tearing. I saw a very large branch on a forked oak tree move horizontally in my direction until it pointed straight at me! Whatever had moved the branch was hidden by the tree's lush summer greenery.

Another crack followed within seconds, and the branch that had swiveled horizontally (I later measured it to be more than thirty feet long and at least eight inches in diameter) was wrenched free from the giant old oak. The branch also looked to be at least thirty feet above the base of the tree, but because I stood on a ridge it was directly at my eye level. I still could not see whatever was moving the branch. As the great limb thudded to the forest floor below, I noted that one end was covered with fresh green leaves, and the wood on both the tree and the splintered end of the branch appeared to be fresh and solid oak.

There was almost no wind and it was a blue-sky, white-cloud kind of day, with great visibility, about eighty degrees Fahrenheit. Dead branches fall off trees naturally all the time, but I could think of no plausible reason for that healthy limb to have cracked off the tree—especially not first twisting horizontally—at that moment when I had so capriciously decided to try to rouse a Bigfoot. That's when I realized that only some truly massive force could have torn this huge branch from a living tree. That's also when I dropped the stick and ran.

CREATURE REVEALED

I didn't stay away long. I wanted to go back before dark with my camera and some other equipment to have a look at the tree limb and reassure myself that it really happened and that the tree limb was not somehow damaged or hollow. My friend Sandra Schwab, an experienced investigator, and her twenty-one-year-old daughter, Natalie, met me at the kettle only about a half hour after the incident.

View of the torn-off, twisted end of the
thirty-five-foot-long, eight-to-nine-inch-
diameter oak limb. *(Photo by author.)*

The three of us slowly made our way down to the bottom of the kettle where the torn branch lay. We were astounded by the size of it and by its obvious freshness. We confirmed it was easily eight to ten inches in diameter at the broken end and more than thirty feet long, including the smaller sections that now lay smashed up against the tree's trunk. The limb had twirled one hundred and eighty degrees in its fall, probably from the way it had been twisted and pushed horizontally before it was finally ripped off the tree. The tree itself sported a freshly broken spur where the branch had been attached. The spur had a slight twist to it, too. There were no saw cut marks or evidence of woodpecker damage. We also realized the big oak tree was ideally situated for a lurking predator to leap down onto the busy deer trail that ran along the ridge of that kettle (where I've also found confirmed elk spoor).

The branch the author saw twisted from a living oak tree,
showing one of two nine-inch, freshly rubbed-off areas
of bark, with one of the recovered bark pieces
held back in place. *(Photo by author.)*

As we examined the branch, we found an oval patch of bark that had very recently been rubbed away leaving fresh wood underneath. It was nine inches long, about the size that I imagine a Bigfoot hand would be, based on many witness observations. Natalie also found a piece of bark that had been rubbed off lying not far from the branch. It was buckled in two places and had shred marks as if something with very strong nails had dug in and applied great force to it. It also stank of a very strong, musky, somewhat skunk-like odor. There was also a matching hand-rub spot on the opposite side of the branch, as if something had leaned over to use both hands to twist the limb.

The branch showing the entire area of the nine-inch fresh bark rub, on torn-off oak limb. *(Photo by author.)*

In fact, the whole area surrounding the tree reeked. We also found bare spots of ground that stank of the same musky urine odor. This discovery only fueled our anxiety to get out of the kettle as the woods grew darker, so we began to climb back out of the kettle to the less vulnerable position of the ridge. We looked for prints as we made our way up the slope, but the ground was too hard. We did see places where the wild ginger and other plants were strangely flattened, and we felt increasingly uneasy. As soon as we had climbed up to the ridge behind the tree, we paused to look down into the adjoining kettle. But the best evidence—and then the shock of our lives—was yet to come.

That's when Natalie screamed and gasped that she saw "it"! Sandra and I both turned toward where she was pointing. But it was too late— whatever she saw had already moved out of our view, behind some dense foliage. Natalie said she saw some sort of large, moving creature bigger than a human and that was partially obscured by brush. She did not see the entire body but said it looked like a tall biped covered in what she described as a gray-beige hue that was much lighter than the numerous reddish-brown deer in this area. She added it was moving quickly into the foliage, but that it wasn't really running or walking exactly like a human, either. The word she finally settled on was "striding," in very long steps, as it disappeared into the brush. I should add that Natalie had been a skeptic on the idea of Bigfoot but is no longer. And she did not know that Bigfoots are reported in a variety of colors, from black to cinnamon to the light color she saw that is often called the blond Bigfoot.

But there's more.

We stood there hoping it might provide a second glimpse when we heard a very low-pitched, menacing growl from somewhere in the kettle below us that was like nothing any of us could recall having heard before. This time I had my camera with me, of course, and could have turned it on and switched the dial to video to record that growl, but the electrifying sound ended too soon. The hair stood on the backs of our necks. The growl had been close enough that we felt whatever it was might come charging up at us at any moment. We left. The last thing we wanted was to be caught in those woods with a creature strong enough to tear a thirty-plus-foot-long branch off a live oak tree.

We returned the next day to have a better peek at the back of that tree. I was looking for fur tufts or other clues that we might have missed. We didn't find any, and the musky, skunky smell was mostly gone. I was left to ponder the improbability of the whole incident.

My original plan for Sunday evening had not included the walk by the kettles. I had wanted to drive to some other active sites but changed my mind and instead ended up being where—and when—something was actually happening. This illustrates the point I often make that both Bigfoot and the dogmen are just as likely to be seen in one favorable habitat as another—whether someone else has seen them there already or not. And yet, most sightings happen when they are least expected. I was lucky.

My luck was not of the overnight variety, however—this incident occurred after twenty-some years of putting myself in likely habitats for unknown creatures. I'm well aware that for many seekers and researchers, it never happens at all.

Because Natalie actually saw some kind of tall, furry creature and the three of us heard that strange growling, I feel a lot more confident thinking that this may have been a Bigfoot rather than some other unknown phenomenon. I don't believe it was a dogman because I think that a canine would have a very difficult time scaling a tree like that much less using its canine arm structure to tear off a giant branch. Bears can climb but also lack the opposable thumbs that would enable them to answer tree knocks with sticks. And it would've been next to impossible for any human to have torn off that branch without using an ax or other equipment that would have left some evidence of itself. Furthermore, I have since found two sixteen-inch, human-like footprints in the area, although the impressions were on slopes and too shallow to photograph well.

I think that I will see and hear that giant branch falling off the oak tree for the rest of my life. I've had more than one nightmare about it. And it has certainly changed the way I think about the woods and creature encounters, in general. There are days I'm not altogether glad for the encounter, because I know without doubt that I was very close to something monstrously large that probably could have hurt me had it wished.

Was it Bigfoot? I can't prove it, but I can't come up with any other explanation. It's remotely possible, I guess, that perhaps the branch was ready to somehow twist and fall on its own at the exact moment that I put myself in place to have a front-row seat to the event, even though there was no apparent reason for the limb to fall right then. But that does not explain the unforgettable smell, the two 9-inch, mitten-shaped bark rubs, the likes of which existed on no other log in the kettle. It offers no rationale for all the rustling sounds in the underbrush, and it utterly fails to explain the insistent, deeply guttural growling that occurred as my friends and I stood on the ridge. Not to mention what Natalie saw.

Another Kettle 'Squatch

As I mentioned, the incident is not an isolated case in this area. There have been numerous other sightings, but I'll mention one in particular because it was also recent and occurred within fifteen miles of my encounter, in an area just south of the Kettle Moraine. I had to pledge not to reveal the road and to keep the witness entirely private, but I consider the witness and the sighting extremely credible.

The witness, "Trish," is a very busy and hardworking woman in her forties and an avid gardener. That is what placed her outdoors at about 10:30 p.m. one warm evening in early September 2011. The property was well lit by powerful yard lights she and her husband had placed around their rural home. It had rained earlier, and she was taking advantage of the man-made illumination and moist earth to weed a flower garden.

A small-business owner who also runs an active household, Trish struck me as a very no-nonsense person as I interviewed her in her living room a few weeks after the incident. She had been on her hands and knees in the garden, she said, when she heard strange noises behind her. The noises were coming from an area of wild grasses that separated her lawn from a small woods.

"I got up and turned," she said, "and saw this creature standing there." She was so shocked, she turned back around and started weeding again, hoping she was imagining things or that it would go away. Instead, the creature emitted a deep rumbling growl followed by a whistling sound. She looked at it again and saw something standing about waist high in the four-foot grasses about fifty feet away from her. "It was light brown or light gray," she said (about the same color as the one I encountered), "and had a round head. Its eyes were round, staring, and reflected yellow. If it had ears, they were not standing up. I could see teeth, lower and upper, and I felt like it was laughing at me. I didn't see a muzzle, the face was almost human, and it had big shoulders."

Trish figured out later that it had to have been between seven and eight feet tall for so much of its body to have shown above the grass.

At that moment she turned for the second time; however, all she felt was panic as she scrambled for her kitchen door and locked herself in the house. She didn't look back and doesn't remember hearing it make any other sounds or seeing it run after her. The incident made her remember that the year before she had seen very large footprints in the snow that led from the woods to her son's bedroom window and back.

There are structures in that small woods that look like what many believe to be blinds or huts constructed by Bigfoot, and some large prints have been found in the area. I had investigated a sighting very close to Trish's about six years earlier, in which a man and a woman saw a dark-furred Bigfoot cross a road ahead of them, and a farmer in the vicinity told me of hearing an unearthly, howling scream at night on a neighboring farm. And interestingly, I also had a sighting of a definite dogman about a quarter of a mile away, a few months after the incident. Busy place!

BLOND BIGFOOTS HAVE MORE FUN

Blond or light-colored Bigfoots may not be rare in Wisconsin. I've had other reports, some going back decades. One arrived in 2005 from a woman who writes for outdoors magazines. The sighting was made by her best friend in the early 1980s, when the girl was about twelve years old. The girl's encounter occurred as she was riding on the back of a snowmobile driven by her older brother through a stretch of woods near Pittsville, a town that skirts the Necedah and Sandhill State Wildlife areas just west of Wisconsin Rapids.

The woman wrote of her friend's experience, "She looked to the side and plainly saw a white Bigfoot that was standing watching them. . . . She said she clearly remembers it and it still gives her the willies. She's still an avid outdoorsman. Her husband is a trapper."

There is also a little-known history of a blond Bigfoot within about fifteen miles of the area where my own encounter occurred. The sighting came from a local police officer, no less, who asked that his name remain confidential. It occurred in 1985 in the vicinity of southeastern Wisconsin's Lima Marsh.

The officer wrote that he graduated from a nearby Jefferson County high school that year and had gone on a traditional prank ride to a remote location looking for an alleged spooky house with some friends one spring night. The plan was to take two underclassmen there and then bring them to a gathering where everyone could laugh at how they were scared by the creepy place.

They set off in one young man's Dodge Charger just after dusk, with the teen who would become the police officer riding jammed into the backseat, and were near an intersection when all five young people saw something that was not on the night's agenda.

"To our right," he wrote, "we saw what at first we thought was a wolf. It was large, had gray/silver thick fur, and a head we later described as almost human-like. Definitely not canine.

"It was in a field about thirty feet off the shoulder. As we slowed, it raised its head, and began loping toward our car. We all screamed like schoolgirls for the driver to go faster, and as he kicked in the powerful V8 engine, the creature raised up on its hind legs and began to run in our direction! I remained fixated on it out through the rear window. As we gained distance the creature quickly gave up the pursuit, and dropped back on all fours, meandering back into the field it was in originally. The thing I remember most vividly besides the facial features were its rear legs; they seemed to be backwards.

"Needless to say, we were all laughing about it by the time we got back to the party. Until, after a few beers, one of the underclassmen who was on the ride started to share the story with a group of friends. A girl stopped him as he got to the point in his story where he described the creature. She, too, saw the thing a few weeks earlier and described exactly what we saw, and there was no way she could have known unless she was there. This burned the image in my mind all these years. Very creepy."

The fur color is described almost exactly as in Natalie's account, but she could not have known about this report since I have never before published it. The reason I think it was a Bigfoot is that the man described its head as human-like, and definitely not canine. That isn't a totally cut-and-dried conclusion, however, because the witness's additional observation that the legs were "turned backwards" usually indicates canine anatomy. But Bigfoots have been known to run on all fours for short distances when necessary, according to many eyewitness accounts I've read elsewhere. They just don't look as graceful as they do on two legs.

Whatever this creature was—and everyone agreed that it could not have been a human—it was the same color as the beast Natalie saw, and it scared five young men, including one who would later become an officer of the law.

It was a perfect monster.

In Closing

Despite the physical evidence and visual and audio confirmation by other witnesses, I still have many unanswered questions about the whys and wherefores of my own encounter with that possible Bigfoot. Why didn't I see the actual creature myself? Where did it go? Was it responsible for subsequent unexplained branch breakings and strange noises heard by other area residents? Had the creature been following me, and did it somehow want me to see it?

These are many of the same questions I've heard other eyewitnesses ask. Of course, the big one is always, what was the creature, really?

That is also the question that drives most researchers to continue the search. There's something about these sightings that teases our understanding of the nature of reality, and hints at the marvelous revelations we might find if only we could puzzle out what all these strange beasts may be.

It's very hard to tell just by looking at them. Some of the oddest—those rotting beach globsters, for instance—are almost always just decrepit carcasses of some known animal. Meanwhile, those that look like physical, sometimes known animals—the Loch Ness monster, upright wolves, and enormous birds—may also belong to some ultradimensional plane or time frame for all we know. I've written elsewhere at great length about theories of shape-shifting nature spirits, demons, extraterrestrials, and more, and there is no end to them. A few people have even asked whether I think this horde of beasts gathering by air, sea, and land will do battle with humankind as part of the evil host of Armageddon. My answer to all of these is the same; I don't know. Perhaps all the theories are right, depending on the case, or maybe none of them are.

That doesn't mean that I think the creatures are all in our heads. There are some cases of eyewitness misperception, certainly, but all these flying, swimming, running things have too much ability to interact physically with us and our environment to dismiss as pure phantoms. Some are undoubtedly flesh and blood. I think the truth about many of them, however, may lie closer to the idea that we share time and space with things that usually live just outside the range of our senses, as a dog whistle is just outside the range of human hearing. Once in a while, the pitch or the light spectrum lowers itself to our level of perception, a moment of flux occurs, and strange creatures happen. That's speculation, not science, but it could certainly explain a lot.

In the end, the only other thing I really know about most of these unknown creatures is that people keep seeing them. Perhaps that is the true mystery, and instead of seeking weird beasts, we should be shining our flashlights upon the nature of our own human perceptions.

String theory physicist Brian Greene says in *The Elegant Universe*, "The history of science teaches us that each time that we think that we have it all figured out, nature has a radical surprise in store for us that requires significant and sometimes drastic changes in how we think the world works."[1]

What that boils down to for me is that none of us yet know exactly how the universe works, and we should therefore expect a few surprises. Some of them may be monsters.

NOTES

Introduction

1 *Newsday*, "Rat Tales: 'Psychotic' Rodents Seize Office Building," *Milwaukee Journal Sentinel*, June 1, 1995.

Chapter 1: Feathered Fiends

1 Michael Edmonds, "Flights of Fancy: Birds and People in the Old Northwest," *Wisconsin Magazine of History* 83, no. 3 (Spring 2000): 165.

2 Charlotte Meredith, "British Archaeologists Unearth Astonishing Collection of Ancient Figurines in Greece," *Express*, http://consciouslifenews.com /british-archaeologists-unearth-astonishing-collection-ancient-figurines -greece/1147042/, accessed January 11, 2013.

3 Roy P. Mackal, *Searching for Hidden Animals: An Inquiry into Zoological Mysteries* (Garden City, NY: Doubleday, 1980), 99.

4 Ibid., 103.

5 Janet Bord and Colin Bord, *Alien Animals: A Worldwide Investigation* (Mechanicsburg, PA: Stackpole Books, 1981), 236.

6 William Janz, "Had to Shoot, Bird Man Says," *Milwaukee Sentinel*, August 2, 1977.

7 Scott Maruna, "Yet Another 1970s Giant Bird Witness Emerges," *Biofort*, October 13, 2006, http://biofort.blogspot.com/2006/10/yet-another-1970s -giant-bird-witness.html.

8 Lon Strickler, "Lawndale, Illinois Thunderbird Witness Comes Forward," *Phantoms & Monsters*, June 19, 2012, http://naturalplane.blogspot.com/2012 /06/lawndale-illinois-thunderbird-witness.html.

9 Sharon Gilfand, "More Report Seeing Bigclaw," *Daily Pantagraph* (Bloomington-Normal, IL), July 31, 1977.

10 UPI, "Mysterious Birds Spotted Again and Filmed in Central Illinois," *Centralia Sentinel* (IL), July 31, 1977.

11 Gilfand, "Bigclaw."

12 Ibid.

13 Brian Seech and Terrie Seech, "Thunderbirds," *Mysterious Mercer County* (privately published, n.d.).

14 Stan Gordon, "The Case of the Phantom Giant Bird—January 1, 2013 South Greensburg, PA," *Stan Gordon's UFO Anomalies Zone*, January 1, 2013, http:// www.stangordon.info/wp/2013/01/11/the-case-of-phantom-giant-bird-january-1-2013-south-greensburg-pa/.

15 Gordon, "Thunderbird Sighting Near South Greensburg, Pennsylvania," *The Gate to Strange Phenomena* 26, no. 3 (January 2011): 10.

16 Gordon, "The Case of the Phantom Giant Bird."

17 Ibid.

18 Reuters, "Paper: Massive Bird Spotted in Alaska," CNN.com/US, October 18, 2002, edition.cnn.com/2002/US/West/10/18/offbeat.alaska.bird.reut/.

19 "Giant Bird Terrorizes Alaskan Villagers," *The Uncoveror*, http://www.un coveror.com/bigbird.htm, accessed January, 21, 2013.

20 UPI, "Radio Station Offers $1000 for Big Bird," *Westfield Evening News* (MA), January 12, 1975.

21 UPI, "Giant Bird Stalks Texas Prairie; or So Some People Claim," *Westfield Evening News* (MA), January 12, 1975.

22 Ken Gerhard, *Big Bird!: Modern Sightings of Flying Monsters* (North Devon, UK: CFZ Press, 2007), 77.

23 Adam Switalski, "The Ecological Effects of Roads in the Brazilian Amazon: Current Status and Prospects for the Future," September, 8, 2005, http:// www.wildlandscpr.org/?q=road-riporter/ecological-effects-of-roads-brazilian-amazon-current-status-and-prospects-future.

24 B. M. Nunnelly, *Mysterious Kentucky: The History, Mystery & Unexplained of the Bluegrass State* (Decatur, IL: Whitechapel Press), 155–56.

25 Ibid., 158.

26 Scott Marlowe, *The Cryptid Creatures of Florida* (North Devon, UK: CFZ Press, 2011), 52.

27 Jackson Judge, "The Bird That Devours Men," *World Explorers* 1, no. 4 (Indianapolis: privately published, 1993), 34–35.

28 Timothy R. Pauketat, *Cahokia: Ancient America's Great City on the Mississippi* (New York: Viking, 2009), 72–73.

29 Edmonds, "Flights of Fancy."

30 Ibid.

31 Steve Mizrach, "Thunderbird and Trickster," *Cyberanthropology*, www.2.fiu .edu/-mizrachs/Thunderbird-and-trickster.html, accessed January 24, 2013.

32 Ibid.

33 Silas Tertius Rand, *Legends of the Micmacs* (Longmans, Green, and Company, 1894; repr. Salt Lake City: Ulan Press, 2012), 82.

34 Scott Maruna, "Witness Claims a Washington Eagle Sighting," *Biofort*, October 23, 2006, http://biofort.blogspot.com/2006/10/witness-claims-washington-eagle.html.

35 Karl Shuker, "Whatever Happened to Washington's Eagle?" *Fortean Times*, May 2010, www.forteantimes.com/features/articles/3484/whatever _happened_to_washingtons_eagle.html.

36 Ben Nottingham, "Giant Bird of Hickory Creek," *News-Palladian* (Benton Harbor, MI), January 31, 1963.

37 Bord and Bord, *Alien Animals*, 114.

38 Ibid., 115.

39 Curt Sutherly, "Pterodactyls and T-birds," *Pursuit* 9, no. 2 (April 1976): 35.

40 Ibid.

41 Mark A. Hall, *Thunderbirds: America's Living Legends of Giant Birds* (New York: Paraview Press, 2004), 153.

42 Ibid., 115.

CHAPTER 2: BATSQUATCH

1 C. R. Roberts, "Mount Rainier–area Youth Has Close Encounter in the Foothills," *News Tribune* (Tacoma, WA), April 24, 1994.

2 Phyllis Benjamin, "Batsquatch, Flap, Flap," *INFO Journal*, International Fortean Organization, no. 73 (Summer 1995): 29–31.

3 "Researchers Believe They Could Be Pterosaurs," *The Gate to Strange Phenomena* 27, no. 2 (October 2011): 12.

4 Paul Dale Roberts, "Batsquatch Sighted at Mt. Shasta," *Unexplained Mysteries*, April 4, 2009, http://www.unexplained-mysteries.com/forum/index.php ?showtopic=150840.

5   Stan Gordon, "Strange Winged Creatures Seen in Butler County," *The Gate to Strange Phenomena* 27, no. 1 (July 2011): 11.

6   Stan Gordon, "Strange Entity Sighted in Ohio and Missouri," *The Gate to Strange Phenomena* 25, no. 3 (January 2010): 13.

7   "Chicago, Illinois—Photograph of Bird or Something Else?" October 13, 2011, *UFO Casebook*, http://www.ufocasebook.com/2011/illinois082211.html.

8   Stan Gordon, "*Moth Man Seen in Chicago*," *The Gate to Strange Phenomena* 27, no. 3 (January 2012): 6.

9   Xavier Ortega, "'Man Bat' Reported in Chihuahua, Mexico," April 8, 2009, http://www.ghosttheory.com/paranormal/man-bat-reported-in-Chihuahua-Mexico.

10 Christine VanPool, "Flight of the Shaman," *Archaeology* 55, no. 1 (January/ February 2002): 42.

11 Ibid., 43.

12 Max A. Rodenfoe, "Mysterious Flying Creature," *FATE* 59, no. 11 (November 2006): 100–01.

13 "Macho Birds, Texas Style," *Pursuit*, 16, no. 4 (1983): 183.

CHAPTER 3: MOTH-MANIA

1   Mark Chorvinsky, "Cryptozoo Conversation with John A. Keel; interviewed by Mark Chorvinsky," *Strange Magazine*, no. 5 (March 1990): 39.

2   John Keel, "UFOs, Mothman, and Me," *FATE* 60, no. 9 (September 2007): 12.

3   Ibid.

4   John A. Keel, *The Complete Guide to Mysterious Beings* (New York: Tor Books, 2002), 265.

5   Sean Casteel, "Hey Mr. Spaceman; Aliens and Rock Stars," *FATE* 52, no. 2 (February 2006): 45–46.

6   Mark A. Hall, *Thunderbirds: America's Living Legends of Giant Birds* (New York: Paraview Press, 2004), 159.

7   "Lock Up Your Pets . . . Eagle Owl on the Loose," *Scotsman* (Scotland), April 12, 2006, http://news.Scotsman.com/index.cfm?id =556602006&format =print.

8   Ibid.

9   Donnie Sergent Jr. and Jeff Wamsley, *Mothman: The Facts Behind the Legend* (Proctorville, OH: Mark S. Phillips Publishing, 2002), 51.

10 William Elsey Connelley, *Wyandot Folk-Lore* (Topeka, KS: Crane & Company, 1900), 86.

11 Sam D. Gill and Irene F. Sullivan, *Dictionary of Native American Mythology* (New York: Oxford University Press, 1992), 288.

12 Peter Brookesmith, ed., *Creatures from Elsewhere: Weird Animals That No One Can Explain* (London: Orbis Publishing, 1984), 30.

13 Ibid.

14 The Church of England, "Mawnan: St. Mawnan, Mawnan," http://www .achurchnearyou.com/venue.php?V=2374, accessed May 1, 2013.

CHAPTER 4: UNTIMELY PTEROSAURS

1 "Introduction to the Pterosauria: The Flying Reptiles," University of California Museum of Paleontology, last updated October, 27, 2005, http://www .ucmp.berkeley.edu/diapsids/pterosauria.html, accessed April 11, 2013.

2 Jonathan David Whitcomb, *Live Pterosaurs in America: Sightings of Apparent Pterosaurs in the United States* (self-published, 2009), 4.

3 Ibid., 53.

4 Ibid.

5 "Don't Get Strung Along by the 'Ropen' Myth," *Dinosaur Tracking: Where Paleontology Meets Pop Culture*, August 16, 2010, http://blogs.smithsonian mag.com/dinosaur/2010/08/dont-get-strung-along-by-the-ropen-myth/.

6 Whitcomb, *Live Pterosaurs in America*, 46–49.

7 David Childress, "Living Pterodactyls Haunt Our Skies," Educate-Yourself, March 30, 2005 http://educate-yourself.org/cn/PterodactylsHauntSkies30mar 05.shtml.

8 Rachel Schleif, "Man Blames Car Wreck on Prehistoric Winged Reptile," *Daily Herald* (Everett, WA), December 29, 2007, http://www.heraldnet.com /article20071229/NEWS02/290431530.

9 Stan Gordon, "Unusual and Unexplained," *The Gate to Strange Phenomena* 24, no. 3 (January 2009): 11.

CHAPTER 5: THE JERSEY DEVIL:
MONSTER OF THE PINES

1 Mark Moran and Mark Sceurman, *Weird N.J.: Your Travel Guide to New Jersey's Local Legends and Best-Kept Secrets* (New York: Barnes & Noble, 2003), 102.

2 Loren Coleman, "On the Trail: Jersey Devil Walks Again," *Fortean Times*, no. 83 (October–November 1995): 49.

3 Ibid.

4 Lon Strickler, "The Mystery of the Pine Barrens," *Phantoms & Monsters*, January 29, 2013, http://naturalplane.blogspot.com/2013/01/the-mystery-of -pine-barrens.html.

5 Gregory McNamee and Luis Urrea, "Hell Monkeys from Beyond: *Chupaca-bras* Comes to the Sonoran Desert," *Tucson Weekly*, May 30, 1996, http:// www.tucsonweekly.com/tw/05-30-96/cover.htm.

CHAPTER 6: CHALLENGE OF THE CHUPACABRAS

1 Ibid.

2 Ibid.

3 Associated Press, "Hunters Kill Big Lynx: Tennessee's 'Kangaroo,'" *New York Times*, January 30, 1934.

4 Linda Godfrey, *Monsters of Wisconsin: Mysterious Creatures in the Badger State* (Mechanicsburg, PA: Stackpole Books, 2011), 41–48.

5 Scott Corrales, "Mystery Animals: Yesterday and Today," *Inexplicata: The Journal of Hispanic Ufology*, September 20, 2010, http://inexplicata.blogspot .com/2010/09/mystery-animals-yesterday-and-today.html.

6 Scott Corrales, *Chupacabras and Other Mysteries* (Murfreesboro, TN: Green-leaf Publications, 1997), 33–34.

7 Ibid., 33–34.

8 Scott Corrales, "Bats Out of Hell: The *Chupacabras* Returns," *FATE* 57, no. 7 (July 2004): 45–46.

9 Alan Brown, *Haunted Texas: Ghosts and Strange Phenomena of the Lone Star State* (Mechanicsburg, PA: Stackpole Books), 53–54.

10 Rhett A. Butler, "Chupacabra Story Is a Hoax; Likely a Xolo Dog Breed," Mongabay, September 4, 2007, news.mongabay.com/2007/0904-chupacabra .html.

11 "Xolo History," K9Gems, http://k9gems.org/id68.html, accessed August 22, 2013.

CHAPTER 7: DRAGONS AND THE AMERICAN GARGOYLE

1 Chiara Piccinini, *Medieval Folklore: A Guide to Myth, Legends, Tales, Beliefs, and Customs*, Carl Lindahl, John McNamara, and John Lindow, eds. (New York: Oxford University Press, 2002), 169.

2 Chad Lewis, Noah Voss, and Kevin Nelson, *The Van Meter Visitor: A True and Mysterious Encounter with the Unknown* (Eau Claire, WI: Unexplained Research Publishing, 2013).
3 David McCormack, "The Unsolved Mystery of the Van Meter Visitor," *Daily Mail Online*, May 4, 2013, http://www.dailymail.co.uk/news/article-2319503/The-unsolved-mystery-Van-Meter-Visitor-winged-creature-glowing-horn-caused-terror-Iowa-town-110-years-ago.html.
4 Jerome Clark, *Unexplained! Strange Sightings, Incredible Occurrences, and Puzzling Phenomena* (Detroit: Visible Ink Press, 1993), 349.
5 Jerome Clark, "Sky Serpents: The Flying Snakes That Terrorized America," *Fortean Times*, July 2009, http://www.forteantimes.com/features/articles/1975/sky_serpents.html.
6 Mark Chorvinsky and Mark Opsasnick, "A Field Guide to the Monsters and Mystery Animals of Maryland," *Strange Magazine*, no. 5 (Fall 1989), 42.
7 Neil Arnold, *Alien Zoo: The A-Z of Zooform Phenomena* (Bideford, UK: Crypto-a-Go-Go, 2005), 52.

CHAPTER 8: QUETZALCOATL AND OTHER DRAGONS OF THE ANCIENT AMERICAS

1 John Bierhorst, ed., *The Red Swan: Myths and Tales of the American Indians* (New York: Indian Head Books, 1976), 65.
2 Jonathan David Whitcomb, "Dragons, Dinosaurs, and Pterosaurs: Are 'Ancient' and Legendary Creatures Somehow Related?" Ropens, http://www.ropens.com/dragons/, accessed August 20, 2013.
3 Jonathan David Whitcomb, "Marfa Lights, Dragons, and Pterosaurs," Ropens, http://www.ropens.com/dragons/, accessed August 20, 2013.
4 Marfa Chamber of Commerce, "Marfa Lights," http://www.marfacc.com/todo/marfalights.php, accessed August 20, 2013.
5 Erich Hoyt, *Creatures of the Deep: In Search of the Sea's "Monsters" and the World They Live In* (Buffalo, NY: Firefly Books, 2001), 18.
6 "New 'Flying White Stingray' Sighting, Hebron, Kentucky," *Phantoms & Monsters*, January 26, 2012.
7 Ibid.
8 Ibid.

Chapter 9: Aquatic Aliens: Unidentified Submarine Objects

1 Teresa Moorey, *Understand Chinese Mythology* (London: Hodder Education, 2012), 23.
2 Bill Hamilton, "Underwater UFOs," *UFO Info*, May 8, 2002, http://www.ufoinfo.com/ufonewsuk/v01/0119.shtml.
3 Preston Dennett, "Is There an Underwater UFO Base off the Southern California Coast?," *FATE* 59, no. 2 (February 2006): 24–31.
4 Ibid., 25.
5 Ibid., 28.
6 Franklin Ruehl, "Are Some UFOs Living Space Beings?" HuffPost Weird News, June 26, 2012, http://www.huffingtonpost.com/dr-franklin-ruehl-phd/are-some-ufos-living-spac_b_1626199.html.
7 Ibid.
8 Ibid.
9 Richard Erdoes and Alfonzo Ortiz, *American Indian Myths and Legends* (New York: Pantheon Books, 1984), 229–30.
10 Ibid., 229.
11 Ibid.

Chapter 10: Mermaids: People Acting Fishy

1 "Tritons," *Theoi Greek Mythology*, http://www.theoi.com/Pontios/Tritones.html, accessed July 7, 2013.
2 Ulrich Magin, "Something Fishy," *Strange Magazine*, no. 10 (Fall–Winter 1992): 13.
3 Joseph Trainor, ed., "Aquaman Spotted in the Caspian Sea," *UFO Roundup* 10, no. 18 (May 4, 2005), http://ufoinfo.com/roundup/v10/rnd1018.shtml.
4 Erdoes and Ortiz, *American Indian Myths and Legends*, 312.
5 Ibid., 355.
6 Magin, "Something Fishy," 51.

Chapter 11: The Florida Gator Man

1 "Dolphins and Porpoises: Pink River Dolphins," *National Geographic Online*, http://video.nationalgeographic.com/video/dolphin-pink-river, accessed July 17, 2013.

2 "Caught on Camera: Is This the World's Only PINK Dolphin?" *Daily Mail*, March 2, 2009, http://www.dailymail.co.uk/news/article-1158494/Caught -camera-Is-worlds-PINK-dolphin.html.

CHAPTER 12: SERPENTS OF THE SEA

1 Laura Helmuth, "Creatures of the Deep!," *Smithsonian* 8, no. 37 (October 2007): 68–75.

2 Richard Ellis, *Monsters of the Sea: The History, Natural History, and Mythology of the Oceans' Most Fantastic Creatures* (New York: Alfred A. Knopf, 1996), 48–49.

3 A. C. Oudemans, *The Great Sea Serpent* (1892; repr., Landisville, PA: Coach-whip Publications, 2007), 363.

4 Ibid., 134.

5 Ibid., 146–47.

6 James B. Sweeney, *A Pictorial History of Sea Monsters and Other Dangerous Marine Life* (New York: Crown Publishers, 1972), 70.

7 James B. Sweeney, *Sea Monsters: A Collection of Eyewitness Accounts* (New York: David McKay Co., Inc., 1977), 64.

8 Ibid., 65.

9 Ibid., 67–68.

10 "Bobo the Sea Monster Appears Again," *News-Sentinel* (Lodi, CA), November 8, 1946, http://news.google.com/newspapers?nid=2245&dat=19461108&id=hqIz AAAAIBAJ&sjid=oO4HAAAAIBAJ&pg=1707,4189021.

11 Ibid.

12 "Monster Swell: The Tale of Bobo, Monterey Bay's Sea Creature, Resurfaces," *Monterey County Weekly*, October 25, 2007, updated May 17, 2013, www .montereycountyweekly.com/news/831_tales/article_5f07cfa2-957b-5549 -a7e9-3c336e110a82.html.

13 Mark Chorvinsky, "Our Strange World," *FATE* 48, no. 1 (January 1995): 24.

14 Ibid.

15 Matt Lake, *Weird Maryland: Your Travel Guide to Maryland's Local Legends and Best Kept Secrets* (New York: Sterling Publishing, 2006), 68–69.

16 Chorvinsky, "Our Strange World," 26.

17 Philip M. Boffey, "'Chessie' Back in the Swim Again," *New York Times*, September 4, 1984, http://www.nytimes.com/1984/09/04/us/chessie-back-in-the -swim-again.html.

18 Chorvinsky, "Our Strange World," 26.

19 Cathy Beck, Rachel Pawlitz, and Jen Bloomer, "Famous Manatee 'Chessie' Sighted in Chesapeake Bay After Long Absence," *Sound Waves* (September–October 2011) http://soundwaves.usgs.gov/2011/10/fieldwork5.html.

CHAPTER 13: AMERICAN KRAKEN: GIANT SQUIDS OF HUMBOLDT BAY

1 Bernard Heuvelmans, *In the Wake of the Sea-Serpents* (New York: Hill and Wang, 1968), 49–50.
2 Erika I. Ritchie and Laylan Connelley, "Huge Squid Cause 'Mayhem': 1,500 Caught on Weekend," *Orange County Register*, January 8, 2013, http://www.ocregister.com/articles/squid-382689-dana-dyke.html.
3 Ibid.
4 Pete Thomas, "Warning Lights of the Sea," *Los Angeles Times*, March 27, 2007, http://articles.latimes.com/2007/mar/26/sports/sp-squid26.

CHAPTER 14: THE ST. AUGUSTINE MONSTER AND OTHER GRUESOME GLOBSTERS

1 Mary Markey, "The Saint Augustine Monster," *Smithsonian*, August 18, 2010, http://siarchives.si.edu/blog/saint-augustine-monster.
2 Mark Chorvinsky, "Gallery of Globsters," *Strange Magazine*, www.strangemag.com/seaserpgallery.html, accessed August 6, 2013.
3 Ibid.
4 "Investigating the Montauk Monster: The Story Deepens!," *New York*, July 30, 2008, http://nymag.com/daily/intelligencer/2008/07/the_monster_of_montauk.html.
5 Ibid.
6 Richard Lawson, "Dead Monster Washes Ashore in Montauk," *Gawker*, July 29, 2008, http://gawker.com/5030531/dead-monster-washes-ashore-in-montauk.
7 Darren Naish, "What was the Montauk Monster?," *Tetrapod Zoology*, August 4, 2008, http://scienceblogs.com/tetrapodzoology/2008/08/04/the-montauk-monster/.
8 Josh Catone, "Top 15 Web Hoaxes of All Time," *Mashable*, July 15, 2009, http://mashable.com/2009/07/15/internet-hoaxes/.

CHAPTER 15: INLAND LAKE MONSTERS

1 Bear Lake Chamber of Commerce, "Bear Lake Monster," www.bearlake chamber.com/bearlakemonster.aspx, accessed August 1, 2013.

2 Bob Mims, "They Are Still Hunting for Bear Lake Monster," *The Spokesman -Review*, January 2, 1984, http://news.google.com/newspapers?nid=1314&da t=19840102&id=4llWAAAAIBAJ&sjid=8-4DAAAAIBAJ&pg=2872% 2C1014969.

3 John A. Keel, *Strange Creatures from Time & Space* (Greenwich, CT: Fawcett Publications, 1970), 263.

4 Ibid., 264.

5 Tabitca Cope, "The Flathead Lake Monster, Sturgeon, Eel, Dinosaur?," *Cryptozoo-oscity*, August 16, 2009, http://cryptozoo-oscity.blogspot.com /2009/08/flathead-lake-monster-sturgeon-eel-or.html.

6 Ibid.

7 Hanzel, Ibid.

8 Matt Naber, "Fishing Guide Shares 'Flathead Lake Monster' Story on National TV Show," *West Shore News*, April 17, 2013, http://www.flatheadnews group.com/bigforkeagle/article_60f487ae-a7ac-11e2-9de5-0019bb2963f4 .html?mode=print, accessed August 2, 2013.

CHAPTER 16: NATIVE AMERICAN WATER SPIRITS

1 Erdoes and Ortiz, *American Indian Myths and Legends*, 182–83.

2 Don Kaufman and Nan Belknap, "A Lake of Many Mysteries," *FATE* 60, no. 2 (February 2007): 66.

3 "Devils Lake Sea Monster," Prairie Public Broadcasting Dakota Datebook, July 11, 2011, www.prairiepublic.org/radio/dakota-datebook/page/9?post =33041.

4 Ibid.

5 Jim Miles, *Weird Georgia: Close Encounters, Strange Creatures, and Unexplained Phenomena* (Nashville, TN: Cumberland House, 2000), 66.

6 Curt Holman, "Stalking Altie: Does Georgia Have Its Own Loch Ness Monster?," *Creative Loafing Atlanta*, June 2, 2011, http://clatl.com/atlanta /stalking-altie-does-georgia-have-its-own-loch-ness-monster/Content?oid =3283993.

7 Gill and Sullivan, *Dictionary of Native American Mythology*, 320.

8 Johann Georg Kohl, *Kitchi-gami: Life Among the Lake Superior Ojibway* (St. Paul, MN: Minnesota Historical Society Press, 1985), 434.

9 Gill and Sullivan, *Dictionary of Native American Mythology*, 331.

Chapter 17: Seeking Aquatic Answers: From Archelon to Zeuglodon

1 "Giant Sea Turtle," *Discovery Channel*, http://dsc.discovery.com/video -topics/other/dinosaur-videos/prehistoric-new-york-giant-sea-turtle.htm, accessed August 11, 2013.
2 David McFadden, "Sea Turtle Comeback: Giant Leatherback Numbers Rebound in Parts of Caribbean," *Huffington Post*, May 18, 2013, http://www .huffingtonpost.com/2013/05/18/sea-turtle-comeback-caribbean_n_3298795 .html.

Chapter 18: Upright Canine Monsters

1 Stan Gordon, "Unusual and Unexplained," *The Gate to Strange Phenomena* 28, no. 3 (January 2013): 11–12
2 Ibid.
3 Linda Godfrey, *Real Wolfmen: True Encounters in Modern America* (New York: Tarcher/Penguin, 2012), 91–93.
4 Linda Godfrey, *Hunting the American Werewolf* (Madison, WI: Trails Books, 2006), 134–38.
5 Rupert Sheldrake, *Dogs That Know When Their Owners Are Coming Home, and Other Unexplained Powers of Animals* (New York: Three Rivers Press, 1999), 168.
6 Andrew Collins, "The Aveley Abduction" (parts 1 and 2), *Flying Saucer Review* (1978): 12–25.
7 Kevin Randle and Russ Estes, *Faces of the Visitors* (New York: Fireside Books, 1997), 220.

Chapter 19: Native American Ice, Bone, and Cannibal Monsters

1 Kohl, *Kitchi-gami*, 356.
2 Ibid., 358.
3 Ibid., 357–58.
4 Ibid., 365.
5 George Nelson, *Orders of the Dreamed: George Nelson on Cree and Northern Ojibwa Religion and Myth, 1823* (St. Paul, MN: Minnesota Historical Press, 1988), 88–90.
6 Ibid., 91–92.

7 Ibid., 93
8 Andrew Hanon, "Bus Beheading Similar to Windigo Phenomenon," Sun Media, August 12, 2008, http://cnews.canoe.ca/CNEWS/Features/2008/08/11/6413481-sun.html, accessed January 5, 2014.
9 Henry R. Schoolcraft, *The Hiawatha Legends: North American Indian Lore* (Philadelphia: Lippincott and Company, 1984), 154.
10 Nelson, *Orders of the Dreamed*, 53.

CHAPTER 20: UNHOLY HYBRIDS AND OTHER MANIMALS

1 Jim Marrs, *Our Occulted History: Do the Global Elite Conceal Ancient Aliens?* (New York: HarperCollins, 2013), 142.
2 "Pigman," *Phantoms & Monsters*, http://www.phantomsandmonsters.com/2010/03/humanoid-cryptid-encounter-reports-10.html, accessed July 3, 2013.
3 Chorvinsky and Opsasnick, "A Field Guide to the Monsters and Mystery Animals of Maryland."
4 Dennis Boyer, *Giants in the Land: Folk Tales and Legends of Wisconsin* (Madison, WI: Prairie Oak Press, 1997), 116–19.
5 Mark Moran and Mark Sceurman, *Weird U.S.: Your Travel Guide to America's Local Legends and Best Kept Secrets* (New York: Barnes & Noble Publishing, 2004), 87.
6 Nunnelly, *Mysterious Kentucky*, 134.

CHAPTER 21: REPTOIDS, COLD-BLOODED CONUNDRUMS

1 "Fifteen Celebrities Who May Be Reptilians," TruTV.com, http://www.trutv.com/conspiracy/hollywood/reptiles/gallery.html, accessed July 6, 2013
2 "Alien Nation," *The Watcher Files*, http://www.thewatcherfiles.com/exposing_reptilians.htm, accessed July 13, 2013.
3 Randles and Estes, *Faces of the Visitors*, 220.
4 Chorvinsky and Opsasnick, "A Field Guide to the Monsters and Mystery Animals of Maryland," 45.
5 Randy Burns, "Police: Murder Victim Lizard Man Witness," June 20, 2009, *Cryptozoology Online*, http://cryptozoologynews.blogspot.com/2009/06/police-murder-victim-lizard-man-witness.html.

6 Ibid.

7 John Hollenhorst, "'Dinosaur' Sightings in Cortez, Colorado?," *KSL TV Eyewitness News*, November 4, 2002, http://archive.today/dRH44.

8 Ibid.

9 "Six Foot Lizard on the Lam in Colorado," CBS News, July 17, 2012, http://www.cbsnews.com/news/6-foot-lizard-on-the-lam-in-colorado/.

10 "Owner of Monitor Lizard Charged," *NBC Connecticut*, September 12, 2013, http://www.nbcconnecticut.com/news/local/Police-Shoot-Monitor-Lizard-in-Ledyard-221185011.html.

CHAPTER 22: FREAKISH FELINES AND ODD DOGS

1 "Were-Jaguar with Half-Mask," Johnson Museum of Art, http://www.museum.cornell.edu/collections/view/were-jaguar-half-mask.html, accessed August 27, 2013.

2 Loren Coleman, "Wampus: Mystery Cat, Swamp Monster, or Booger Bigfoot?" *Cryptomundo*, June 12, 2012, http://www.cryptomundo.com/crypto zoo-news/wampus/.

3 Amy Hotz, "Have You Seen This Creature?" *The Wilmington Star* archived at *Star News Online*, October 29, 2006, http://www.starnewsonline.com/arhclc/20061029/NEWS/61027007/1051.

4 Margaret Worley, "Strange Encounter," *FATE* 61, no. 6 (June 2008): 99–100.

5 Tal H. Branco, "Franklin County's Wild Crypto Zoo," *Charleston Express*, January 10, 2006, http://www.charlestonexpress.com/articles/2006/01/11/news/news01.txt, accessed January 11, 2006.

6 Ivan Sanderson, "The Dire Wolf," *Pursuit*, no. 6 (October 1974): 91–94.

7 "Ear-eating Monster Gets a Head," *Jasper County News* (IN), January 26, 1977.

CHAPTER 23: WATCH FOR THE SASQUATCH

1 Erdoes and Ortiz, *American Indian Myths and Legends*, 191.

2 Ivan T. Sanderson, *Abominable Snowmen: Legend Come to Life* (Kempton, IL: Adventures Unlimited Press, [1961] 2006), 120.

3 Ibid.

4 Darwin Porter and Danforth Prince, Frommer's ShortCuts, *Bimini, the Berry Islands & Andros, Bahamas* (Hoboken, NJ: John Wiley and Sons, 2012).

5 Karl Shuker, "Death Birds and Dragonets—In Search of Forgotten Monsters," *FATE* 46, no. 11 (November 1993): 174.

6 Scott Corrales, "History Lessons: Bigfoot, the Viceroyalty and the Natives of Nootka," *Inexplicata: The Journal of Hispanic UFOlogy*, April 29, 2013, http://inexplicata.blogspot.com/2013/04/history-lessons-Bigfoot-viceroy alty-and.html.

7 Marian T. Place, *On the Track of Bigfoot* (New York: Dodd, Mead, and Co., 1974), 86–87.

8 Michael T. Shoemaker, "Searching for the Historical Bigfoot," *Strange Magazine*, no. 5 (January 1990): 18–23.

9 Bord and Bord, *Alien Animals*, 144.

10 Ibid.

11 "Fight with a Wild Man," *Hillsdale Standard* (MI), January 26, 1869.

12 Ted Van Arsdol, "Wild-eyed Rifleman fleeing Devils of Peak, Launches Legend of Mt. St. Helen's Apes," *Longview Times* (WA), http://www.bigfooten counters.com/articles/longview1924.htm, accessed August 4, 2013.

13 Loren Coleman, *Bigfoot!: The True Story of Apes in America* (New York: Paraview Pocket Books, 2003), 68–69.

14 Place, *On the Track of Bigfoot*, 50.

15 Ibid.

16 Charlie Carlson, *Weird Florida: Your Travel Guide to Florida's Local Legends and Best Kept Secrets* (New York: Sterling Publishing, 2005), 80.

17 Linda Florea, "Woman Says 'Skunk Ape' Stood Up Beside Highway," *Orlando Sentinel*, November 20, 2004.

18 Marlowe, *The Cryptid Creatures of Florida*, 90–93.

19 Jason Van Hoose, "Number 80," UFOinfo.com, http://www.ufoinfo.com/humanoid/humanoid2005.shtml, accessed February 27, 2013.

20 Scott Sandsberry, "True Believers: People of All Types Are Certain They Have Encountered Sasquatch," *Yakima Herald Republic*, July 3, 2012, http://sportsyakima.com/2012/07/trues-believers-people-of-all-types-are-certain-they-have-encountered-sasquatch/.

21 Ibid.

Chapter 24: Author Encounters

1 Brian Greene, *The Elegant Universe: Superstrings, Hidden Dimensions, and the Quest for the Ultimate Theory* (New York: Vintage Books, 2003), 373.

INDEX

ABOUT THE AUTHOR

Nationally recognized author, award-winning journalist, and investigator of mystery creatures, Linda S. Godfrey has researched hundreds of case studies, beginning with her 1992 news story, "The Beast of Bray Road." Godfrey has been featured on *MonsterQuest, Monsters and Mysteries in America, Sean Hannity's America, Inside Edition, Lost Tapes, Haunted Highway,* and many other TV and radio shows. She has published fifteen books on strange creatures, eccentric people, and unusual and haunted places.

Godfrey lives with her husband and Lhasa apso in rural Wisconsin. Visit her Web site at http://lindagodfrey.com.